BEGINNERS GUIDE TO POWERSHELL SCRIPTING

Paul Kell

For my wife...

TABLE OF CONTENTS

Preface

If you've ever spent hours clicking through the same mind-numbing menus, repeating the same administrative tasks day after day, you're not alone. I've been there—managing users, rebooting servers, installing software, cleaning up logs—all with a creeping sense that there had to be a better way. That's when I found PowerShell.

At first, it was intimidating. A black screen. Strange syntax. Cryptic error messages. But as I pushed through the learning curve, something incredible happened: I stopped working *for* my computer and started making it work *for me*. Tasks that took hours became one-liners. Repetitive processes became scripts. Suddenly, I had more time, fewer mistakes, and a powerful new skill that boosted my confidence—and my career.

I wrote this book for people like you:

- **Beginners** who have no scripting experience
- **IT pros** stuck in GUI hell looking to break free
- **Learners** who want real-world examples, not theory
- **Future engineers** who want to automate everything

You don't need a computer science degree. You don't need to know how to code. You just need curiosity, a keyboard, and the drive to make your life easier.

This guide walks you step-by-step from the very basics all the way through practical PowerShell scripting in real environments—Windows, Active Directory, cloud platforms like AWS and Azure, and beyond. It's packed with scripts, projects, and insights that I wish I had when I started. Most importantly, this isn't just a book. It's a toolkit for your future.

By the time you finish, you'll be scripting with confidence, solving real problems, and creating value in ways that set you apart.

Here's to writing your first script—and the thousands that will follow.

Paul Kell

Cloud Security Engineer & Self-Taught Scripting Addict

Introduction to PowerShell

WHAT IS POWERSHELL?

PowerShell is a powerful task automation and configuration management framework from Microsoft, consisting of a command-line shell and a scripting language built on the .NET framework. Introduced in 2006, PowerShell was designed to address the limitations of traditional Windows command-line interfaces and to give administrators a more robust tool for managing computers locally and remotely.

In recent years, PowerShell has evolved into a cross-platform tool, known as PowerShell Core, which runs on Windows, Linux, and macOS. Its widespread use in enterprise environments and its deep integration with Microsoft products have made it an essential skill for system administrators, DevOps professionals, and IT support staff.

The Origins and Evolution of PowerShell

PowerShell was born out of a need to modernize Windows scripting and administration. Before PowerShell, Windows administrators relied primarily on graphical tools and the traditional Command Prompt (cmd.exe), which offered limited functionality and poor scripting capabilities.

Jeffrey Snover, a Microsoft engineer, led the initiative that became PowerShell. His vision, described in the "Monad Manifesto," proposed a new model for managing systems using a command-line interface combined with a powerful scripting language. That vision culminated in PowerShell 1.0, which shipped with Windows Server 2008 and was also available as a separate download for earlier versions of Windows.

As PowerShell matured, new versions added more features, better error handling, and deeper integration with Windows Management

Instrumentation (WMI), the .NET framework, and later, Common Information Model (CIM). With the release of PowerShell Core 6 in 2016, Microsoft made PowerShell open-source and cross-platform. PowerShell 7, the successor to PowerShell Core, further improved compatibility with existing Windows PowerShell scripts while maintaining cross-platform capabilities.

Shell + Scripting Language

PowerShell combines the interactivity of a shell with the power of a programming language. This hybrid nature makes it ideal for both quick one-liners and complex scripts.

Unlike traditional shells that treat everything as text, PowerShell is object-oriented. Commands (called cmdlets) return .NET objects, not raw text. This allows for precise data manipulation, filtering, and formatting.

For example, consider the following PowerShell command:

```
Get-Process | Where-Object { $_.CPU -gt 100 } | Sort-Object
CPU -Descending
```

This command gets a list of processes, filters those that use more than 100 CPU units, and sorts them in descending order by CPU usage. Each command in the pipeline receives and outputs objects, making it far more powerful than traditional text-based pipelines.

Key Features of PowerShell

Cmdlets

PowerShell uses small, single-purpose commands known as cmdlets. These follow a Verb-Noun naming convention, such as Get-Process, Set-Service, or New-Item. This consistent syntax makes it easier to learn and predict the purpose of a cmdlet.

Pipelining

One of PowerShell's most powerful features is the pipeline. Output from one command can be passed as input to another, allowing for complex operations to be composed in a readable and modular way.

Scripting and Automation

PowerShell scripts are plain text files with a .ps1 extension.

Scripts can automate nearly any administrative task, including file manipulation, user management, system configuration, and software installation. Because scripts are composed of the same cmdlets used in the shell, users can easily graduate from interactive use to automation.

Remote Management

PowerShell supports remote execution of commands using PowerShell Remoting, based on Windows Remote Management (WinRM). This allows administrators to manage multiple machines from a central location.

Object-Based Output

Unlike many shells, which process and output only text, PowerShell outputs structured objects. These objects can be filtered, sorted, and formatted without complex parsing.

Extensibility

PowerShell supports modules and snap-ins to extend its functionality. You can create your own modules or use those published by the community and Microsoft in the PowerShell Gallery.

Cross-Platform Support

With the introduction of PowerShell Core, PowerShell can now run on Windows, Linux, and macOS. This makes it a viable tool for managing heterogeneous environments.

PowerShell vs. Command Prompt

While both PowerShell and Command Prompt are command-line interfaces, they differ significantly in capabilities and design philosophy. The Command Prompt is based on MS-DOS and is limited in terms of scripting and automation. PowerShell, on the other hand, is built on the .NET framework, supports object-oriented programming, and offers far more powerful tools for system management.

For example, listing the contents of a directory in Command Prompt looks like this:

```
dir
```

In PowerShell, the equivalent is:

```
Get-ChildItem
```

But unlike dir, Get-ChildItem returns a collection of objects representing files and directories. This allows for rich manipulation using further cmdlets or script logic.

Who Uses PowerShell?

PowerShell is used by a wide range of professionals, including:

- **System Administrators**: Automate administrative tasks, manage servers, configure services, and schedule regular jobs.
- **Helpdesk Technicians**: Troubleshoot systems, gather diagnostics, and deploy configurations.
- **DevOps Engineers**: Integrate PowerShell into CI/CD pipelines, deploy infrastructure as code (IaC), and manage cloud resources.
- **Security Professionals**: Perform forensic analysis, audit logs, and detect anomalies.
- **Developers**: Manage development environments, configure systems, and integrate with APIs and build tools.

Whether managing a single workstation or an entire enterprise network, PowerShell offers tools that scale.

Real-World Use Cases

PowerShell is used in countless real-world scenarios, such as:

- Creating new Active Directory users in bulk.
- Deploying software across hundreds of machines.
- Monitoring system performance and logging results.
- Querying installed software and checking compliance.
- Automatically generating reports for audits.
- Interacting with REST APIs.
- Automating Azure or AWS cloud infrastructure tasks.

PowerShell in the Cloud Era

PowerShell has adapted to the rise of cloud computing. Modules like Az for Azure and AWS Tools for PowerShell allow users to manage cloud resources directly. For example, you can spin up a new virtual machine or configure storage accounts without leaving the PowerShell interface.

Additionally, PowerShell integrates with CI/CD tools like Azure DevOps, GitHub Actions, and Jenkins. Scripts can be used in build and deployment pipelines, bringing automation and consistency to development workflows.

Getting Started with PowerShell

If you're new to PowerShell, the best way to get started is to open a PowerShell console and begin experimenting. The integrated help system is a powerful ally. For example, try:

```
Get-Help Get-Process
```

You can also discover available cmdlets with:

```
Get-Command
```

And explore how objects work by using:

```
Get-Process | Get-Member
```

These commands reveal the capabilities of PowerShell and demonstrate its consistency and discoverability.

Conclusion

PowerShell is far more than just a replacement for Command Prompt. It's a full-featured automation and configuration platform that empowers users to manage systems more effectively, securely, and at scale. Its deep integration with Windows, its object-oriented pipeline, and its cross-platform nature make it an invaluable tool for anyone working in IT today.

Whether you're looking to automate repetitive tasks, manage a complex network, or integrate with modern cloud platforms, PowerShell provides the tools to do the job. By mastering PowerShell, you're investing in a skill that opens doors across systems administration, DevOps, cloud computing, and beyond.

HISTORY AND EVOLUTION (WINDOWS POWERSHELL → POWERSHELL CORE)

PowerShell is not just a shell—it is a powerful scripting language and automation engine that has played a pivotal role in modern system administration. The story of PowerShell's evolution is a tale of strategic innovation, community feedback, and the drive to unify administrative tools across platforms. From its proprietary Windows beginnings to its current open-source, cross-platform form, PowerShell's journey illustrates the shifting landscape of IT needs and Microsoft's responsiveness to a rapidly changing world.

The Birth of Windows PowerShell

PowerShell's origin dates back to the early 2000s when Windows administrators faced increasing complexity in managing systems. Graphical User Interfaces (GUIs) were the norm, but they often lacked the power and scalability needed for enterprise environments. Microsoft recognized this gap and began work on a project initially codenamed "Monad."

Monad was conceived as a task-based command-line shell and scripting language designed to automate system management. Its formal release came in 2006 as **Windows PowerShell 1.0**, bundled with the Windows Management Framework for Windows XP, Windows Server 2003, and Windows Vista.

Windows PowerShell was built on the .NET Framework and introduced key concepts that set it apart:
- **Cmdlets**: Lightweight commands built on .NET.
- **Pipeline**: Allowing objects—not just text—to pass between commands.
- **Verb-Noun Naming Convention**: Standardized, self-descriptive command names like Get-Process.
- **Providers**: Tools that let users access different data stores like the registry or file system as if they were file structures.
- **Scripting Language**: A robust, object-oriented language suitable for both small tasks and complex automation.

Windows PowerShell quickly gained traction among system administrators who valued its flexibility and power.

The Maturing Tool: Versions 2.0 to 5.1

PowerShell evolved rapidly after its initial release. Each subsequent version added critical features:

PowerShell 2.0 (2009)

Included in Windows 7 and Windows Server 2008 R2, version 2.0 added:

- Remoting capabilities via WS-Management.
- The Integrated Scripting Environment (ISE).
- Background jobs and script debugging.

These additions significantly broadened PowerShell's utility in enterprise environments.

PowerShell 3.0 (2012)

Released with Windows 8 and Server 2012, PowerShell 3.0 improved scripting with:

- Simplified syntax (e.g., Where-Object shorthand).
- Improved cmdlet discovery with Show-Command.
- Robust workflows for long-running tasks.

PowerShell 4.0 (2013)

Came with Windows 8.1 and Server 2012 R2 and introduced:

- Desired State Configuration (DSC), a declarative platform for managing configuration.
- Enhanced debugging tools.

PowerShell 5.0 and 5.1 (2016)

The final versions under the Windows PowerShell name, included in Windows 10 and Server 2016:

- OneGet (PackageManagement) and PowerShellGet (for module management).
- Class-based object-oriented programming.
- Enhanced logging and security features.

PowerShell 5.1 marked the pinnacle of Windows PowerShell's development. However, it was still tethered to Windows and the .NET Framework.

The Paradigm Shift: PowerShell Core and Open Source

In 2016, Microsoft announced a seismic shift: PowerShell would become open-source and cross-platform. This decision aligned with Microsoft's broader embrace of open-source technologies and its commitment to supporting diverse computing environments.

PowerShell Core, based on **.NET Core**, was born. This stripped-down, modular version of PowerShell was designed to run on:

- Windows
- Linux (various distros)
- macOS

The initial release, **PowerShell Core 6.0**, launched in January 2018. This version aimed to offer a consistent scripting experience across platforms. Key aspects included:

- Modular design with reduced footprint.
- Compatibility with existing cmdlets (where possible).
- New cmdlets tailored for cross-platform functionality.

Despite being a new product line, PowerShell Core coexisted with Windows PowerShell, which remained in use—particularly for features not yet ported to Core (e.g., some Windows-specific modules).

PowerShell 7: The Unified Future

Microsoft listened to community feedback about fragmentation between Windows PowerShell and PowerShell Core. The solution was **PowerShell 7**, launched in March 2020.

This version, based on **.NET 5**, brought massive improvements:

- Unified support for Windows, Linux, and macOS.
- Improved backward compatibility with existing Windows PowerShell modules.
- New operators (??, ||, &&), parallel ForEach-Object, and pipeline chaining.
- Better error handling and simplified scripting.

PowerShell 7 also marked the return to a single, cohesive scripting platform. It bridged the gap between old and new while leveraging the speed and flexibility of the latest .NET Core releases.

Subsequent releases, including **PowerShell 7.1, 7.2 (LTS)**, and **7.3**, have continued this trend, focusing on:

- Performance optimization.
- Cloud-native development and automation.

- DevOps tooling enhancements.

From Windows-Only to Everywhere

The evolution from Windows PowerShell to PowerShell Core represents a fundamental shift in philosophy:

- **From Proprietary to Open Source**: PowerShell's code is now available on GitHub, encouraging community contributions and transparency.
- **From Windows-Only to Cross-Platform**: Native support for Linux and macOS has made PowerShell a first-class citizen in modern IT ecosystems.
- **From Admin Tool to Automation Framework**: PowerShell is now foundational in CI/CD, cloud automation (especially with Azure), and configuration management.

This change has also impacted the user base. PowerShell is no longer just for system administrators—it is now widely used by developers, DevOps engineers, cloud architects, and security professionals.

Community and Ecosystem Growth

The PowerShell community has played a significant role in shaping the language's direction. Initiatives such as:

- **PowerShell Gallery** (for sharing modules).
- **PSReadLine** (enhanced shell interactivity).
- **Pester** (testing framework for scripts).
- **PlatyPS** (documentation generator).

...have all helped mature the ecosystem. In addition, projects like **Azure PowerShell** and **AWS Tools for PowerShell** highlight PowerShell's importance in multi-cloud environments.

Conclusion: A Living, Evolving Platform

PowerShell has transformed from a Windows-centric scripting tool to a global, cross-platform automation solution. As of PowerShell 7 and beyond, Microsoft has committed to regular updates and long-term support (LTS) versions, ensuring stability for enterprises and flexibility for innovators.

Whether you're managing local systems, automating cloud infrastructure, or integrating CI/CD pipelines, PowerShell provides a reliable, expressive, and extensible toolset. Understanding this evolution is key to appreciating PowerShell's current capabilities—and its promising future.

This historical perspective lays a strong foundation for the scripting journey ahead. The next chapters will dive into practical applications, syntax mastery, and real-world automation scenarios.

WHY LEARN POWERSHELL?

PowerShell is a powerful and flexible command-line shell and scripting language designed specifically for system administration and automation. If you're new to IT, development, or scripting, you might wonder why PowerShell is worth your time and effort. The answer is simple: learning PowerShell can dramatically boost your efficiency, reduce repetitive tasks, enhance system management capabilities, and open doors to automation that are critical in modern IT environments. This chapter will delve into why learning PowerShell is not just beneficial—but essential—for anyone working with Windows systems and beyond.

A Tool Designed for Administrators

Unlike traditional command-line tools or scripting languages like VBScript or Bash, PowerShell was created with system administrators in mind. Its design philosophy revolves around giving IT professionals a consistent, powerful interface to manage local and remote systems, manipulate system objects, and automate administrative tasks.

PowerShell provides access to the full power of the .NET framework, making it capable of performing tasks far beyond the limitations of older tools. It uses cmdlets (pronounced "command-lets"), which are simple, task-oriented commands that follow a verb-noun naming pattern (e.g., Get-Process, Start-Service, Set-ExecutionPolicy). This naming convention makes it easier to discover and remember commands.

Consistency and Discoverability

One of PowerShell's most significant advantages is its consistency. Each cmdlet follows a standardized syntax, which means once you understand how one command works, you can easily understand others. For example, the use of Get-, Set-, Start-, Stop-, and Remove- in command names creates a predictable and logical structure.

PowerShell also includes powerful discovery tools like Get-Command, Get-Help, and Get-Member. These commands help users explore available functionality, learn command syntax, and inspect the properties and methods of objects returned by cmdlets. This built-in guidance system is invaluable for beginners who are learning the ropes.

Object-Oriented Output

Unlike traditional command shells that output plain text, PowerShell works with .NET objects. This distinction is crucial. Because cmdlets return rich objects rather than just text, you can easily access properties and methods of those objects for further manipulation or filtering.

For instance, running Get-Service doesn't just display a list of services in text—it returns a collection of service objects that you can filter, sort, and manipulate programmatically:

```
Get-Service | Where-Object {$_.Status -eq 'Running'} | Sort-Object DisplayName
```

This object-based pipeline makes it possible to chain commands in powerful ways that are simply not possible with traditional shell scripting.

Automation and Scripting

One of PowerShell's most celebrated features is its scripting capability. Whether you're writing a one-liner to restart a group of services or building a complex script to automate user account provisioning, PowerShell makes it possible to streamline repetitive tasks and reduce human error.

Scripts can be saved as .ps1 files and reused or scheduled via Task Scheduler. PowerShell also supports parameters, conditionals, loops, and error handling—making it a full-fledged programming language tailored for automation.

Here's a simple script example to check disk space and send an alert:

```
$drives = Get-PSDrive -PSProvider FileSystem
foreach ($drive in $drives) {
    if ($drive.Free -lt 1GB) {
        Write-Output "Warning: Low space on $($drive.Name)
drive."
    }
}
```

Remote Management and Scalability

PowerShell remoting allows you to execute commands on remote systems as if you were sitting in front of them. This feature is invaluable in enterprise environments where managing hundreds or thousands of machines individually is not feasible.

With a single line, you can manage multiple computers:

```
Invoke-Command -ComputerName Server01, Server02 -ScriptBlock
{ Get-Process }
```

Combined with tools like Desired State Configuration (DSC) and Windows Admin Center, PowerShell enables scalable infrastructure management and configuration enforcement.

Cross-Platform Capabilities

With the introduction of PowerShell Core (now simply referred to as PowerShell 7+), the language became truly cross-platform. You can now run PowerShell on Windows, macOS, and Linux, making it an increasingly versatile tool in heterogeneous environments.

This also means scripts can be more portable and integrated with diverse systems—especially beneficial for DevOps workflows and cloud environments.

Integration with Modern Tools and Cloud Services

PowerShell integrates tightly with modern management platforms such as Microsoft Azure, Microsoft 365, and AWS. It has dedicated modules (e.g., Az, AWSPowerShell) that allow you to manage cloud resources directly from your terminal or scripts.

Need to spin up a virtual machine in Azure? PowerShell can do that. Want to bulk-update users in Microsoft 365? PowerShell has your back. This integration empowers you to orchestrate complex environments efficiently.

Active Community and Abundant Learning Resources

PowerShell enjoys robust community support. From official documentation to community-contributed modules on the PowerShell Gallery, help is never far away. Websites like Stack Overflow, Reddit, and the PowerShell Discord channel are full of experienced professionals who can provide assistance.

Additionally, Microsoft Learn, Pluralsight, Udemy, and YouTube offer high-quality tutorials for every skill level.

A Stepping Stone to DevOps and Infrastructure as Code

PowerShell is often the first step toward mastering DevOps practices. Tools like Azure DevOps, GitHub Actions, and CI/CD pipelines often incorporate PowerShell scripts. Infrastructure as Code (IaC) tools such as Terraform or Ansible often work alongside PowerShell for configuration and orchestration.

By learning PowerShell, you're laying the groundwork for modern, agile, automated infrastructure management.

Career Advancement and Marketability

In today's IT job market, knowing PowerShell is a significant advantage. Many job postings for system administrators, DevOps engineers, and IT support professionals list PowerShell proficiency as a requirement or preferred skill.

Demonstrating your ability to write efficient scripts and automate tasks can make you stand out to employers and improve your prospects for promotions, raises, and more advanced roles.

Final Thoughts

Learning PowerShell isn't just about writing scripts. It's about transforming how you interact with your systems. It's about saving time, reducing errors, gaining control, and positioning yourself for long-term success in a tech-driven world. Whether you're managing a single Windows PC or thousands of cloud instances, PowerShell gives you the tools to work smarter, not harder.

In the chapters to come, we'll guide you from the very basics of launching the PowerShell console to writing powerful automation scripts that can revolutionize your workflow. Get ready to empower your career—one command at a time.

Installing and Setting Up PowerShell

INSTALLING POWERSHELL ON WINDOWS, LINUX, MACOS

PowerShell has evolved from a Windows-only scripting language to a powerful cross-platform automation and configuration management framework. Whether you're a system administrator, developer, or enthusiast, PowerShell can be a critical tool in your toolkit. This section will guide you through the process of installing PowerShell on the three major operating systems: Windows, Linux, and macOS. By the end of this section, you will have PowerShell installed and ready to use, regardless of your platform.

Windows

Windows PowerShell vs. PowerShell (Core)

Before we begin, it's essential to differentiate between **Windows PowerShell** (the legacy version built into Windows) and **PowerShell 7+** (also called PowerShell Core), which is cross-platform. Windows PowerShell is installed by default on most Windows systems but is no longer actively developed beyond version 5.1. PowerShell 7+ is the future of PowerShell and should be used for new development and cross-platform compatibility.

Method 1: Installing via Microsoft Store (Recommended)

The Microsoft Store provides the easiest method to install PowerShell on supported Windows versions (Windows 10 and later).

1. Open the **Microsoft Store**.
2. Search for **PowerShell**.
3. Click **Get** or **Install**.
4. After installation, you can open PowerShell from the Start Menu.

The Microsoft Store version is automatically updated, ensuring you're always using the latest release.

Method 2: Installing via MSI Installer

For systems without access to the Microsoft Store (e.g., Windows Server), use the MSI installer:

1. Visit the official GitHub repository for PowerShell: https://github.com/PowerShell/PowerShell
2. Navigate to the **Releases** section.
3. Download the latest .msi file for your system architecture (x64 or x86).
4. Run the installer and follow the prompts.
5. Choose the option to add PowerShell to your PATH environment variable.
6. Launch PowerShell via Start Menu or Command Prompt using pwsh.

Method 3: Installing via Winget

If you have Windows Package Manager (winget), you can use it to install PowerShell:

```
winget install --id Microsoft.PowerShell --source winget
```

This is a great option for scriptable installations or automated deployments.

Linux

PowerShell is supported on most major Linux distributions, including Ubuntu, Debian, CentOS, Red Hat, Fedora, and Arch Linux. Microsoft provides package repositories to simplify the installation process.

General Instructions

All Linux installations require root or sudo access.

Ubuntu and Debian

1. Update the package list and install prerequisites:

```
sudo apt update
sudo apt install -y wget apt-transport-https software-
properties-common
```

2. Download and register the Microsoft repository:

```
wget -q https://packages.microsoft.com/config/ubuntu/20.04/
packages-microsoft-prod.deb
```

```
sudo dpkg -i packages-microsoft-prod.deb
```
3. Install PowerShell:
```
sudo apt update
sudo apt install -y powershell
```
4. Launch PowerShell:
```
pwsh
```

Red Hat and CentOS

1. Register the Microsoft repository:
```
sudo rpm --import https://packages.microsoft.com/keys/
microsoft.asc
sudo curl -o /etc/yum.repos.d/microsoft.repo https://
packages.microsoft.com/config/rhel/7/prod.repo
```
2. Install PowerShell:
```
sudo yum install -y powershell
```
3. Start PowerShell:
```
pwsh
```

Fedora

Fedora users can follow similar steps:

1. Add the Microsoft repository:
```
sudo rpm --import https://packages.microsoft.com/keys/
microsoft.asc
sudo curl -o /etc/yum.repos.d/microsoft.repo https://
packages.microsoft.com/config/fedora/38/prod.repo
```
2. Install PowerShell:
```
sudo dnf install -y powershell
```
3. Launch PowerShell:
```
pwsh
```

Arch Linux

On Arch, PowerShell is available via the AUR (Arch User Repository).

1. Use an AUR helper such as yay:
```
yay -S powershell-bin
```
2. Run PowerShell:
```
pwsh
```

macOS

macOS users can install PowerShell using Homebrew, a package manager for macOS.

Prerequisites

Ensure Homebrew is installed. If not, install it:

```
/bin/bash -c "$(curl -fsSL https://
raw.githubusercontent.com/Homebrew/install/HEAD/install.sh)"
```

Installing PowerShell

1. Tap the cask for Microsoft tools:

```
brew tap microsoft/powershell
```

2. Install PowerShell:

```
brew install --cask powershell
```

3. Launch PowerShell:

```
pwsh
```

Alternatively, you can download and install the .pkg file from GitHub:

1. Go to: https://github.com/PowerShell/PowerShell/releases
2. Download the latest .pkg installer for macOS.
3. Double-click the installer and follow the prompts.
4. Launch PowerShell via Terminal using pwsh.

Verifying Your Installation

After installation, confirm the version of PowerShell:

```
$PSVersionTable.PSVersion
```

This command will return the version number and confirm that pwsh is functional.

Updating PowerShell

To stay current with the latest features and security patches, update PowerShell regularly:

- **Windows (Microsoft Store)**: Updates automatically.
- **Windows (MSI)**: Download and reinstall newer versions manually.
- **Linux/macOS**: Use the same commands to reinstall, which upgrades to the latest version.

You can also use PowerShell to check for updates programmatically in scripts.

Uninstalling PowerShell

Uninstall methods vary by platform:
- **Windows**: Use "Apps & Features" or `winget uninstall Microsoft.PowerShell`
- **Linux**: Use your package manager: `sudo apt remove powershell`
- **macOS**: If installed via Homebrew, use `brew uninstall powershell`

Conclusion

Installing PowerShell is a straightforward process on all major operating systems. Microsoft has made significant strides to ensure the process is seamless and consistent across platforms. Whether you prefer graphical installers or command-line tools, you can get PowerShell up and running quickly.

Once installed, you'll unlock a powerful environment for scripting, automation, and configuration management across systems. Next, we'll explore configuring your PowerShell environment for productivity and customization.

SETTING EXECUTION POLICY

PowerShell is a powerful scripting environment designed to help system administrators and power users automate administrative tasks and configuration management. One of the foundational components of using PowerShell securely and effectively is understanding and configuring the **Execution Policy**. This chapter covers what execution policies are, why they exist, how to set them, and best practices to follow.

What is an Execution Policy?

The PowerShell **Execution Policy** is a security feature that determines the conditions under which PowerShell loads configuration files and runs scripts. It acts as a gatekeeper to help prevent the accidental execution of malicious scripts. It's not a security system in itself like antivirus software, but rather a way to protect users from unintentionally running untrusted code.

Microsoft introduced the execution policy to balance security with flexibility, especially in enterprise environments. It is important to note that the execution policy is not a foolproof security boundary — users with sufficient privileges can always override it. However, it is a valuable first line of defense.

Types of Execution Policies

PowerShell supports several execution policies, each offering a different level of script execution control:

1. **Restricted**
   - This is the default policy on Windows client systems.
   - It does not allow any scripts to run.
   - Only interactive commands can be executed.
2. **AllSigned**
   - Scripts can run, but they must be digitally signed by a trusted publisher.
   - This helps ensure that the script has not been altered since it was signed.
   - Useful in environments with strict script security requirements.
3. **RemoteSigned**
   - Scripts created on the local computer can run.
   - Scripts downloaded from the internet must be signed by a trusted publisher.
   - This policy helps prevent running potentially unsafe remote code.
4. **Unrestricted**

- Allows all scripts to run, but warns the user before running downloaded scripts.
- Not recommended for production environments.

5. **Bypass**
- Nothing is blocked or warned.
- This policy is typically used when a script is run by an application that manages its own security.

6. **Undefined**
- No policy is set at the specified scope.
- If all scopes are Undefined, PowerShell reverts to Restricted on Windows clients.

Scopes of Execution Policy

Execution policies can be set at various scopes, allowing fine-grained control depending on the context:

1. **MachinePolicy**: Set by Group Policy for all users on the computer. Cannot be overridden by users.
2. **UserPolicy**: Set by Group Policy for the current user. Also cannot be overridden.
3. **Process**: Applies only to the current PowerShell session. Once the session is closed, the policy is gone.
4. **CurrentUser**: Affects only the current user.
5. **LocalMachine**: Affects all users on the computer.

When multiple policies are set, the one with the highest precedence takes effect. The order of precedence (from highest to lowest) is:

1. MachinePolicy
2. UserPolicy
3. Process
4. CurrentUser
5. LocalMachine

Viewing the Current Execution Policy

To check the current effective policy, use the following command:

```
Get-ExecutionPolicy
```

To view policies for all scopes:
```
Get-ExecutionPolicy -List
```

This command displays a list of all defined policies across the different scopes, helping administrators understand where policies are being enforced.

Setting the Execution Policy

To change the execution policy, use the Set-ExecutionPolicy cmdlet. Here is an example:
```
Set-ExecutionPolicy RemoteSigned
```

You can also specify the scope:
```
Set-ExecutionPolicy -ExecutionPolicy RemoteSigned -Scope
CurrentUser
```

This command sets the policy to RemoteSigned for only the current user, leaving the system-wide policy unchanged.

To bypass prompts, add the -Force parameter:
```
Set-ExecutionPolicy -ExecutionPolicy RemoteSigned -Scope
CurrentUser -Force
```

Best Practices

- **Use the Least Permissive Policy That Still Allows You to Work**
- Avoid setting policies like Unrestricted or Bypass unless absolutely necessary.
- RemoteSigned offers a good balance for most users.
1. **Sign Your Scripts**
- Especially in enterprise environments, digitally signing your scripts adds a layer of trust and integrity.
2. **Leverage Group Policy in Enterprise Environments**
- Set MachinePolicy or UserPolicy using Group Policy Objects (GPOs) to enforce policies across your organization.

3. **Understand the Source of Your Scripts**
- Scripts downloaded from the internet are marked as such via the NTFS "Zone.Identifier" metadata. Use Unblock-File to remove the marker if you trust the source:

```
Unblock-File -Path .\yourscript.ps1
```

4. **Don't Rely Solely on Execution Policy for Security**
- Always pair execution policy with good security hygiene: antivirus, user access control, and regular script auditing.

Common Use Cases

- **Developers on Local Machines**: May choose RemoteSigned to allow running and testing locally written scripts without being overly permissive.
- **CI/CD Pipelines**: Often set to Bypass temporarily in the script to ensure execution in controlled environments.
- **Enterprise Admins**: Use AllSigned with GPO enforcement to ensure that only approved scripts run in production.

Troubleshooting Execution Policy Errors

Sometimes you may run into errors such as:

```
File .\myscript.ps1 cannot be loaded because running scripts
is disabled on this system.
```

This typically occurs under the Restricted policy. Use the Set-ExecutionPolicy cmdlet to allow script execution.

For example:

```
Set-ExecutionPolicy RemoteSigned -Scope CurrentUser
```

You may also see this when running scripts via double-click or from another application. In such cases, consider launching a PowerShell session with the appropriate policy or embedding policy changes within the script (not recommended unless in fully trusted environments).

Temporarily Changing Execution Policy for a Single Session

If you want to run a script without changing the policy system-wide, start PowerShell with a temporary execution policy:

```
powershell.exe -ExecutionPolicy Bypass -File .\myscript.ps1
```

This is especially useful in CI/CD or automation scenarios where you want to avoid persistent changes.

Summary

The PowerShell Execution Policy is an essential concept for script security. It helps administrators enforce safe scripting practices while providing enough flexibility for development and automation. By understanding the different policy types, scopes, and best practices, you can ensure your PowerShell environment remains secure and functional.

Whether you are a beginner just writing your first script or an enterprise administrator managing hundreds of systems, configuring the right execution policy is a critical step toward mastering PowerShell scripting.

USING POWERSHELL CONSOLE VS POWERSHELL ISE VS VS CODE

When getting started with PowerShell scripting, one of the first decisions you'll need to make is which environment to use for writing and executing your scripts. While all PowerShell environments can run the same commands and scripts, each tool offers different benefits depending on your skill level, scripting needs, and personal preferences. In this section, we'll explore the three primary interfaces used by PowerShell users: the traditional PowerShell Console, the PowerShell Integrated Scripting Environment (ISE), and Visual Studio Code (VS Code). We'll compare their features, strengths, and weaknesses to help you decide which is right for your workflow.

PowerShell Console

The PowerShell Console is the most basic and lightweight way to interact with PowerShell. It comes preinstalled with Windows and offers a simple, no-frills command-line interface.

Features

- **Fast startup**: Since it's a lightweight command-line application, the PowerShell Console loads quickly.
- **Direct command execution**: You can run ad-hoc commands and scripts directly without needing to save them to a file.
- **Built-in history**: The console retains your command history, allowing you to scroll through previous commands using the arrow keys.

Strengths

- **Minimal system resources**: The console uses very little memory and CPU, making it ideal for low-resource environments.
- **Simplicity**: For users who prefer a straightforward interface or are executing quick administrative tasks, the console gets the job done without distractions.
- **Remote accessibility**: It's often the easiest tool to use on remote systems accessed via SSH or Remote Desktop.

Weaknesses

- **Lack of advanced editing**: The PowerShell Console has very limited support for script editing, with no syntax highlighting, IntelliSense, or debugging capabilities.
- **No integrated help tools**: You won't find tooltips, parameter hints, or function auto-completion.
- **Not ideal for large scripts**: Managing long scripts in the console can be tedious and error-prone.

PowerShell ISE

PowerShell ISE is a GUI-based environment specifically designed for writing and testing PowerShell scripts. It comes installed with Windows PowerShell (up to version 5.1) but has been deprecated in favor of more modern tools.

Features

- **Multi-tab scripting panes**: ISE allows you to have multiple scripts open at once in separate tabs.
- **Color-coded syntax**: Keywords, variables, and strings are color-

coded to improve readability.

- **Built-in debugger**: You can set breakpoints, step through code, and watch variable values in real-time.
- **IntelliSense**: Auto-completion and tooltips help guide your scripting with available cmdlets and syntax.

Strengths

- **User-friendly interface**: Beginners often find ISE more approachable due to its visual layout and integrated features.
- **Inline script testing**: Scripts can be run directly in the editor, and output appears in the lower pane.
- **Great for learning**: Its interactive experience helps new scripters understand the structure and flow of PowerShell code.

Weaknesses

- **Limited extensibility**: Compared to VS Code, ISE lacks plugin and extension support.
- **Performance issues**: For very large scripts or extended sessions, ISE may experience slowdowns or crashes.
- **Deprecated status**: Microsoft is no longer developing new features for ISE, and future updates will focus on bug fixes only.

Visual Studio Code (VS Code)

Visual Studio Code has rapidly become the editor of choice for PowerShell professionals. It's a free, open-source editor developed by Microsoft with support for hundreds of languages and features, including PowerShell.

Features

- **Highly customizable**: VS Code supports themes, extensions, keyboard shortcuts, and settings tailored to individual preferences.
- **PowerShell extension**: This extension brings IntelliSense, syntax highlighting, code snippets, and rich debugging tools to VS Code.
- **Git integration**: Source control is built-in, allowing you to commit and push changes to repositories without leaving the editor.
- **Terminal support**: An integrated terminal allows you to run

PowerShell scripts and other shell commands side by side.

Strengths

- **Cross-platform compatibility**: VS Code runs on Windows, macOS, and Linux, making it ideal for users working in diverse environments.
- **Modern interface**: The UI is sleek, responsive, and intuitive for both new and advanced users.
- **Rich ecosystem**: Thousands of extensions enable integration with Azure, Docker, Python, and other tools used in DevOps and cloud operations.
- **Robust debugging**: Breakpoints, watches, stack traces, and variable inspection are easy to use and offer a seamless troubleshooting experience.

Weaknesses

- **Initial learning curve**: New users may find the number of options and settings overwhelming at first.
- **Requires setup**: To use PowerShell effectively in VS Code, you need to install the PowerShell extension and configure a few settings.
- **Heavier resource usage**: Compared to the console or ISE, VS Code uses more memory and CPU.

Which Should You Use?

The answer depends on your goals, environment, and experience level. Here are a few guidelines:

- **Just starting out?** Try **PowerShell ISE**. It's beginner-friendly and provides a solid set of tools to help you learn the basics without overwhelming you.
- **Need something simple and quick?** Use the **PowerShell Console**. It's fast and sufficient for running a few commands or small scripts.
- **Looking to go pro?** Embrace **VS Code**. While it takes some time to set up and get comfortable, it offers the most powerful feature set and is the most future-proof option.

If you're managing multiple systems, working with cloud services, building modules, or writing production-ready scripts, VS Code will become your best friend. On the other hand, if you're just automating basic admin tasks or learning the language, ISE still holds its own — just be aware of its limitations and eventual obsolescence.

Transitioning Between Tools

As you gain confidence in PowerShell scripting, it's natural to progress from one tool to the next. Many users begin in ISE and move to VS Code as their needs grow. Knowing how to use all three tools can give you the flexibility to adapt to any environment or task.

- Start with **ISE** for learning and prototyping small scripts.
- Use the **Console** when working directly on servers or in restricted environments.
- Adopt **VS Code** when you're ready to take scripting seriously and need version control, debugging, and modular script organization.

Final Thoughts

Each PowerShell interface serves a purpose. The key is not to choose one and stick with it rigidly, but rather to understand their respective strengths and use the right tool for the job. For beginners writing simple scripts or exploring the language, ISE remains a solid choice. For advanced scripting, module creation, or integration with CI/CD pipelines, VS Code offers a full development environment with virtually limitless potential.

No matter which environment you start with, the fundamentals of PowerShell remain the same. Choose the interface that supports your learning curve and productivity, then evolve your toolset as your scripting journey unfolds.

PowerShell Basics

CMDLETS, PARAMETERS, AND PIPELINING

PowerShell is a powerful scripting language and automation framework built on .NET, designed primarily for system administrators and advanced users. One of the cornerstones of PowerShell is its use of **cmdlets**, **parameters**, and **pipelining** to create highly efficient and readable scripts. This chapter breaks down these essential concepts in a beginner-friendly manner.

What Are Cmdlets?

Cmdlets (pronounced "command-lets") are lightweight commands used in the PowerShell environment. Unlike traditional executable programs or scripts, cmdlets are .NET classes that perform a single function. PowerShell includes a rich set of built-in cmdlets, and you can also create your own or install third-party modules.

Characteristics of Cmdlets
- **Verb-Noun Naming Convention**: Cmdlets follow a strict naming convention of Verb-Noun, such as Get-Process, Set-Item, or Remove-User.
- **Consistency**: This naming pattern ensures readability and predictability.
- **Output**: Cmdlets typically return objects, not plain text, which allows for further manipulation through the pipeline.

Examples of Common Cmdlets
- Get-Help: Displays help information about cmdlets and concepts.
- Get-Command: Lists all available cmdlets and functions.
- Get-Service: Retrieves the status of services on the system.
- Set-ExecutionPolicy: Changes the user preference for the PowerShell script execution policy.

Understanding Parameters

Parameters are values you can pass to cmdlets to customize their behavior. They add flexibility and power to each command by allowing users to fine-tune what a cmdlet does.

Types of Parameters

1. **Positional Parameters**: These can be entered without specifying the parameter name, based on the position in the command.
2. **Named Parameters**: Require the parameter name and an associated value, providing clarity.
3. **Switch Parameters**: Boolean values that are either present or not. Example: -Force, -Verbose.

Example: Using Parameters with Cmdlets

```
Get-Process -Name notepad -Verbose
```

In this example:

- -Name is a named parameter.
- notepad is the value passed to the -Name parameter.
- -Verbose is a switch parameter that provides detailed execution messages.

Getting Parameter Info

Use Get-Help to explore available parameters:

```
Get-Help Get-Process -Full
```

This will show a comprehensive list of all parameters, their aliases, and how to use them.

Introduction to Pipelining

Pipelining allows you to pass the output of one cmdlet as input to another. This is done using the | (pipe) symbol. Pipelines enhance readability and reduce the need for temporary variables or extra steps.

Basic Pipeline Example

```
Get-Process | Where-Object { $_.CPU -gt 100 }
```

Explanation:

- Get-Process retrieves all running processes.

- The pipe (|) passes the output to Where-Object, which filters based on CPU usage.
- $_ represents the current object in the pipeline.

Advantages of Pipelining

- **Efficiency**: Processes objects one at a time, reducing memory usage.
- **Readability**: Chains logical steps together in a linear fashion.
- **Modularity**: Each cmdlet does one job, making debugging and reuse easier.

Chaining Multiple Cmdlets

```
Get-Service | Where-Object { $_.Status -eq "Running" } |
Sort-Object DisplayName
```

This command:

1. Gets all services.
2. Filters only running services.
3. Sorts them alphabetically by display name.

Working with Objects in the Pipeline

PowerShell treats everything as an object. Cmdlets emit structured data (objects), not plain text. This makes it easier to filter, sort, and transform data.

Accessing Object Properties

You can access properties of objects passed in the pipeline using dot notation:

```
Get-Process | Select-Object Name, CPU
```

Here, only the Name and CPU properties of each process are selected.

Filtering with Where-Object

```
Get-EventLog -LogName Application | Where-Object {
$_.EntryType -eq "Error" }
```

This filters application logs to show only error entries.

Advanced Parameter Techniques

Parameter Aliases

Aliases offer shorthand versions of parameter names:

```
Get-ChildItem -Recurse
# Equivalent to:
Get-ChildItem -r
```

Use Get-Alias to view cmdlet aliases:

```
Get-Alias
```

Parameter Sets

Some cmdlets have multiple parameter sets that change the behavior of the cmdlet. Each set is mutually exclusive.

Mandatory Parameters

Some parameters must be provided for a cmdlet to execute:

```
Read-Host -Prompt "Enter your name"
```

Best Practices

Use Get-Help Often

Help is always available and should be your first stop when learning a new cmdlet.

Leverage Pipelining for Clarity

Instead of writing complex logic inside a script block, use the pipeline to break tasks into discrete steps.

Be Explicit with Parameters

Even when positional parameters are allowed, being explicit improves readability and helps when sharing scripts.

Use Aliases Sparingly

Avoid using aliases in scripts intended for others, as it reduces readability.

Real-World Example: Cleaning Up Temp Files

```
Get-ChildItem -Path "C:\Temp" -Recurse -Force | Where-Object
{ !$_.PSIsContainer } | Remove-Item -Force
```

This script:

1. Retrieves all items in C:\Temp, including hidden ones.
2. Filters out folders (keeps only files).
3. Deletes them forcefully.

Conclusion

Cmdlets, parameters, and pipelining are the building blocks of PowerShell scripting. Understanding how they work individually—and together—enables users to write efficient, readable, and powerful scripts. As you grow more comfortable with these tools, you'll find that even complex administrative tasks can be accomplished with just a few lines of code.

Keep exploring, try variations, and use the help system liberally. With practice, PowerShell scripting becomes second nature—and cmdlets, parameters, and pipelines will be your most trusted allies.

WORKING WITH HELP AND GET-COMMAND

PowerShell is a powerful tool for both beginners and seasoned administrators alike. One of the key reasons it has become such a dominant force in the scripting and automation space is because of how self-documenting it is. For those new to PowerShell scripting, understanding how to find help, explore cmdlets, and discover functionality is one of the most important skills to develop. This chapter is focused on two foundational components of that process: Get-Help and Get-Command.

Why Documentation is a Superpower

Before diving into the technical details of Get-Help and Get-Command, let's understand why these two cmdlets matter so much.

In traditional programming or scripting environments, finding information about how a command or function works often requires reading through external documentation, searching online forums, or digging into long manuals. PowerShell turns this process into an integrated, seamless experience.

PowerShell's built-in help system means that every cmdlet comes with documentation that is accessible right from the shell. That means no need to minimize your terminal or switch to a browser to find examples or understand syntax. When used effectively, Get-Help and Get-Command can make the learning process intuitive and efficient.

Introduction to Get-Help

Get-Help is your gateway to understanding any command, concept, or function in PowerShell. It's like a built-in encyclopedia tailored to your specific environment.

Basic Syntax

```
Get-Help <command-name>
```

This returns the basic help entry for the command.

Example

```
Get-Help Get-Process
```

This will return a description of the Get-Process cmdlet, its syntax, and available parameters.

Understanding the Output

When you run Get-Help, the output includes:

- **Name**: The name of the cmdlet.
- **Synopsis**: A brief description.
- **Syntax**: Different ways the cmdlet can be used.
- **Parameters**: Each available parameter with its description.
- **Remarks**: Notes about functionality and usage.

Getting Examples

To see real-world usage examples:

```
Get-Help Get-Process -Examples
```

This is especially useful when learning a new command.

Getting Full Details

```
Get-Help Get-Process -Detailed
```

Provides all parameter descriptions and usage scenarios.

See Everything

```
Get-Help Get-Process -Full
```

This displays the complete help file for the command.

Update-Help

When first using PowerShell, you may notice that the help files are not installed locally. To download them:

```
Update-Help
```

This command pulls the latest help documentation from Microsoft and caches it for offline access.

Using Get-Command to Discover Cmdlets

Get-Command is the other side of the coin. While Get-Help explains how to use a known command, Get-Command helps you find the command you *need*.

Basic Syntax

```
Get-Command
```

Running this by itself lists every available cmdlet, function, and external command. That's overwhelming, so it's best to filter it down.

Filtering by Verb

```
Get-Command -Verb Get
```

This filters commands that perform a "get" operation. Useful for exploring.

Filtering by Noun

```
Get-Command -Noun Service
```

Lists commands that deal with services, like Get-Service, Start-Service, etc.

Finding Commands by Name

```
Get-Command *service*
```

Wildcard searches help locate all commands with 'service' in their name.

Show Command Types

Get-Command returns several types:

- Cmdlet
- Function
- Alias
- Application

You can filter these too:

```
Get-Command -CommandType Cmdlet
```

Finding Function Definitions

```
Get-Command Get-MyCustomFunction | Select-Object -
ExpandProperty Definition
```

If a function is defined in your session, this retrieves the script code itself.

Combining Get-Help and Get-Command

The real power of these two cmdlets shines when they're used together. For example, suppose you want to manage services but don't know the exact commands.

Step 1: Use Get-Command to discover possibilities.

```
Get-Command *service*
```

Step 2: Use Get-Help to learn how to use each one.

```
Get-Help Start-Service -Full
```

This process helps you go from "I want to manage services" to "I know how to stop, start, and configure services with confidence."

Bonus: Get-Help for Concepts and About Topics

PowerShell also includes conceptual help articles under the about_ namespace. These cover broader topics like scripting techniques, common practices, and advanced features.

```
Get-Help about_*
```

This lists all conceptual help topics.

Examples:

```
Get-Help about_If
Get-Help about_ForEach
Get-Help about_Functions
```

These entries are vital when you're learning the PowerShell language, not just individual commands.

Practical Exercise: Exploring Services

Let's walk through a mini-lab to solidify your understanding.

Goal: Explore how to find and use commands related to system services.

1. **Discover Commands**

```
Get-Command *service*
```

1. **Read Help for Key Commands**

```
Get-Help Get-Service -Full
Get-Help Start-Service -Examples
```

1. **Try Them Out**

```
Get-Service
Start-Service -Name wuauserv
Stop-Service -Name wuauserv
```

1. **Learn More**

```
Get-Help about_Services
```

This type of exploration builds both muscle memory and confidence.

Summary

- Get-Help is your built-in manual for any command or concept.
- Get-Command helps you discover available commands by name, verb, noun, or wildcard.
- Use Update-Help to get the latest local documentation.
- Use conceptual about_ topics to deepen your scripting knowledge.
- Combine both tools for a powerful, self-directed learning experience.

Mastering Get-Help and Get-Command early in your PowerShell journey means you'll never feel lost or stuck. These cmdlets transform PowerShell into a self-learning environment where curiosity is rewarded with instant, actionable answers.

In the next chapter, we'll explore **cmdlet parameters** in more detail, learning how to pass data, filter results, and create efficient scripts that do exactly what you want them to.

UNDERSTANDING THE VERB-NOUN SYNTAX

PowerShell, as a scripting language and interactive shell, is built around a design philosophy that emphasizes readability, consistency, and discoverability. One of the most critical and foundational elements that supports these goals is its *verb-noun syntax*. Understanding this syntax is essential for writing effective, efficient, and standardized PowerShell scripts. This chapter will delve into the purpose, structure, best practices, and benefits of the verb-noun syntax, offering examples and guidance for beginners to master this core concept.

What Is Verb-Noun Syntax?

In PowerShell, all cmdlets (pronounced *command-lets*) follow a standardized naming convention: they consist of a **verb**, followed by a **noun**, separated by a hyphen. This syntax is not just a naming preference—it is a carefully crafted rule that ensures consistency across the scripting language.

Examples:
- Get-Process
- Set-Item
- New-User
- Remove-Item
- Start-Service

Each cmdlet name is designed to clearly express its intent through this pairing. The **verb** specifies the action, and the **noun** identifies the target of that action.

Why Verb-Noun Matters

The use of a consistent verb-noun structure provides several advantages:

1. Discoverability

PowerShell includes built-in mechanisms for discovering commands, and the consistent naming format makes it easier to find what you need. For example, using the Get-Command cmdlet with a wildcard:

```
Get-Command -Verb Get
```

This command lists all cmdlets that use the Get verb. Similarly:

```
Get-Command -Noun Process
```

This will show all cmdlets that deal with processes.

2. Readability

Scripts become self-documenting. When a reader sees Start-Service, it's immediately clear that the command is starting a service. There's no need to decipher complex or abbreviated names.

3. Consistency

Because PowerShell uses a standard set of approved verbs, scripts remain consistent across different modules and teams. This standardization improves collaboration and reduces confusion.

4. Tab Completion and Predictability

The uniform structure enables efficient tab-completion. Typing Get- and pressing TAB cycles through all available cmdlets that start with that verb.

Understanding Verbs

Verbs in PowerShell should come from the **approved list of standard verbs** maintained by Microsoft. These verbs fall into logical categories and are designed to reflect common actions in IT administration and development tasks.

Examples of common approved verbs include:
- Get: Retrieve data
- Set: Modify data or configuration
- New: Create a new object or resource
- Remove: Delete or remove an item
- Start: Begin an operation or process
- Stop: End an operation or process
- Invoke: Perform a specific action (often one that initiates execution)
- Enable / Disable: Toggle a state on or off

You can view the full list using:

```
Get-Verb
```

This command returns all approved verbs along with their associated groups.

Guidelines for Choosing Verbs
- **Use standard verbs**: Stick to the approved list unless you have a compelling reason not to.
- **Be precise**: Choose the verb that most accurately describes the action being performed.
- **Be consistent**: If you're writing a module, ensure all functions use a coherent verb style.

Understanding Nouns

While verbs come from a standardized list, **nouns are user-defined** and specific to the object or resource being acted upon. They should be singular, clear, and concise.

Examples:
- User instead of Users
- File instead of Files
- Service instead of Services

The noun should describe the data or resource that the verb is targeting.

Guidelines for Choosing Nouns
- **Use singular form**: Always use the singular version of a word unless plural is inherent to the noun (e.g., Statistics).
- **Be descriptive**: The noun should clearly represent what the cmdlet acts on.
- **Avoid ambiguity**: Ensure the noun does not conflict with system-reserved or unrelated terms.

Examples of Verb-Noun Pairs

Let's look at some common cmdlets and break down their components:

Example 1: Get-Process
- **Verb**: Get – Retrieve information
- **Noun**: Process – Refers to system processes

Purpose: Lists running processes on the system.

Example 2: Set-Date
- **Verb**: Set – Modify or update
- **Noun**: Date – System date and time

Purpose: Changes the system's date and time.

Example 3: New-Item
- **Verb**: New – Create something
- **Noun**: Item – A generic object in a data store (file, folder, registry key)

Purpose: Creates a new item in a data store.

Example 4: Remove-Variable
- **Verb**: Remove – Delete something
- **Noun**: Variable – A stored value in PowerShell

Purpose: Deletes a variable from the current session.

Writing Custom Functions with Verb-Noun Syntax

When you create your own functions, adopting the verb-noun syntax is strongly encouraged. It aligns your code with PowerShell's native style and ensures your functions integrate well with help systems, tab completion, and module exports.

Example:
```
function Get-Greeting {
    param([string]$Name)
    return "Hello, $Name!"
}
```

This function follows the Get-<Noun> convention and is immediately intuitive.

Adding to the Help System

Using standard verbs allows your function to be discoverable via Get-Help, Get-Command, and other documentation tools.
```
Get-Help Get-Greeting
```

Making Your Function Compliant

You can use the CmdletBinding attribute and [OutputType()] to further integrate your function:
```
function Get-Greeting {
    [CmdletBinding()]
    [OutputType([string])]
    param(
        [Parameter(Mandatory=$true)]
        [string]$Name
    )
    "Hello, $Name!"
}
```

Naming Pitfalls to Avoid

1. Non-Standard Verbs

Avoid verbs that are not in the approved list unless absolutely necessary. Fetch, Retrieve, Execute are all examples of non-standard verbs that should be replaced with their standard counterparts like Get or Invoke.

2. Abbreviations

Don't shorten verbs or nouns. Use Remove-Item instead of Del-File, for example.

3. Plural Nouns

Always use singular nouns to maintain consistency with native cmdlets.

Final Thoughts

The verb-noun syntax is more than just a stylistic choice in PowerShell—it is a guiding principle that shapes how scripts are written and understood. For beginners, mastering this convention early sets a solid foundation for scripting practices that are clean, professional, and in line with community and enterprise standards.

By adhering to this structure, you'll create scripts that are:

- Easier to read and maintain
- Easier to discover and document
- Consistent with PowerShell's core principles

Understanding and applying verb-noun syntax will make you a more effective PowerShell user and script author. As you build your skillset, this simple rule will serve as a touchstone for clarity and quality in every command you write.

First Scripts and Automation Mindset

CREATING AND RUNNING .PS1 SCRIPTS

PowerShell scripts, saved as .ps1 files, are at the heart of automation in Windows environments. Whether you're managing user accounts, configuring system settings, or orchestrating complex IT workflows, the ability to create and execute .ps1 scripts is an essential skill for any aspiring PowerShell scripter. In this chapter, we'll explore how to create these scripts, configure your system to run them securely, and manage script execution with best practices for beginners.

What is a .ps1 File?

A .ps1 file is simply a plain-text file that contains PowerShell commands. The .ps1 file extension tells Windows that the file is a PowerShell script. Like batch files (.bat) or shell scripts in Unix-based systems, .ps1 scripts allow you to automate repetitive tasks and execute multiple commands in a sequence.

Creating a .ps1 Script

1. Choosing a Script Editor

To write PowerShell scripts, you can use any text editor, but using a purpose-built tool can make scripting much easier. Here are some common options:

- **Windows PowerShell ISE (Integrated Scripting Environment)**: Comes preinstalled on many versions of Windows. Great for beginners.
- **Visual Studio Code**: A powerful, extensible code editor with a PowerShell extension for syntax highlighting, IntelliSense, and debugging.
- **Notepad++ or Notepad**: Simple editors if you just want to write

a few quick commands.

2. Writing Your First Script

Start by opening your editor and typing a few simple PowerShell commands. For example:

```
# My first PowerShell script
Write-Host "Hello, World!"
Get-Date
```

This script prints "Hello, World!" and then displays the current date and time.

Save this script with the .ps1 extension, such as MyFirstScript.ps1.

Running a PowerShell Script

Method 1: Running from the PowerShell Console

Navigate to the directory where your script is saved. For example:

```
cd C:\Users\YourName\Documents\Scripts
```

Then run the script with:

```
.\MyFirstScript.ps1
```

The .\ prefix tells PowerShell to look in the current directory.

Method 2: Running with Full Path

You can also run a script directly by specifying its full path:

```
C:\Users\YourName\Documents\Scripts\MyFirstScript.ps1
```

If the execution policy is too restrictive, PowerShell will warn you and block the script.

Method 3: Right-Click and Run with PowerShell

Windows Explorer provides a handy right-click option: **Run with PowerShell**. This opens a new PowerShell window, executes the script, and closes the window automatically.

Note: This method is less ideal for scripts requiring user input or that produce lengthy output.

Adding Comments and Documentation

Use comments generously in your scripts to make them understandable to others and your future self. Start a line with # to comment:

```
# This script checks for system updates and displays the
result
Get-WindowsUpdateLog
```

To include help documentation, use the comment block format:

```
<#
.SYNOPSIS
    Displays system update logs
.DESCRIPTION
    This script retrieves the Windows Update log and
displays it in the console.
#>
```

Script Parameters and User Input

You can make your script more flexible by adding parameters:

```
param(
    [string]$UserName
)


Write-Host "Hello, $UserName!"
```

Run the script with:

```
.\MyScript.ps1 -UserName "Paul"
```

Or ask for user input during execution:

```
$name = Read-Host "Enter your name"
Write-Host "Hello, $name!"
```

Logging and Output

Use output redirection or file logging to capture script results:

```
Get-Process > processes.txt
```

Or write custom logs within your script:

```
$date = Get-Date -Format "yyyy-MM-dd HH:mm:ss"
"$date - Script started" | Out-File log.txt -Append
```

Error Handling

Basic error handling improves reliability. Use try/catch blocks:

```
try {
    Get-Content "nonexistent.txt"
```

```
} catch {
    Write-Host "An error occurred: $_"
}
```

Use $ErrorActionPreference = 'Stop' to treat all errors as terminating within a script.

Scheduling Scripts with Task Scheduler

You can automate script execution using Windows Task Scheduler:

1. Open Task Scheduler and create a new task.
2. On the **Actions** tab, choose *Start a program*.
3. In the **Program/script** field, enter:

```
powershell.exe
```

4. In the **Add arguments** field, add:

```
-File "C:\Path\To\YourScript.ps1"
```

5. Configure triggers (e.g., daily, at startup) as needed.

Best Practices for Script Writing

- **Always comment your code**: This helps others (and your future self) understand your logic.
- **Use meaningful variable names**: Instead of $x, use $userName.
- **Test incrementally**: Run parts of the script before executing the whole thing.
- **Validate input**: Check user-supplied values to prevent unexpected results.
- **Use version control**: Store your scripts in Git for tracking changes and collaboration.

Conclusion

PowerShell scripting unlocks the full power of automation on Windows systems. Learning to create and run .ps1 files is a foundational step in becoming a proficient PowerShell user. With just a text editor and a few commands, you can start building tools that save time, reduce errors, and simplify IT tasks. By following the practices in this chapter, you'll be well on your way to writing clean, secure, and efficient scripts.

UNDERSTANDING OUTPUT AND REDIRECTION

In PowerShell scripting, **output** and **redirection** are foundational concepts that enable users to interact with, manipulate, and route data in flexible and powerful ways. Whether you're displaying information for users, logging data for future analysis, or directing errors to a file for troubleshooting, mastering output and redirection will make your scripts more efficient and easier to debug. This chapter explores these features in depth.

Standard Output in PowerShell

Standard output refers to the data that a command returns. In PowerShell, this typically includes objects that are displayed in the console. Unlike many traditional shells that return only plain text, PowerShell returns rich .NET objects.

```
Get-Process
```

The above command returns a list of running processes as objects. These objects contain properties such as ProcessName, Id, CPU, etc. This distinction is vital: because PowerShell outputs objects, you can manipulate, filter, and format them with high precision.

```
Get-Process | Where-Object {$_.CPU -gt 100}
```

This command filters the list of processes to only those using more than 100 CPU time units.

Output Streams in PowerShell

PowerShell has multiple output streams. Understanding these streams is key to effective redirection:

1. **Output (Success) Stream (1)**: Standard output, which contains

the data you expect.

2. **Error Stream (2)**: Contains error messages.
3. **Warning Stream (3)**: Contains warning messages.
4. **Verbose Stream (4)**: Contains detailed messages intended for debugging.
5. **Debug Stream (5)**: Contains debug messages.
6. **Information Stream (6)**: Used for general informational output (PowerShell 5+).

Each stream has a numeric identifier, which you'll use when performing redirection.

Redirecting Output

Redirecting Errors

To redirect output to a file, use the > or >> operators:

```
Get-Process > processes.txt
```

This saves the output of Get-Process to a file named processes.txt, overwriting the file if it exists. To append instead of overwrite:

```
Get-Process >> processes.txt
```

Redirecting Errors

You can redirect error messages separately:

```
Get-Process xyz 2> errors.txt
```

The above command attempts to get a process named xyz (which doesn't exist), and redirects the error message to errors.txt.

To append error messages:

```
Get-Process xyz 2>> errors.txt
```

Redirect All Output (Success + Error)

```
Get-Process xyz *> all_output.txt
```

The *> operator redirects all streams (output, error, warning, etc.) to a file.

Combining Streams

You can merge streams when redirecting:

```
Get-Process xyz 2>&1 > combined.txt
```

This command merges the error stream (2) with the output stream (1), then redirects all to combined.txt. The order of redirection matters. Reversing it would produce different results.

Out-File Cmdlet

For more control, use Out-File:

```
Get-Service | Out-File -FilePath services.txt -Encoding UTF8
```

This writes the output to a file with specified encoding, giving you more flexibility than the > operator.

You can append with -Append:

```
Get-Service | Out-File -FilePath services.txt -Append
```

Output Formatting

PowerShell provides several cmdlets for formatting output:

- Format-Table: Format output as a table.
- Format-List: Format output as a list.
- Format-Wide: Format output in a wide format (single property across columns).

Example:

```
Get-Process | Format-Table Name, Id, CPU
```

Use these formatting tools to enhance readability, especially for reports.

Exporting Output

You often need to export data for use in other tools:

Export to CSV:

```
Get-Process | Select-Object Name, Id, CPU | Export-Csv -Path processes.csv -NoTypeInformation
```

Export to JSON:

```
Get-Process | ConvertTo-Json | Out-File processes.json
```

Export to XML:

```
Get-Process | Export-Clixml -Path processes.xml
```

These exports make it easy to analyze PowerShell data in Excel, web applications, or APIs.

Capturing Output in a Variable

To work with output in your script later, capture it in a variable:
```
$services = Get-Service
$services | Where-Object {$_.Status -eq 'Running'}
```

Displaying Output to Console

Sometimes you want to write messages directly to the console, such as logs or status updates:

Using Write-Output:
```
Write-Output "The script has started."
```
Using Write-Host (for display only):
```
Write-Host "Processing..." -ForegroundColor Green
```
Note: Write-Host outputs directly to the screen and does not write to the output stream, so it's not captured in redirection.

Using Write-Verbose:
```
Write-Verbose "This is a verbose message." -Verbose
```
Use -Verbose to enable output from Write-Verbose. It's ideal for debugging.

Using Write-Error, Write-Warning, Write-Debug, Write-Information:
```
Write-Error "Something went wrong."
Write-Warning "This is a warning."
Write-Debug "Debug info here."
Write-Information "Info message."
```
Each of these targets a specific stream and helps categorize output.

Silencing Output

Sometimes you don't want to display any output. Use $null:
```
$null = Get-Process
```
This suppresses the output, which is useful when you only care about the side effects of a command (e.g., updating a setting).

Conclusion

PowerShell's output and redirection capabilities make it vastly more powerful than traditional command-line tools. By understanding and mastering streams, redirection, and formatting, you can build scripts that are clean, maintainable, and suitable for both production and debugging purposes. Whether you're writing a simple utility or a complex automation workflow, being in control of what your script outputs—and where it goes—is essential. Practice with the examples in this chapter and experiment with different redirection strategies to develop an intuitive grasp of these powerful tools.

REAL-WORLD EXAMPLES: HELLO WORLD, DISK CLEANUP

In this section, we'll transition from foundational PowerShell knowledge to practical application. These examples—*Hello World* and *Disk Cleanup*—demonstrate how to implement basic scripting techniques in real-world scenarios. Whether you're automating a simple greeting or maintaining system hygiene by freeing up disk space, these examples show just how powerful even the most basic PowerShell scripts can be.

Part 1: The "Hello World" Script

Purpose
The "Hello World" program is a rite of passage for anyone learning a programming or scripting language. It's a minimal yet effective way to demonstrate how to write, execute, and validate code.

Writing the Script
Here's the simplest PowerShell script you can write:

```
Write-Output "Hello, World!"
```

Or even shorter:

```
"Hello, World!"
```

How It Works
- Write-Output is a cmdlet that sends the specified string to the output stream.
- PowerShell automatically outputs strings not assigned to variables or piped to other cmdlets.

Saving and Running the Script
1. Open **Notepad** or your preferred text editor.
2. Type the script above.
3. Save it as HelloWorld.ps1.
4. Open PowerShell and navigate to the directory where the script is saved.
5. Run the script using:

.\HelloWorld.ps1

If your execution policy prevents scripts from running, you may need to change it temporarily:

```
Set-ExecutionPolicy -Scope Process -ExecutionPolicy Bypass
```

Modifying the Script
Let's add a bit more logic to personalize the message:

```
$name = Read-Host "Enter your name"
Write-Output "Hello, $name! Welcome to PowerShell scripting."
```

Now when you run the script, it prompts you to enter your name, and then outputs a personalized message.

Real-World Application
While the "Hello World" script may seem trivial, its significance lies in understanding the scripting flow, syntax, and PowerShell environment. You'll use the same structure—input, processing, and output—in more complex scripts.

Part 2: Disk Cleanup Script

Purpose
Disk cleanup is a common task for both system administrators and home users. Over time, temporary files, system logs, and browser caches consume valuable disk space. Automating this task saves time and ensures consistency.

Goals of the Script
- Delete files from specific temporary folders.
- Remove old files (older than X days).

- Generate a log of deleted files.

Initial Version of the Script

```
$TempFolders = @(
    "$env:TEMP",
    "$env:SystemRoot\Temp"
)


$LogFile = "CleanupLog.txt"
$DaysOld = 7

foreach ($folder in $TempFolders) {
    if (Test-Path $folder) {
        Get-ChildItem -Path $folder -Recurse -Force -
ErrorAction SilentlyContinue |
        Where-Object { !$_.PSIsContainer -and
$_.LastWriteTime -lt (Get-Date).AddDays(-$DaysOld) } |
        ForEach-Object {
            try {
                Remove-Item $_.FullName -Force -ErrorAction
Stop
                Add-Content -Path $LogFile -Value "Deleted:
$($_.FullName)"
            } catch {
                Add-Content -Path $LogFile -Value "Failed to
delete: $($_.FullName) - $_"
            }
        }
    }
}
```

Explanation of Components

- **$TempFolders**: An array of temporary directories to clean.
- **$LogFile**: Path to the log file.
- **$DaysOld**: Files older than this many days will be deleted.
- **Get-ChildItem**: Lists files in the folder and subfolders.
- **Where-Object**: Filters files based on age.
- **Remove-Item**: Deletes the file.
- **Add-Content**: Appends log entries to a text file.

Enhancements

1. User Confirmation Prompt

```
$response = Read-Host "Do you want to proceed with disk
cleanup? (Y/N)"
```

```
if ($response -ne 'Y') {
    Write-Output "Disk cleanup aborted by user."
    exit
}
```

2. Parameterized Script

Add parameters to make it reusable:

```
param(
    [string[]]$Paths = @("$env:TEMP",
"$env:SystemRoot\Temp"),
    [int]$Days = 7,
    [string]$Log = "CleanupLog.txt"
)
```

Use these values in place of hard-coded variables.

3. Email Notification (Optional Advanced Feature)

For enterprise use:

```
Send-MailMessage -To "admin@example.com" -From
"script@example.com" -Subject "Disk Cleanup Report" -Body
(Get-Content $Log -Raw) -SmtpServer "smtp.example.com"
```

Scheduling the Script

You can automate this task using Task Scheduler:

1. Open **Task Scheduler**.
2. Create a new **Basic Task**.
3. Set the schedule (daily, weekly, etc.).
4. Choose **Start a Program**.
5. Point to powershell.exe and add the script path as an argument:

```
-ExecutionPolicy Bypass -File "C:\Scripts\DiskCleanup.ps1"
```

Best Practices

- **Always test scripts** in a controlled environment.
- **Avoid deleting critical system directories.**
- **Use logging** to track script performance and errors.
- **Backup important files** or use a dry-run flag for first-time executions.

Real-World Use Case: IT Department Weekly Cleanup

In many organizations, helpdesk teams manually clean temp files from shared workstations. By scheduling the above script across all systems using Group Policy or System Center Configuration Manager (SCCM), teams can automate this task and reduce manual labor, free up resources, and ensure systems perform optimally.

Real-World Use Case: Developer Workstation Maintenance

Software developers often build and test applications that leave behind artifacts in temp folders. Automating disk cleanup helps prevent performance degradation and frees up valuable SSD space. Developers can customize this script to exclude folders critical to their build systems while still targeting large junk files.

Conclusion

The "Hello World" and "Disk Cleanup" scripts are more than beginner exercises—they are gateways to understanding how PowerShell can solve real problems. These examples reinforce the fundamental scripting flow: input, process, and output. With just a few lines of code, you can perform tasks that save time, enhance system health, and streamline your workflow.

As you progress, build on these foundations by incorporating more advanced features like error handling, parameter validation, reporting, and integration with other systems. Whether you're writing scripts for personal convenience or enterprise automation, the skills you gain here will serve as the bedrock for more powerful solutions.

Variables and Data Types

STRINGS, INTEGERS, BOOLEANS, ARRAYS, HASHTABLES

In PowerShell, everything is an object. Understanding how PowerShell handles basic data types such as strings, integers, booleans, arrays, and hashtables is foundational to becoming proficient in scripting. This chapter will introduce these essential building blocks, demonstrate how to work with them, and explore best practices for their usage.

Strings

Strings in PowerShell are sequences of characters enclosed in either single or double quotes. They are among the most common data types used in scripting.

Declaring Strings

```
$singleQuoted = 'This is a string'
$doubleQuoted = "This is a string with $($env:USERNAME)"
```

The key difference between single and double quotes is that variables and expressions are *interpolated* in double-quoted strings but not in single-quoted strings.

String Operations

```
$string = "Hello, World!"

# Length
$length = $string.Length

# Uppercase
$upper = $string.ToUpper()

# Lowercase
$lower = $string.ToLower()
```

```
# Substring
$substring = $string.Substring(7, 5)  # Output: World

# Replace
$replaced = $string.Replace("World", "PowerShell")

# Split
$words = $string.Split(',')

# Trim
$trimmed = "  padded string  ".Trim()
```

Strings are objects of the .NET System.String class and offer many built-in methods.

String Formatting

```
$name = "Alice"
$age = 30

# Concatenation
$message = "Name: " + $name + ", Age: " + $age

# Format operator
$message = "Name: {0}, Age: {1}" -f $name, $age

# Here-Strings (multiline strings)
$hereString = @"
Hello,
My name is $name.
"@
```

Booleans

Booleans represent logical values: $true and $false.

Declaring Booleans

```
$boolTrue = $true
$boolFalse = $false
```

Boolean Logic

```
$a = $true
$b = $false
```

```
# AND
$result = $a -and $b  # False

# OR
$result = $a -or $b   # True

# NOT
$result = -not $a     # False
```

Boolean Evaluation

PowerShell treats some values as $false in conditional expressions:

- $null
- 0 (zero)
- "" (empty string)
- $false

Everything else is treated as $true.

```
if ("Hello") {
    "This is true"
}


if ("") {
    "This won't show"
}
```

Arrays

Arrays are collections of elements that can be of any type. PowerShell arrays are strongly typed only when explicitly declared.

Declaring Arrays

```
$fruits = @("apple", "banana", "cherry")
```

Accessing Elements

```
$firstFruit = $fruits[0]   # apple
$lastFruit = $fruits[-1]   # cherry
```

Modifying Arrays

Arrays in PowerShell are immutable; to add elements, use the +

operator or cast to an ArrayList:

```
$fruits = $fruits + "date"


# Using ArrayList for efficiency
$arrayList = New-Object System.Collections.ArrayList
$arrayList.Add("apple") | Out-Null
$arrayList.Add("banana") | Out-Null
```

Array Operations

```
$numbers = 1..5
$sum = ($numbers | Measure-Object -Sum).Sum


# Filtering
$even = $numbers | Where-Object { $_ % 2 -eq 0 }


# Mapping
$squared = $numbers | ForEach-Object { $_ * $_ }
```

Multidimensional and Jagged Arrays

```
# Multidimensional array
$matrix = New-Object 'int[,]' 3,3
$matrix[0,0] = 1


# Jagged array (array of arrays)
$jagged = @( @(1,2), @(3,4) )
```

Hashtables

Hashtables (dictionaries in other languages) store key-value pairs. They are widely used for storing structured data.

Declaring Hashtables

```
$person = @{ Name = "John"; Age = 34; City = "Austin" }
```

Accessing Values

```
$name = $person["Name"]
$age = $person.Age
```

Adding and Removing Keys

```
$person["State"] = "Texas"
```

```
$person.Remove("City")
```

Looping Through Hashtables

```
foreach ($key in $person.Keys) {
    "$key: $($person[$key])"
}
```

Sorting Hashtables

```
$sorted = $person.GetEnumerator() | Sort-Object Name
```

Nested Hashtables

```
$employee = @{
    Name = "Alice"
    Address = @{
        Street = "123 Main St"
        City = "Houston"
    }
}

$city = $employee["Address"]["City"]
```

Integers

PowerShell supports various numeric types, but the most commonly used for whole numbers is the 32-bit integer (Int32).

Declaring Integers

```
$intValue = 42
```

Arithmetic Operations

```
$a = 10
$b = 3

$sum = $a + $b
$diff = $a - $b
$product = $a * $b
$quotient = $a / $b
$remainder = $a % $b
```

Type Casting

```
$asString = "123"
$asInt = [int]$asString   # Casts string to integer
```

Integer Comparison

```
$a = 10
$b = 20

$a -eq $b   # False
$a -lt $b   # True
$a -gt $b   # False
```

You can use other comparison operators such as -le, -ge, and -ne for less than or equal, greater than or equal, and not equal.

Best Practices

- **Use descriptive variable names** to make scripts readable.
- **Prefer double quotes** when variables need interpolation.
- **Cast explicitly** to prevent unexpected behaviors.
- **Avoid using arrays when performance matters**, and opt for ArrayList instead.
- **Use hashtables for structured data** and nested hashtables to represent complex objects.
- **Remember that everything is an object.** You can call methods and access properties directly on variables.

Conclusion

Understanding PowerShell's basic data types—strings, integers, booleans, arrays, and hashtables—is the first step in writing powerful and effective scripts. These types form the backbone of almost all scripting tasks, from simple automation to complex data manipulation. By mastering their syntax, operations, and best practices, you'll be better prepared to take on more advanced topics and create scripts that are both robust and maintainable.

TYPE CASTING AND VALIDATION

PowerShell is a robust scripting language built on the .NET Framework, which means it inherits a strong type system. Understanding type casting and validation is essential for writing reliable scripts that behave as expected and are resilient to user input or system variation. This chapter will cover the basics and advanced use cases for type casting and validation, including how they contribute to writing clean, predictable, and efficient code.

What is Type Casting?

Type casting is the process of converting a variable from one data type to another. PowerShell automatically performs many type conversions behind the scenes (implicit casting), but it also allows for manual type conversions (explicit casting).

Implicit Casting

PowerShell attempts to automatically convert types when it deems it appropriate. For example:

```
$number = "123"
$sum = $number + 10
Write-Output $sum  # Output: 133
```

In this case, PowerShell automatically converts the string "123" to an integer for the arithmetic operation.

Explicit Casting

Explicit casting is when you manually convert a variable to a specific type using square brackets:

```
[string]$text = 456
[int]$value = "789"
```

This gives you more control and helps prevent unexpected behavior, especially in complex scripts.

Common Data Types in PowerShell

Understanding which types are most commonly used in PowerShell will make casting easier and more intuitive. Here are a few:

- [string]: Text
- [int]: Integer
- [float]: Floating-point number
- [bool]: Boolean ($true or $false)
- [datetime]: Date and time values
- [array]: Collections of items
- [hashtable]: Key-value pairs

Type Conversion Examples

Let's look at some common scenarios where type casting is essential:

String to Integer

```
[int]$number = "42"
```

String to Boolean

```
[bool]$flag = "true"
```

String to DateTime

```
[datetime]$date = "2025-04-11"
```

Array from CSV

```
[array]$lines = Get-Content "file.csv"
```

Type Constraints in Function Parameters

PowerShell allows you to enforce type constraints in function parameters. This ensures the correct data types are passed to your functions, reducing bugs and increasing clarity.

```
function Add-Numbers {
    param (
        [int]$a,
        [int]$b
    )
    return $a + $b
}


Add-Numbers -a 5 -b "7"  # Implicit cast will occur for the
string "7"
```

For stricter validation, you can use [ValidateScript()], [ValidateRange()], and other attributes.

Validation Attributes

Validation attributes provide a mechanism to verify that inputs meet specific conditions. They work well with parameter declarations.

ValidateNotNullOrEmpty

Ensures the parameter is not null or an empty string.

```
param (
    [ValidateNotNullOrEmpty()]
    [string]$Name
)
```

ValidateRange

Ensures a numeric parameter falls within a given range.

```
param (
    [ValidateRange(1, 100)]
    [int]$Age
)
```

ValidateSet

Limits the acceptable values to a predefined set.

```
param (
    [ValidateSet("Red", "Green", "Blue")]
    [string]$Color
)
```

ValidatePattern

Validates input based on a regular expression.

```
param (
    [ValidatePattern("^[a-zA-Z0-9]+$")]
    [string]$Username
)
```

ValidateScript

Runs a custom script block to validate input.

```
param (
    [ValidateScript({$_ -gt 0})]
    [int]$PositiveNumber
)
```

Custom Type Validation with Classes

PowerShell 5.0 and newer support class-based programming. This can help enforce strong typing in more complex scripts.

```
class Person {
    [string]$Name
    [int]$Age

    Person ([string]$name, [int]$age) {
        $this.Name = $name
        $this.Age = $age
    }
}

$john = [Person]::new("John", 30)
```

Using classes helps encapsulate data and ensures type safety by design.

Try-Catch for Type Casting Failures

Sometimes, casting can fail. It's wise to wrap casting operations in a try/catch block to handle potential errors gracefully.

```
try {
    [int]$num = "abc"   # Will throw an error
} catch {
    Write-Error "Failed to convert input to integer: $_"
}
```

This kind of error handling is vital when accepting user input or working with unpredictable data sources.

Practical Use Case: Input Validation in a Script

Suppose you're writing a script that accepts user input for processing employee records. Input validation and type casting help ensure the script behaves as expected:

```
param (
    [ValidatePattern("^[a-zA-Z]+$")]
    [string]$FirstName,

    [ValidateRange(18, 65)]
    [int]$Age,
```

```
    [ValidateSet("HR", "IT", "Finance")]
    [string]$Department
)
```

```
Write-Output "Processing record for $FirstName, age $Age,
department $Department."
```

This script ensures that the name consists only of letters, the age is within working limits, and the department is among accepted values.

Conclusion

Mastering type casting and validation is foundational for writing robust PowerShell scripts. Type casting helps control and convert data for correct operations, while validation ensures that only suitable data is processed. Whether you're writing a quick utility or a complex automation system, applying these principles will lead to cleaner, safer, and more professional code.

In the next chapter, we will explore **Loops and Control Structures** —key elements that allow scripts to make decisions and repeat actions dynamically.

Operators and Expressions

ARITHMETIC, COMPARISON, LOGICAL, ASSIGNMENT

PowerShell, as a full-fledged scripting language, provides a wide array of operators to perform calculations, comparisons, logic processing, and value assignment. Understanding these operators is fundamental to effective scripting, whether you're performing calculations, making decisions, or assigning values to variables.

In this chapter, we will explore four categories of PowerShell operators:

1. Arithmetic Operators
2. Comparison Operators
3. Logical Operators
4. Assignment Operators

Each of these groups plays a critical role in scripting and automation tasks.

Arithmetic Operators

Arithmetic operators are used to perform mathematical operations such as addition, subtraction, multiplication, and division. These are often employed in scripts that involve counters, calculations, or manipulating numerical data.

Here are the most commonly used arithmetic operators in PowerShell:

- + (Addition)
- - (Subtraction)
- * (Multiplication)
- / (Division)
- % (Modulus)

Examples:

```
$a = 10
```

```
$b = 4

$sum = $a + $b          # 14
$diff = $a - $b         # 6
$product = $a * $b      # 40
$quotient = $a / $b     # 2.5
$remainder = $a % $b    # 2
```

PowerShell handles these operations much like any standard programming language, with support for both integers and floating-point numbers. This makes it particularly useful when dealing with storage sizes, time calculations, or any numeric metric.

Comparison Operators

Comparison operators are used to evaluate the relationship between two values. These are extremely useful in if statements, loops, and filters.

Key comparison operators include:
- -eq (Equal to)
- -ne (Not equal to)
- -gt (Greater than)
- -lt (Less than)
- -ge (Greater than or equal to)
- -le (Less than or equal to)

Examples:

```
$x = 5
$y = 10

$x -eq $y       # False
$x -ne $y       # True
$x -lt $y       # True
$x -gt $y       # False
$x -le $y       # True
$x -ge $y       # False
```

PowerShell also supports string comparisons with -eq, -ne, and others. For instance:

```
$name = "Alice"
$name -eq "Alice"    # True
$name -ne "Bob"      # True
```

Comparison operators are especially important in conditional logic. They allow scripts to branch or loop based on user input, file existence, service states, or other parameters.

Logical Operators

Logical operators allow you to combine multiple conditions. These are crucial when decisions need to be made based on more than one condition.

The logical operators in PowerShell include:

- -and (Logical AND)
- -or (Logical OR)
- -not (Logical NOT)
- ! (Alias for -not)

Examples:

```
$a = 5
$b = 10

($a -lt 10) -and ($b -gt 5)    # True
($a -lt 3) -or ($b -gt 5)      # True
-not ($a -lt 10)               # False
!($a -eq 5)                    # False
```

These operators are typically used in if statements or while loops:

```
if (($user -eq "admin") -and ($access -eq "granted")) {
    Write-Output "Access Approved"
} else {
    Write-Output "Access Denied"
}
```

By combining logical operators, you can construct highly precise and complex decision-making criteria.

Assignment Operators

Assignment operators are used to assign values to variables. The simplest and most common is the = operator, but PowerShell provides several compound assignment operators to combine operations and assignment in one step.

Standard assignment operator:

- =

Compound assignment operators:

- += (Addition assignment)
- -= (Subtraction assignment)
- *= (Multiplication assignment)
- /= (Division assignment)
- %= (Modulus assignment)

Examples:
```
$count = 5
$count += 2     # count is now 7
$count -= 1     # count is now 6
$count *= 2     # count is now 12
$count /= 3     # count is now 4
$count %= 3     # count is now 1
```

Compound assignments are shorthand and help make code cleaner, especially in loops or counters:
```
for ($i = 0; $i -lt 10; $i += 2) {
    Write-Output $i
}
```

Understanding how assignment works is vital, as PowerShell variables are strongly tied to data manipulation throughout your scripts. Variables in PowerShell are loosely typed, but assignment still governs how data is stored and updated.

Best Practices and Tips

- Always use parentheses to group logical expressions for clarity.
- Use comparison operators inside if conditions to make your scripts dynamic.
- Prefer +=, -=, etc., in loops to avoid repetition and improve readability.
- When debugging, output intermediate values to verify that

operators are returning the expected results.

- Be careful with division and modulus when working with integers vs floats.

Understanding these operator types gives you the building blocks for constructing dynamic scripts. Whether you're looping through arrays, filtering logs, or performing system checks, arithmetic, comparison, logical, and assignment operators will be part of the core syntax you'll use daily.

These concepts may appear basic, but mastering them allows you to write clean, efficient, and powerful scripts. In later chapters, you'll see these operators come together in complex scenarios like user creation automation, data transformation, and system auditing. So make sure you're comfortable with them before moving forward.

Next, we'll build on these fundamentals and look into conditional statements, where many of these operators find their most common use. This will open the door to building scripts that can think and adapt based on input or system state.

REGULAR EXPRESSIONS BASICS

Regular expressions, often abbreviated as *regex*, are a powerful tool in PowerShell (and many other programming and scripting languages) that allow you to search, match, and manipulate strings based on specific patterns. Understanding regex is an essential skill for any PowerShell scripter who wants to efficiently parse logs, validate user inputs, extract data from strings, or perform advanced find-and-replace operations.

What is a Regular Expression?

A regular expression is a string that defines a search pattern. You can think of it like a flexible and powerful version of the typical Find function you might use in a text editor, but with far more capability. For example, you can use regex to find all instances of a word, numbers that match a certain pattern, or even email addresses and IP addresses from a body of text.

Regex in PowerShell

PowerShell integrates regex natively through several mechanisms:

- The -match, -notmatch, and -replace operators
- The [regex] .NET class
- The Select-String cmdlet

Example:

```
"Hello123" -match "\d+"    # Returns True because it matches
one or more digits
```

Regex Syntax Basics

Understanding the building blocks of regex syntax is critical. Here are some of the most commonly used elements:

- . – Matches any single character except newline.
- ^ – Anchors the match at the start of a string.
- $ – Anchors the match at the end of a string.
- * – Matches zero or more occurrences of the preceding character.
- + – Matches one or more occurrences of the preceding character.
- ? – Matches zero or one occurrence of the preceding character.
- \d – Matches any digit (0–9).
- \w – Matches any word character (alphanumeric plus underscore).
- \s – Matches any whitespace character.
- [...] – Matches any one of the characters inside the brackets.
- [^...] – Matches any character *not* inside the brackets.
- (abc) – Groups expressions. Also used for capturing.
- | – Acts like a logical OR.

Anchors and Boundaries

Anchors are useful when you're trying to match patterns at the start or end of lines or words:

- ^Hello matches any string that starts with "Hello"
- World$ matches any string that ends with "World"
- \b represents a word boundary. For example, \bword\b ensures that "word" is not matched within another word like

"sword"

Character Classes and Quantifiers

Character classes let you define sets of characters to match, while quantifiers specify how many times you want to match those characters.

Character Classes:
- [aeiou] matches any vowel
- [0-9] matches any digit
- [a-zA-Z] matches any letter, regardless of case

Quantifiers:
- {n} – Exactly n times
- {n,} – n or more times
- {n,m} – Between n and m times

Grouping and Capturing

Parentheses () not only group patterns together but also capture the matched text so you can reference or extract it later.

Example:
```
$string = "My phone number is 123-456-7890"
if ($string -match "(\d{3})-(\d{3})-(\d{4})") {
    $matches[0]   # Entire match
    $matches[1]   # First group: 123
    $matches[2]   # Second group: 456
    $matches[3]   # Third group: 7890
}
```

This is invaluable when dealing with structured text data such as logs, filenames, or data exports.

Regex with -match and -replace

PowerShell provides -match and -replace operators to work seamlessly with regex patterns.

-match Example:
```
"Server2025" -match "Server\d{4}"   # True
```

-replace Example:

```
"Error: Code 500" -replace "\d+", "XXX"  # Outputs: Error:
Code XXX
```

Using the [regex] Class

The [regex] class in .NET gives you even more control, such as finding multiple matches and advanced replacements.

Example – Finding All Matches:

```
$text = "Error 401, Error 404, Error 500"
$pattern = "\d{3}"
[regex]::Matches($text, $pattern) | ForEach-Object {
$_.Value }
```

Practical Examples

Validating an Email Address

```
$email = "user@example.com"
if ($email -match "^[\w.-]+@[\w.-]+\.\w{2,4}$") {
    "Valid Email"
} else {
    "Invalid Email"
}
```

Extracting Dates from a Log File

```
$log = "[2025-04-10] User login"
if ($log -match "\[(\d{4}-\d{2}-\d{2})\]") {
    $matches[1]  # Output: 2025-04-10
}
```

Replacing IP Addresses

```
$input = "Login from 192.168.1.100"
$output = $input -replace "\b\d{1,3}(\.\d{1,3}){3}\b",
"[REDACTED]"
```

Tips for Writing and Testing Regex

1. **Start simple**: Build your regex in small parts.
2. **Use online testers**: Tools like regex101.com provide real-time feedback and explanations.

3. **Escape special characters**: Characters like ., *, +, ?, |, and () have special meanings and must be escaped with a backslash if you want to match them literally.
4. **Use comments when patterns get complex**: Consider using the (?x) mode in .NET regex for free-spacing and inline comments.

Common Pitfalls

- **Greedy Matching**: By default, quantifiers are greedy, which means they match as much as possible. To make them lazy (i.e., match as little as possible), append ? to the quantifier.
- Greedy: "<.*>" matches the entire string "<tag>value</tag>"
- Lazy: "<.*?>" matches just "<tag>"
- **Escaping in PowerShell**: PowerShell requires double escaping backslashes in strings. So \d in regex must be written as "\d" in PowerShell strings.
- **Performance**: Complex regex on large text files can be slow. Optimize by anchoring or using more specific patterns when possible.

Conclusion

Regular expressions may seem intimidating at first, but mastering them can dramatically increase your effectiveness in PowerShell scripting. From parsing log files to sanitizing input, regex provides a concise and powerful way to work with text. While the syntax can be tricky, especially with escaping and grouping, consistent practice and real-world application will help solidify your understanding. As you continue your PowerShell journey, regular expressions will become an indispensable part of your scripting toolkit.

Conditional Logic

IF, ELSEIF, ELSE, SWITCH

Conditional logic is one of the foundational building blocks of any programming or scripting language, and PowerShell is no exception. Understanding how to use if, elseif, else, and switch statements effectively will empower you to create scripts that can make decisions based on dynamic data. In this section, we'll explore each of these conditional statements, explain how they work, and provide examples of how to use them in real-world scenarios.

The if Statement

The if statement evaluates a condition and executes a block of code only if the condition is $true. This is the most basic form of decision-making in PowerShell.

Syntax:

```
if (<condition>) {
    # Code to execute if condition is true
}
```

Example:

```
$age = 18
if ($age -ge 18) {
    Write-Host "You are eligible to vote."
}
```

In this example, the script checks if the variable $age is greater than or equal to 18. If the condition is true, it outputs a message stating that the person is eligible to vote.

The elseif Statement

The elseif statement lets you test additional conditions if the initial if condition is false. You can have multiple elseif branches to test various scenarios.

Syntax:

```
if (<condition1>) {
    # Code to execute if condition1 is true
} elseif (<condition2>) {
    # Code to execute if condition2 is true
} elseif (<condition3>) {
    # Code to execute if condition3 is true
} else {
    # Code to execute if none of the above conditions are
true
}
```

Example:

```
$score = 85
if ($score -ge 90) {
    Write-Host "Grade: A"
} elseif ($score -ge 80) {
    Write-Host "Grade: B"
} elseif ($score -ge 70) {
    Write-Host "Grade: C"
} else {
    Write-Host "Grade: F"
    }
```

This script evaluates a test score and outputs a grade based on the score. If the score is not high enough for any of the defined categories, it defaults to an F.

The else Statement

The else statement provides a fallback option when all previous conditions are false. It should always be the last block in an if-elseif-else chain.

Use Case:

The else block is essential when you want to ensure that some code runs if none of the earlier conditions are met. It is a catch-all for any unanticipated values.

Example:

```
$weather = "rainy"
if ($weather -eq "sunny") {
    Write-Host "Go for a walk."
```

```
} elseif ($weather -eq "cloudy") {
    Write-Host "Maybe take an umbrella just in case."
} else {
    Write-Host "Stay indoors and watch a movie."
}
```

This script determines an action based on weather conditions. If the weather doesn't match any of the specified conditions, the script executes the default behavior.

Using if, elseif, and else for Input Validation

These conditional statements are especially useful for input validation and user interaction.

Example:
```
$name = Read-Host "Enter your name"
if ([string]::IsNullOrWhiteSpace($name)) {
    Write-Host "Name cannot be empty."
} else {
    Write-Host "Hello, $name!"
}
```

This script prompts the user for their name and checks if the input is empty. If the name is valid, it proceeds with a greeting.

The switch Statement

While if and elseif are great for evaluating a few specific conditions, the switch statement is better suited for evaluating a single expression against multiple potential matches. It is cleaner and more efficient for handling many discrete values.

Syntax:
```
switch (<expression>) {
    <value1> { # code }
    <value2> { # code }
    default { # code }
}
```

Example:
```
$day = "Wednesday"
switch ($day) {
    "Monday" { Write-Host "Start of the work week." }
```

```
    "Wednesday" { Write-Host "Midweek checkpoint." }
    "Friday" { Write-Host "Almost the weekend!" }
    default { Write-Host "Just another day." }
}
```

In this example, $day is checked against several possible values. The switch statement executes the matching block of code.

Case Sensitivity in switch

By default, switch is case-insensitive. However, if you need to make a case-sensitive comparison, you can use the -CaseSensitive parameter.

Example:
```
$letter = "a"
switch -CaseSensitive ($letter) {
    "A" { Write-Host "Uppercase A" }
    "a" { Write-Host "Lowercase a" }
}
```

This script differentiates between uppercase and lowercase input.

When to Use if vs. switch

Understanding when to use if vs. switch is crucial:
- Use if, elseif, and else when comparing multiple different conditions or expressions.
- Use switch when comparing one expression to multiple static values.

Example Scenario:
If you're checking if a number is both positive and even, use if. If you're checking what day of the week it is, use switch.

Matching Patterns with switch

The switch statement can also be used to match wildcard patterns or even regular expressions with the -Wildcard and -Regex parameters.

Wildcard Example:
```
$name = "admin-user"
switch -Wildcard ($name) {
```

```
    "admin-*" { Write-Host "Administrator account detected."
}
    "user-*" { Write-Host "Standard user account." }
    default { Write-Host "Unknown account type." }
}
```

Regex Example:

```
$input = "abc123"
switch -Regex ($input) {
    "^[a-z]+\d+$" { Write-Host "Lowercase letters followed
by digits." }
    default { Write-Host "Input format not recognized." }
}
```

These options greatly increase the power of switch, allowing it to be used for more advanced decision-making.

Real-World Script Example

Let's look at a practical PowerShell script that uses both if and switch to decide what action to take on a file.

Example:

```
$filePath = "C:\Reports\summary.txt"
if (Test-Path $filePath) {
    $extension = [System.IO.Path]::GetExtension($filePath)
    switch ($extension) {
        ".txt" { Write-Host "Opening with Notepad...";
notepad $filePath }
        ".docx" { Write-Host "Opening with Word..."; Start-
Process winword $filePath }
        ".xlsx" { Write-Host "Opening with Excel..."; Start-
Process excel $filePath }
        default { Write-Host "Unknown file type." }
    }
} else {
    Write-Host "File does not exist."
}
```

This script first checks whether a file exists, then uses a switch block to determine the appropriate application to open it based on its extension.

Summary

The if, elseif, else, and switch statements are indispensable tools in PowerShell scripting. They give your scripts the power to respond dynamically to inputs and conditions, making them far more useful and robust.

By mastering these conditional structures, you unlock the ability to write flexible, readable, and intelligent scripts that can adapt to a wide variety of scenarios. As you move forward, you'll find these control structures at the core of nearly every script you write.

Keep experimenting with different conditions, nesting logic, and using switch with wildcard or regex patterns to become truly proficient in PowerShell decision-making.

REAL-WORLD EXAMPLES

PowerShell scripting isn't just an academic exercise or a tool reserved for enterprise environments—it's a real-world problem-solver that IT professionals, system administrators, and power users depend on daily. In this section, we'll explore several real-world scenarios that highlight how PowerShell scripts can automate tasks, enforce consistency, improve security, and save time.

Example 1: Automating User Account Creation in Active Directory

The Problem:

When onboarding new employees, IT staff often have to manually create Active Directory (AD) user accounts. This process typically includes setting usernames, passwords, group memberships, and home directories. Manual repetition increases the chances of human error and takes up valuable time.

The PowerShell Solution:

```
Import-Module ActiveDirectory

$users = Import-Csv "C:\Scripts\new_users.csv"
```

```
foreach ($user in $users) {
    New-ADUser -Name $user.Name `
                -GivenName $user.FirstName `
                -Surname $user.LastName `
                -SamAccountName $user.Username `
                -UserPrincipalName "$
($user.Username)@yourdomain.com" `
                -Path "OU=Employees,DC=yourdomain,DC=com" `
                -AccountPassword (ConvertTo-SecureString
$user.Password -AsPlainText -Force) `
                -Enabled $true

    Add-ADGroupMember -Identity "Employees" -Members
$user.Username
}
```

This script reads user details from a CSV file and automatically provisions accounts, ensuring standardization and reducing workload.

Example 2: Monthly Disk Cleanup on Servers

The Problem:

Over time, temporary files and logs accumulate on servers, consuming valuable disk space. Without regular cleanup, performance can degrade, and critical services may fail.

The PowerShell Solution:

```
$paths = @("C:\Temp", "C:\Windows\Temp", "C:\Logs")

foreach ($path in $paths) {
    Get-ChildItem -Path $path -Recurse -Force |
    Where-Object { $_.LastWriteTime -lt (Get-
Date).AddDays(-30) } |
    Remove-Item -Force -Recurse
}
```

This script finds and deletes files older than 30 days from specified directories. Scheduled via Task Scheduler, this script can help maintain server health with minimal effort.

Example 3: Checking for Missing Windows Updates

The Problem:

Security updates are essential, but manually checking each machine is time-consuming and impractical in larger environments.

The PowerShell Solution:

```
Install-Module PSWindowsUpdate -Force
Import-Module PSWindowsUpdate

Get-WindowsUpdate -ComputerName (Get-Content "C:
\Scripts\servers.txt") -Verbose |
Out-File "C:\Scripts\update_report.txt"
```

This script installs a PowerShell module to scan multiple computers for missing updates and logs the results, helping administrators identify vulnerabilities proactively.

Example 4: Scheduled Reboots for Patch Management

The Problem:

Some updates require reboots, but doing so during working hours can be disruptive. Admins need a way to automate reboots during off-hours.

The PowerShell Solution:

```
$computers = Get-Content "C:\Scripts\servers.txt"

foreach ($computer in $computers) {
    Restart-Computer -ComputerName $computer -Force -Delay
60 -Credential (Get-Credential)
}
```

With this script, you can schedule a reboot across all listed servers, ensuring updates take effect with minimal user disruption.

Example 5: Automated Backups of Critical Files

The Problem:

Data loss is a constant threat. Backing up files manually is inefficient and easy to forget.

The PowerShell Solution:

```
$source = "C:\ImportantData"
$destination = "D:\Backups\$(Get-Date -Format yyyy-MM-dd)"

New-Item -ItemType Directory -Path $destination
Copy-Item -Path $source -Destination $destination -Recurse -
Force
```

This script creates a dated backup of critical data folders. You can integrate it with Windows Task Scheduler to run daily or weekly.

Example 6: Monitoring Event Logs for Critical Errors

The Problem:

When critical errors go unnoticed in event logs, they can spiral into major issues.

The PowerShell Solution:

```
$events = Get-WinEvent -FilterHashtable @{LogName='System';
Level=1} -MaxEvents 50

foreach ($event in $events) {
    Write-Output "$($event.TimeCreated) - $($event.Message)"
}
```

This script retrieves the 50 most recent critical events from the System log and prints them for review, enabling proactive diagnostics.

Example 7: Detecting Inactive Active Directory Users

The Problem:

Inactive accounts can be a security risk and unnecessary clutter.

The PowerShell Solution:

```
Search-ADAccount -AccountInactive -UsersOnly -TimeSpan
90.00:00:00 |
Export-Csv "C:\Scripts\inactive_users.csv" -
NoTypeInformation
```

This script identifies AD user accounts inactive for 90 days and exports the list to a CSV for further action.

Example 8: Sending Custom Email Alerts

The Problem:

Admins often need notifications about system health, but monitoring tools may be limited.

The PowerShell Solution:

```
$smtpServer = "smtp.yourdomain.com"
$msg = new-object Net.Mail.MailMessage
$msg.From = "admin@yourdomain.com"
$msg.To.Add("itteam@yourdomain.com")
$msg.Subject = "Disk Space Alert"
$msg.Body = "Server XYZ has less than 10% disk space
remaining."
$smtp = new-object Net.Mail.SmtpClient($smtpServer)
$smtp.Send($msg)
```

This script sends a custom email alert when paired with a disk monitoring script. It's a flexible and portable solution.

Example 9: Inventory of Installed Software

The Problem:

Organizations need an accurate inventory of installed software for licensing and compliance.

The PowerShell Solution:

```
Get-ItemProperty HKLM:
\Software\Wow6432Node\Microsoft\Windows\CurrentVersion\Unins
tall\* |
Select-Object DisplayName, DisplayVersion, Publisher |
Export-Csv "C:\Scripts\software_inventory.csv" -
NoTypeInformation
```

This script lists all installed software from the Windows registry and saves it for analysis.

Final Thoughts

These real-world examples demonstrate the true power of PowerShell scripting across various IT domains. From automation and monitoring to compliance and backups, PowerShell provides robust tools to enhance your workflow. By mastering these kinds of tasks, even beginner scripters can quickly become valuable assets in their environments. As you continue learning, try adapting these scripts to your own scenarios—customization is where the magic truly begins.

Loops and Iteration

FOR, FOREACH, WHILE, DO-WHILE

Looping structures are fundamental building blocks in programming, allowing scripts to repeat actions based on specific conditions or across data collections. PowerShell, like many other scripting languages, provides several types of loop constructs to cater to different scenarios: for, foreach, while, and do-while. Understanding the appropriate use case and structure of each is key to writing efficient and readable PowerShell scripts.

For Loop

The for loop in PowerShell is ideal when you need to iterate a specific number of times. It is commonly used when the number of iterations is known beforehand, such as incrementing through numbers or indexes.

Syntax:
```
for (<initialization>; <condition>; <iteration>) {
    # Code block to execute
}
```

Example:
```
for ($i = 0; $i -lt 5; $i++) {
    Write-Host "Iteration number: $i"
}
```

How It Works:
1. **Initialization**: $i = 0 sets the starting point.
2. **Condition**: $i -lt 5 continues the loop while true.
3. **Iteration**: $i++ increments the counter after each loop.

When to Use:
- When working with index-based arrays or lists.
- When the total number of iterations is known.

Foreach Loop

The foreach loop iterates through each item in a collection, making it ideal for working with arrays, lists, or objects where the number of items might not be known.

Syntax:
```
foreach ($item in $collection) {
    # Code block to execute
}
```

Example:
```
$servers = @("Server01", "Server02", "Server03")
foreach ($server in $servers) {
    Write-Host "Pinging $server"
    Test-Connection -ComputerName $server -Count 1
}
```

How It Works:
- PowerShell automatically assigns each item in the collection to the loop variable $server during each iteration.

When to Use:
- Working with items in arrays, files, or results from a command.
- You want to perform the same operation on each item in a list.

While Loop

The while loop runs as long as the specified condition evaluates to $true. It's a top-tested loop, meaning it checks the condition before running the loop body.

Syntax:
```
while (<condition>) {
    # Code block to execute
}
```

Example:
```
$count = 0
while ($count -lt 3) {
    Write-Host "Count is $count"
    $count++
```

}

How It Works:
- Before each loop iteration, PowerShell evaluates the condition.
- If the condition is true, the loop body executes.
- The loop continues until the condition becomes false.

When to Use:
- When repeating an action until a certain state or condition is reached.
- When it is possible the loop may not run at all.

Do-While Loop

The do-while loop is similar to the while loop, but it is a bottom-tested loop. This means the loop body executes at least once, regardless of the condition.

Syntax:
```
do {
    # Code block to execute
} while (<condition>)
```

Example:
```
$count = 0
do {
    Write-Host "Running with count $count"
    $count++
} while ($count -lt 3)
```

How It Works:
- Executes the loop body first.
- Then evaluates the condition.
- If the condition is true, it loops again.

When to Use:
- When the loop should run at least once, even if the condition is false initially.

Key Differences and Best Practices

Each looping construct serves a unique purpose and offers flexibility for various scripting needs.

for vs foreach:
- Use for when you require control over an index or are manipulating data structures based on numerical iteration.
- Use foreach for direct iteration over items, especially objects or strings in a collection.

while vs do-while:
- Use while when it is possible the loop should not execute if the condition fails initially.
- Use do-while when at least one execution is guaranteed before condition checking.

Efficiency Tips:
- Avoid infinite loops by ensuring loop conditions eventually evaluate to $false.
- Minimize logic inside the loop if performance is critical—especially in larger datasets.
- Use break to exit a loop early if a specific condition is met.
- Use continue to skip the current iteration and move to the next one.

Example Using All Loops:

```
# Using for loop to create an array
$numbers = @()
for ($i = 1; $i -le 5; $i++) {
    $numbers += $i
}


# Using foreach to double each number
foreach ($number in $numbers) {
    Write-Host "Double of $number is $($number * 2)"
}


# Using while to count down
$countdown = 5
while ($countdown -gt 0) {
    Write-Host "Countdown: $countdown"
    $countdown--
```

```
}

# Using do-while for user input
$input = ""
do {
    $input = Read-Host "Type 'exit' to quit"
    Write-Host "You typed: $input"
} while ($input -ne "exit")
```

This script highlights how each loop construct has a distinct use case. Together, they give PowerShell the flexibility to adapt to a wide range of scripting challenges.

Summary

Understanding the differences between for, foreach, while, and do-while loops allows you to write cleaner and more effective PowerShell scripts. Choosing the right loop not only makes your code more readable but also improves maintainability and performance. Whether you're looping through arrays of server names, waiting for a service to start, or prompting user input, there's a loop structure in PowerShell perfectly suited for the task.

As you become more comfortable with these constructs, you'll find that combining them with conditional statements and functions makes your scripts much more dynamic and powerful. Experiment with different loops in real scenarios to strengthen your intuition and scripting abilities.

LOOP CONTROL (BREAK, CONTINUE)

PowerShell, like most scripting languages, includes powerful mechanisms for controlling the flow of execution within loops. Among the most essential control keywords are break and continue. These keywords allow scripters to make decisions dynamically during loop execution, offering flexibility and precision in how iterations are managed.

This section will explore the use of break and continue in

PowerShell, examine real-world scenarios, and provide best practices to help beginners become proficient with loop control logic.

Understanding Loop Control Basics

Before diving into how break and continue work, it's important to understand the context in which they are used. Loop control keywords are utilized within loops such as for, foreach, while, and do-until.

Common Loop Structures in PowerShell

1. **for loop** – Repeats a block of code a specific number of times.

```
for ($i = 0; $i -lt 10; $i++) {
    Write-Output $i
}
```

2. **foreach loop** – Iterates over a collection of items.

```
foreach ($item in 1..5) {
    Write-Output $item
}
```

3. **while loop** – Continues executing as long as a condition is true.

```
$i = 0
while ($i -lt 5) {
    Write-Output $i
    $i++
}
```

4. **do-until loop** – Executes at least once and continues until a condition becomes true.

```
$i = 0
do {
    Write-Output $i
    $i++
} until ($i -eq 5)
```

These loops form the backbone of automation and iteration in scripts. Controlling their flow intelligently is key to writing clean and efficient code.

The break Statement

The break keyword immediately exits the nearest enclosing loop. It's typically used when a certain condition has been met, and continuing the loop is unnecessary or inefficient.

Syntax
break

Example: Exiting on a Condition

```
foreach ($number in 1..10) {
    if ($number -eq 5) {
        break
    }
    Write-Output $number
}
```

Output:

```
1
2
3
4
```

The loop stops entirely once $number equals 5.

Practical Use Case

Imagine scanning a list of server names and exiting the loop once you find the first one that is offline:

```
$servers = @("Server1", "Server2", "Server3", "Server4")

foreach ($server in $servers) {
    if (-not (Test-Connection -ComputerName $server -Count 1
-Quiet)) {
        Write-Output "$server is offline. Exiting loop."
        break
    }
    Write-Output "$server is online."
}
```

This avoids unnecessary checks once the critical failure is found.

The continue Statement

Unlike break, which stops the loop entirely, the continue keyword skips the current iteration and proceeds with the next one. This is useful for ignoring certain conditions without halting the loop.

Syntax

continue

Example: Skipping Specific Values

```
foreach ($number in 1..10) {
    if ($number % 2 -eq 0) {
        continue
    }
    Write-Output $number
}
```

Output:

```
1
3
5
7
9
```

Only odd numbers are printed; even numbers are skipped.

Real-World Scenario: Processing Files with Exceptions

Imagine looping through a list of file paths but skipping any that are system files.

```
$files = Get-ChildItem -Path "C:\Temp"

foreach ($file in $files) {
    if ($file.Attributes -match "System") {
        continue
    }
    Write-Output "Processing file: $($file.Name)"
}
```

This lets you ignore specific cases without breaking the flow of the script.

Combining break and continue

These control statements can also be used together to create finely tuned logic.

Example: Break on Error, Continue on Warning

```
$logEntries = @("INFO", "INFO", "WARNING", "INFO", "ERROR",
"INFO")

foreach ($entry in $logEntries) {
    if ($entry -eq "WARNING") {
        Write-Output "Warning encountered. Skipping."
        continue
    }
    if ($entry -eq "ERROR") {
        Write-Output "Error encountered. Exiting loop."
        break
    }
    Write-Output "Processing log: $entry"
}
```

Output:
```
Processing log: INFO
Processing log: INFO
Warning encountered. Skipping.
Processing log: INFO
Error encountered. Exiting loop.
```

Best Practices

1. **Use break sparingly** – Exiting a loop prematurely can be powerful, but make sure it aligns with the script's goal.
2. **Use continue for filtering** – When working with large datasets, continue helps ignore unimportant cases cleanly.
3. **Avoid nested loop confusion** – In nested loops, break and continue only affect the innermost loop. Consider adding comments or using functions for clarity.
4. **Validate logic paths** – Always test your loops to ensure break or continue conditions don't result in unexpected behavior.

Conclusion

Loop control using break and continue is essential for building scripts that respond dynamically to real-time data and conditions. These keywords can simplify your logic, reduce unnecessary processing, and make your PowerShell scripts more efficient and easier to maintain.

Understanding when and how to use them appropriately is a foundational skill for every PowerShell scripter. Practice with real-world scenarios—like skipping log files, terminating scans on errors, or filtering out known bad data—and you'll soon gain a natural intuition for these tools.

In the next section, we'll explore **return statements** and how they compare and interact with break and continue, especially within functions and script blocks.

Functions and Scoping

DEFINING FUNCTIONS

One of the most powerful features of PowerShell is its support for user-defined functions. Functions are essential for writing clean, reusable, and modular code. They allow you to encapsulate blocks of logic into a single unit that can be executed whenever needed. In this section, we will explore what functions are, how to define and use them, and best practices for making them efficient and easy to maintain.

What is a Function?

A function in PowerShell is a named block of code that performs a specific task. It can take input, process data, and return output. Functions help reduce code duplication, simplify complex scripts, and make your scripts more readable.

The basic syntax of a PowerShell function is:

```
function FunctionName {
    # Code block
}
```

Or, with parameters:

```
function FunctionName {
    param (
        [string]$Param1,
        [int]$Param2
    )
    # Code block
}
```

Creating Your First Function

Let's start by creating a simple function that prints a message:
```
function Say-Hello {
    Write-Output "Hello, World!"
}


Say-Hello  # Output: Hello, World!
```

This function, Say-Hello, doesn't take any parameters. It simply outputs a message. To run the function, you call it by name.

Adding Parameters to Functions

Functions become much more powerful when you add parameters. Parameters allow you to pass data into the function for processing.
```
function Greet-User {
    param (
        [string]$Name
    )
    Write-Output "Hello, $Name!"
}


Greet-User -Name "Alice"  # Output: Hello, Alice!
```

This example shows how to accept input via the $Name parameter and use it in the output message.

Return Values

A function can return values using the return keyword or simply by outputting data.
```
function Add-Numbers {
    param (
        [int]$A,
        [int]$B
    )
    return $A + $B
}


$result = Add-Numbers -A 5 -B 7
```

```
Write-Output $result  # Output: 12
```

In PowerShell, any object not captured or suppressed is returned by default. However, using return can make your intentions clearer.

Advanced Function Features

PowerShell offers many advanced features for functions:

Default Parameter Values

You can assign default values to parameters:

```
function Greet-User {
    param (
        [string]$Name = "Guest"
    )
    Write-Output "Hello, $Name!"
}


Greet-User              # Output: Hello, Guest!
Greet-User -Name "Bob" # Output: Hello, Bob!
```

Type Enforcement

You can enforce specific data types:

```
function Multiply-Numbers {
    param (
        [int]$A,
        [int]$B
    )
    return $A * $B
}
```

Passing a non-integer to this function will cause an error.

Mandatory Parameters

You can make parameters mandatory:

```
function Greet-User {
    param (
        [Parameter(Mandatory = $true)]
        [string]$Name
    )
    Write-Output "Hello, $Name!"
```

```
}
```

If you call Greet-User without the -Name parameter, PowerShell will prompt you for it.

Scoping in Functions

PowerShell has a concept called **scope**, which defines the visibility of variables. By default, variables defined inside a function are local to that function:

```
function Set-Message {
    $message = "This is local"
    Write-Output $message
}


Set-Message
Write-Output $message  # Will produce an error if $message
is not defined globally
```

If you need a function to modify a global variable, you can use the global: scope:

```
function Set-GlobalMessage {
    $global:message = "This is global"
}


Set-GlobalMessage
Write-Output $message  # Output: This is global
```

ScriptBlocks and Inline Functions

PowerShell also supports script blocks and inline functions (anonymous functions):

```
$adder = {
    param ($x, $y)
    $x + $y
}


&$adder 3 4  # Output: 7
```

This flexibility allows you to treat functions as variables, pass them around, and execute them dynamically.

Function Naming Conventions

PowerShell encourages the **Verb-Noun** naming convention for functions (e.g., Get-Data, Start-Process). This helps maintain consistency and readability.

You can see approved verbs by running:

```
Get-Verb
```

Aliases for Functions

You can create aliases for your functions using the Set-Alias cmdlet:

```
function Get-DateTime {
    Get-Date
}

Set-Alias gdt Get-DateTime

gdt  # Calls Get-DateTime
```

Best Practices for Defining Functions

1. **Use meaningful names**: Stick to the Verb-Noun format.
2. **Add comments and help documentation**: Use comments and Get-Help metadata.
3. **Avoid global variables**: Try to keep variable scope local unless necessary.
4. **Validate input**: Use type enforcement and parameter attributes.
5. **Return only what is needed**: Avoid writing unnecessary output.
6. **Use begin, process, and end blocks** for pipeline functions.

Example: A Real-World Utility Function

Here's an example function that checks if a computer is online:

```
function Test-ComputerOnline {
    param (
        [string]$ComputerName
    )

    if (Test-Connection -ComputerName $ComputerName -Count 1
-Quiet) {
        return "$ComputerName is online."
    } else {
        return "$ComputerName is offline."
    }
}


Test-ComputerOnline -ComputerName "localhost"
```

This function is reusable, easy to understand, and uses proper
PowerShell practices.

Summary

Defining functions in PowerShell is a cornerstone of writing efficient,
maintainable scripts. By encapsulating logic into functions, you create
a cleaner structure and reduce redundancy. With the ability to define
parameters, enforce types, manage scope, and add documentation,
PowerShell functions are as powerful as those in any modern
programming language. As you continue your journey, focus on
building libraries of well-written functions to accelerate your
scripting and automation efforts.

In the next section, we'll dive into **Modules**, which allow you to
group and share your functions more efficiently.

PARAMETERS, RETURN, AND SCOPING RULES

PowerShell scripting offers a highly flexible and powerful approach to
task automation and system administration. Understanding how to
define and work with **parameters**, how to use **return values**, and how
scoping rules affect variable behavior is critical to writing efficient
and maintainable scripts. In this section, we'll explore these three

foundational elements in detail.

Parameters: Accepting Input in Functions and Scripts

Parameters allow scripts and functions to accept input dynamically, making them reusable and adaptable. PowerShell provides several ways to define parameters depending on the complexity of your needs.

Basic Parameter Declaration

The simplest way to define parameters is by using the param keyword within a function or script block:

```
function Get-Greeting {
    param ($Name)
    "Hello, $Name!"
}
```

This function takes a single argument $Name and returns a greeting. You can call it like so:

```
Get-Greeting -Name "Alice"
```

Strongly Typed Parameters

PowerShell supports strongly typed parameters to enforce the type of input expected:

```
function Add-Numbers {
    param ([int]$A, [int]$B)
    return $A + $B
}
```

This ensures that only integers are passed, reducing the risk of runtime errors.

Parameter Attributes

You can enhance parameters using attributes like [Parameter()], which allow you to control aspects such as mandatory input, parameter sets, and position.

```
function Show-Info {
    param (
        [Parameter(Mandatory=$true)]
        [string]$Name,
```

```
        [Parameter(Position=1)]
        [int]$Age
    )
    "Name: $Name, Age: $Age"
}
```

Default Values and Validation

Default values can be assigned, and input can be validated using attributes such as [ValidateRange()] or [ValidateSet()]:

```
function Set-Level {
    param (
        [ValidateSet("Low", "Medium", "High")]
        [string]$Level = "Medium"
    )
    "Level is set to: $Level"
}
```

This restricts input to specific values, helping catch user errors early.

Return: Sending Data Back from Functions

PowerShell functions can return data implicitly or explicitly. Understanding the nuances of how data is returned is essential for effective scripting.

Implicit Return

Any output produced by a function that is not captured or suppressed will be returned automatically:

```
function Multiply {
    $Result = 2 * 5
    $Result
}
```

Explicit Return

You can also use the return keyword to exit the function and return a specific value:

```
function Get-Double {
    param ($Number)
    return $Number * 2
```

}

Note that using return stops the execution of the function immediately. Anything after return is ignored.

Returning Multiple Values

Functions can return multiple values by outputting objects or using arrays:

```
function Get-Stats {
    $cpu = Get-Counter '\\Processor(_Total)\\% Processor
Time'
    $mem = Get-Counter '\\Memory\\Available MBytes'
    return @($cpu, $mem)
}
```

Or, better yet, return a custom object:

```
function Get-SystemStats {
    [PSCustomObject]@{
        CPUUsage = (Get-Counter '\\Processor(_Total)\\%
Processor Time').CounterSamples[0].CookedValue
        FreeMemory = (Get-Counter '\\Memory\\Available
MBytes').CounterSamples[0].CookedValue
    }
}
```

This makes the result easier to work with and more readable.

Scoping Rules: Managing Variable Visibility

Scope determines the visibility and lifetime of variables. Misunderstanding scope can lead to bugs that are hard to trace. PowerShell includes several types of scope:

Types of Scope

- **Global**: Accessible from anywhere in the session.
- **Script**: Visible throughout the script file where the variable is declared.
- **Local**: The default scope; visible only in the current function or block.
- **Private**: Similar to local but hidden from child scopes.

Declaring Variables with Scope

```
$Global:UserName = "Alice"
$Script:AppName = "PowerTool"
$Local:Count = 10
$Private:SessionToken = "XYZ123"
```

Use these prefixes carefully—especially $Global:—as they can create conflicts or unexpected behavior when reused.

Scope Inheritance

Child scopes inherit variables from parent scopes, but not vice versa:

```
function Parent {
    $message = "Hello from parent"
    Child
}


function Child {
    Write-Output $message  # Works due to scope inheritance
}
```

However, variables declared in a child scope are not available to the parent unless explicitly passed or declared in a shared scope.

Scope Modifiers and Best Practices

When modifying global or script-scope variables within functions, use caution:

```
function Update-Global {
    $Global:Counter += 1
}
```

This is useful but can lead to difficult debugging situations if not well-documented. A better approach is often to return the value and assign it explicitly outside the function:

```
function Increment {
    param($Value)
    return $Value + 1
}


$Counter = Increment -Value $Counter
```

Summary

- **Parameters** let functions accept input and be more versatile.
- Use **validation and attributes** to improve input quality and enforce logic.
- **Return values** can be implicit or explicit; returning objects improves clarity.
- Understanding **scoping rules** helps manage where and how variables are accessible.

Mastering these concepts will empower you to build PowerShell scripts that are clean, powerful, and maintainable. In the next chapter, we'll dive into looping constructs and conditional logic to further enhance your automation capabilities.

SCRIPT VS GLOBAL SCOPE

Understanding the concept of **scope** in PowerShell is crucial for writing efficient, maintainable, and secure scripts. Scope determines the visibility and lifespan of variables, functions, aliases, and other elements. Two of the most commonly referenced scopes in PowerShell are **Script Scope** and **Global Scope**. Knowing how and when to use each is essential for both beginners and seasoned scripters alike.

This section will explore these two scopes in depth, comparing their behaviors, use cases, and potential pitfalls. By the end, you should have a strong grasp of how to control scope effectively in your PowerShell scripts.

What is Scope in PowerShell?

In PowerShell, scope refers to the context in which a variable or function is defined and accessed. When you define something in PowerShell, it exists within a certain boundary. These boundaries are known as scopes, and they control whether something can be seen or modified from another part of your code.

There are several types of scope in PowerShell:
- **Global**
- **Script**
- **Local**

- **Private**

For this section, we will focus on Global and Script scopes specifically.

Global Scope

The **Global Scope** is the top-level scope in PowerShell. Anything defined in the Global Scope is accessible from anywhere in the session —whether in scripts, functions, or the command line. This makes the Global Scope both powerful and potentially dangerous.

Characteristics of Global Scope:

- Variables and functions defined in the Global Scope remain available throughout the PowerShell session.
- Changes to global variables affect all parts of the session.
- Useful for session-wide configuration or state.

When to Use Global Scope:

- When defining settings or variables that must be accessed across multiple scripts or functions.
- When initializing modules that will share state or resources.
- For debugging or testing purposes.

Example:

```
# Define a global variable
global:MyGlobalVar = "This is a global variable"

function Show-GlobalVar {
    Write-Output $global:MyGlobalVar
}

Show-GlobalVar  # Output: This is a global variable
```

In this example, MyGlobalVar is defined in the global scope and is accessible within the function Show-GlobalVar.

Pitfalls of Global Scope:

- Can lead to **variable pollution**, where too many variables clutter the session.
- High risk of **naming conflicts**, especially in larger scripts or when using third-party modules.

- Difficult to manage and debug, as changes in one script may affect others unintentionally.

Script Scope

The **Script Scope** is specific to the script file in which elements are defined. Items declared in the Script Scope are accessible anywhere within that script, but not outside of it.

Characteristics of Script Scope:

- Variables and functions are only available to the script in which they are defined.
- Script Scope is ideal for modular and reusable code.
- It prevents unintentional modification of values outside the script.

When to Use Script Scope:

- When creating self-contained scripts that should not alter or be altered by the global environment.
- To avoid polluting the Global Scope with temporary or internal-use variables.
- In automation tasks where script integrity and isolation are key.

Example:

```
# In MyScript.ps1
script:MyScriptVar = "This is a script-scoped variable"

function Show-ScriptVar {
    Write-Output $script:MyScriptVar
}

Show-ScriptVar  # Output: This is a script-scoped variable
```

Here, MyScriptVar is defined within the script scope and used throughout the script without affecting the global environment.

Benefits of Script Scope:

- Reduces the risk of conflicts and unexpected behavior.
- Keeps code modular and easier to maintain.
- Enhances readability and reliability of the script.

Comparing Script Scope and Global Scope

Let's take a moment to highlight the differences:

- **Lifetime**:
- Global: Persists for the entire session.
- Script: Lives only for the duration of the script's execution.
- **Visibility**:
- Global: Visible everywhere in the session.
- Script: Visible only within the script file.
- **Best for**:
- Global: Configuration, state-sharing, debugging.
- Script: Encapsulation, isolation, reusable scripts.
- **Risk**:
- Global: Higher risk of side effects.
- Script: Lower risk due to isolation.

Best Practices for Scope Management

Here are some best practices to follow when managing scope in your PowerShell scripts:

1. **Prefer local or script scope** over global whenever possible.
2. **Only use global scope** when absolutely necessary, such as for shared settings or module-wide configuration.
3. **Use consistent naming conventions** to avoid accidental conflicts.
4. **Initialize variables in the narrowest scope** needed for their functionality.
5. **Document your use of scope**, especially when using global variables or complex functions.
6. **Avoid modifying global variables from within functions or scripts** unless that is your explicit intent.
7. **Use Get-Variable -Scope** to audit variable scopes when debugging.

Practical Scenario: Why Scope Matters

Consider you're developing a PowerShell script to automate a deployment pipeline. You initialize some configuration values and authentication tokens.

If you place them in the global scope, and another script runs concurrently or afterward in the same session, those values may be overwritten or misused. This could lead to accidental deployments to the wrong environment, or security vulnerabilities.

On the other hand, using script scope ensures those values are only valid for the duration and context of that specific script. This makes your automation more robust, predictable, and secure.

Summary

Understanding the difference between Script and Global scopes in PowerShell is fundamental for writing clean, reliable scripts. The Global Scope gives you broad access and persistent variables but should be used sparingly due to its far-reaching consequences. The Script Scope, by contrast, is well-suited for contained, modular scripting and should be your go-to for most scripting tasks.

Managing scope effectively not only improves your code's functionality but also enhances its maintainability and security. By applying the best practices outlined in this section, you'll be well-equipped to handle scope-related challenges in any PowerShell project.

Error Handling

TRY/CATCH/FINALLY

When scripting in PowerShell, one of the most important skills a scripter can develop is the ability to handle errors gracefully. Rather than allowing your script to crash or behave unpredictably, PowerShell provides robust mechanisms to catch and manage exceptions using the try, catch, and finally blocks. This section will explore these constructs in depth, offering beginner-friendly guidance, practical examples, and best practices for effective error handling in PowerShell.

Understanding the Basics

The try/catch/finally structure in PowerShell is similar to that found in other programming languages like C# or JavaScript. It is used to define a block of code that may throw an error (try), a block to handle the error if one occurs (catch), and a block of code that should always execute regardless of whether an error occurred (finally).

Syntax

```
try {
    # Code that might throw an exception
}
catch {
    # Code to handle the exception
}
finally {
    # Code that will always run
}
```

All three blocks are optional except try, but they are most powerful when used together. Now let's break down each component.

114

The try Block

The try block contains the code that you want to monitor for exceptions. This can be anything from reading a file to querying a database or accessing a web API. If an error occurs in this block, PowerShell immediately stops execution within the block and transfers control to the catch block, if one is defined.

Example

```
try {
    Get-Content "C:\nonexistentfile.txt"
    Write-Output "File read successfully."
}
```

If the file doesn't exist, PowerShell throws an error, and because we haven't defined a catch, the error will be displayed to the user.

The catch Block

This is where you define how to handle the error. The catch block executes only if an error occurs within the associated try block. You can also use multiple catch blocks for different types of exceptions, but this is more advanced and rarely needed in basic scripts.

Example

```
try {
    Get-Content "C:\nonexistentfile.txt"
}
catch {
    Write-Output "An error occurred: $_"
}
```

The special variable $_ holds the current error object, which contains details about the error that occurred. This allows you to log errors, notify users, or take corrective actions.

Filtering Exceptions

You can also specify the type of exception you want to catch. This is useful for scripts that may encounter multiple types of exceptions and you want to handle each one differently.

```
try {
    # Attempt to divide by zero
```

```
    $result = 5 / 0
}
catch [System.DivideByZeroException] {
    Write-Output "You can't divide by zero!"
}
catch {
    Write-Output "A general error occurred: $_"
}
```

In this example, if a divide-by-zero error occurs, it's caught by the first catch block. If another kind of error occurs, it's caught by the second block.

The finally Block

The finally block always runs, whether an error occurred or not. This is commonly used to clean up resources like closing file handles or disconnecting from a remote session.

Example

```
try {
    $stream = [System.IO.StreamReader]::new("C:
\example.txt")
    $content = $stream.ReadToEnd()
    Write-Output $content
}
catch {
    Write-Output "An error occurred while reading the file."
}
finally {
    if ($stream) { $stream.Close() }
    Write-Output "File stream closed."
}
```

Even if the file doesn't exist and an error occurs, the finally block ensures that the script attempts to close the stream and notify the user.

Why Use Try/Catch/Finally?

Handling errors gracefully provides multiple benefits:
1. **Improved User Experience**: Instead of crashing, your script can provide meaningful error messages.
2. **Robustness**: Scripts that handle errors are more reliable and easier to maintain.
3. **Debugging**: You can log errors for troubleshooting.
4. **Automation**: Automated scripts that crash midway can cause cascading failures. Error handling prevents this.

Common Mistakes and How to Avoid Them

1. Forgetting $ErrorActionPreference
PowerShell doesn't treat all errors as terminating by default. Some errors are non-terminating and won't trigger catch. To ensure try/catch works as expected, set:
```
$ErrorActionPreference = "Stop"
```
Or add -ErrorAction Stop to individual commands:
```
Get-Content "C:\nonexistentfile.txt" -ErrorAction Stop
```

2. Overusing try/catch
Not every line of code needs to be wrapped in try/catch. Use it where errors are likely or where failure needs to be handled explicitly.

3. Ignoring the Error Object
Don't just write catch {} and move on. Use the error object $_ to diagnose problems or log them.

4. Not Cleaning Up in finally
Failing to use finally for cleanup can lead to resource leaks like open file handles or persistent connections.

Real-World Use Case

Let's say you're writing a script to backup logs from a directory and archive them. You want to ensure that even if one part fails, the script logs the error and continues or exits cleanly.
```
$source = "C:\Logs"
$destination = "D:\Backups\Logs.zip"

try {
```

```
    Compress-Archive -Path $source -DestinationPath
$destination -ErrorAction Stop
    Write-Output "Logs backed up successfully."
}
catch {
    Write-Output "Backup failed: $_"
    # Log to file
    Add-Content -Path "C:\Logs\backup_errors.txt" -Value "[$
(Get-Date)] $_"
}
finally {
    Write-Output "Backup script execution complete."
}
```

Summary and Best Practices

- Always use -ErrorAction Stop if you expect to catch non-terminating errors.
- Use try/catch to control script behavior when things go wrong.
- Use finally to clean up resources, even if no errors occurred.
- Don't swallow errors silently. Always log or notify.
- Write specific catch blocks if you need tailored error responses.

PowerShell scripts, like any form of automation, must be dependable. With try/catch/finally, you gain the tools to write resilient scripts that handle failure like a pro. The sooner you incorporate error handling into your scripting practices, the smoother your automation journey will be.

$ERROR, $?, AND ERRORACTION

In PowerShell, effective error handling is essential for writing reliable scripts that can gracefully handle unexpected conditions, provide meaningful output, and continue operation when possible. Three crucial components of error handling are the automatic variables $Error, $?, and the -ErrorAction common parameter. Understanding how these elements function and interact can greatly improve your PowerShell scripting capabilities.

Understanding $Error

The $Error variable in PowerShell is an automatic array-like variable that stores a collection of error objects generated during the current session. This array is ordered with the most recent error at index 0. Each time an error occurs, it is appended to the top of the $Error array.

Key Characteristics:

- **Array Behavior**: $Error[0] gives the most recent error.
- **Session Lifetime**: Errors persist in $Error until the session ends or until explicitly cleared.
- **Manual Clearing**: Use $Error.Clear() to remove all entries.
- **Error Objects**: Each entry is a System.Management.Automation.ErrorRecord object, which contains rich metadata like the message, category, target object, and the exception type.

Example:

```
Get-Item "C:\nonexistentfile.txt"
$Error[0].Exception.Message
```

This will show the exception message related to the failed Get-Item command.

Inspecting Errors:

```
$lastError = $Error[0]
$lastError.Exception.GetType().FullName
$lastError.FullyQualifiedErrorId
```

These lines help you understand the type and identity of the error, which is especially useful for conditional logic and logging.

Understanding $?

The $? variable is a Boolean that reflects the success or failure of the **last command** that was executed. If the last command was successful, $? is True. If it failed, $? is False.

Common Use Cases:

- **Flow Control**: Determine what to do next based on whether the last command succeeded.
- **Scripting Logic**: Conditionally execute steps only if the prior

command was successful.

Example:

```
Remove-Item "C:\nonexistentfile.txt"
if (-not $?) {
    Write-Host "Command failed."
}
```

This conditional block executes if Remove-Item fails.

Important Notes:

- $? checks only whether the command **completed successfully in PowerShell's eyes**, not necessarily whether the operation logically succeeded. For instance, a command might return a non-zero exit code but not throw an error.

Combining $? and $Error:

While $? tells you **if** the last command failed, $Error tells you **what** went wrong. Together, they are a powerful duo.

```
Some-Command
if (-not $?) {
    Write-Warning "Something went wrong: $
($Error[0].Exception.Message)"
}
```

The -ErrorAction Common Parameter

-ErrorAction allows you to control how PowerShell responds to non-terminating errors. Many cmdlets throw errors that do **not** stop script execution; -ErrorAction gives you the power to change that behavior.

Available Values:

- Continue *(default)*: Display the error and continue executing the script.
- Stop: Treat the error as a terminating error and stop execution.
- SilentlyContinue: Suppress the error message and continue.
- Ignore: Suppress the error and do not add it to the $Error array.
- Inquire: Prompt the user for action before continuing.
- Suspend *(for workflows only)*: Pause the workflow.

Example:

```
Get-Item "C:\nonexistentfile.txt" -ErrorAction
SilentlyContinue
if (-not $?) {
```

```
    Write-Host "The item could not be found."
}
```

Here, the error message won't display, but you can still react to the failure using $? or $Error.

Making Errors Terminating:

Sometimes you want an error to stop the script immediately. Using -ErrorAction Stop converts non-terminating errors into terminating ones.

```
try {
    Get-Item "C:\nonexistentfile.txt" -ErrorAction Stop
} catch {
    Write-Host "Caught an error: $_"
}
```

This try/catch block works because the error was converted into a terminating error.

Putting It All Together

Robust Error Handling Example:

```
function Test-FileAccess {
    param (
        [string]$Path
    )

    try {
        Get-Item $Path -ErrorAction Stop
        Write-Host "File exists and is accessible."
    } catch {
        Write-Warning "Could not access file: $
($_.Exception.Message)"
        # Optionally log the error
        Add-Content -Path "C:\Logs\ErrorLog.txt" -Value $_
    }

    if (-not $?) {
        Write-Host "Command failed, examining \$Error
stack..."
        $Error[0] | Format-List *
```

```
    }
}


Test-FileAccess -Path "C:\nonexistentfile.txt"
```

Error Recovery Example:
```
$files = @("C:\file1.txt", "C:\file2.txt", "C:
\missingfile.txt")
foreach ($file in $files) {
    try {
        Remove-Item $file -ErrorAction Stop
        Write-Host "$file removed successfully."
    } catch {
        Write-Warning "Failed to remove $file: $
($_.Exception.Message)"
    }
}
```

This ensures that the script continues even if some files are missing.

Best Practices

Always Handle Expected Failures

Use try/catch with -ErrorAction Stop when dealing with file system, network, or user input operations that are prone to failure.

Use $Error.Clear() in Loops or Repeated Checks

This ensures your error logic is checking only fresh errors, avoiding false positives from earlier issues.
```
$Error.Clear()
Do-Something
if ($Error.Count -gt 0) {
    Write-Host "Error occurred: $
($Error[0].Exception.Message)"
}
```

Avoid Relying Only on $? in Critical Scripts

Since $? evaluates success from PowerShell's perspective, it might be True even when a command returns a non-zero exit code.
```
$proc = Start-Process ping -ArgumentList "127.0.0.1 -n 1" -
PassThru -Wait
```

```
if ($proc.ExitCode -ne 0) {
    Write-Warning "Ping failed even though \$? was $($?)."
}
```

Summary

PowerShell provides a robust and flexible error handling system through $Error, $?, and -ErrorAction. By mastering these tools, you can:

- Detect when and why errors occur
- Respond dynamically to failures
- Suppress or escalate errors based on context
- Maintain cleaner, more maintainable, and more reliable scripts

Whether you're writing a simple automation script or building an advanced deployment pipeline, integrating proper error handling techniques is essential to building production-quality PowerShell code.

Files and Directories

COPYING, MOVING, RENAMING, DELETING

One of the most common tasks in PowerShell scripting involves managing files and directories. Whether you're backing up important data, organizing content into structured folders, or cleaning up redundant files, you'll often need to copy, move, rename, or delete files. PowerShell makes these operations straightforward and powerful, offering a wide range of options for both manual and automated workflows.

Copying Files and Directories

The Copy-Item cmdlet is used to copy files and directories in PowerShell. This command allows you to duplicate a file or folder from one location to another.

Basic Syntax

```
Copy-Item -Path "source" -Destination "destination"
```

Example: Copy a Single File

```
Copy-Item -Path "C:\Reports\report1.txt" -Destination "D:
\Backups"
```

This command copies report1.txt to the D:\Backups directory.

Copying Directories

To copy a folder and all its contents, use the -Recurse parameter:

```
Copy-Item -Path "C:\Reports" -Destination "D:\Backups" -
Recurse
```

Overwriting Files

By default, Copy-Item does not overwrite existing files. To force an overwrite, you can use -Force in combination with logic to remove the destination file first or wrap the copy command in a conditional script.

Moving Files and Directories

Move-Item is used to move files and folders from one location to another. This command is especially useful when reorganizing a file structure or archiving old data.

Basic Syntax

```
Move-Item -Path "source" -Destination "destination"
```

Example: Move a File

```
Move-Item -Path "C:\Temp\notes.txt" -Destination "C:
\Documents"
```

Moving and Overwriting

Like Copy-Item, Move-Item does not overwrite existing files. To handle overwrites, you may need to check if the destination file exists and delete it beforehand:

```
if (Test-Path "C:\Documents\notes.txt") {
    Remove-Item "C:\Documents\notes.txt" -Force
}
Move-Item "C:\Temp\notes.txt" "C:\Documents"
```

Moving Folders

To move an entire folder and its contents:

```
Move-Item -Path "C:\OldProjects" -Destination "D:\Archives"
```

Renaming Files and Directories

Renaming files and directories in PowerShell is handled by the Rename-Item cmdlet. This is useful for standardizing file names, batch-renaming files based on patterns, or organizing content.

Basic Syntax

```
Rename-Item -Path "currentName" -NewName "newName"
```

Example: Rename a File

```
Rename-Item -Path "C:\Documents\notes.txt" -NewName
"meeting_notes.txt"
```

Rename with Wildcards and Loops

You can rename multiple files using loops. For instance, to rename all .txt files in a folder to have a _2025 suffix:

```
Get-ChildItem -Path "C:\Logs" -Filter "*.txt" | ForEach-
Object {
    $newName = $_.BaseName + "_2025" + $_.Extension
    Rename-Item -Path $_.FullName -NewName $newName
}
```

Renaming Directories

```
Rename-Item -Path "C:\OldFolder" -NewName "ArchivedFolder"
```

Deleting Files and Directories

Deleting is a potentially dangerous operation, especially when done programmatically. PowerShell's Remove-Item cmdlet should be used carefully.

Basic Syntax

```
Remove-Item -Path "target"
```

Example: Delete a File

```
Remove-Item -Path "C:\Temp\oldfile.txt"
```

Deleting Directories

Use the -Recurse parameter to delete a folder and its contents:

```
Remove-Item -Path "C:\OldBackups" -Recurse
```

Force Deletion

To delete read-only or hidden files, include the -Force parameter:

```
Remove-Item -Path "C:\Temp\lockedfile.txt" -Force
```

Deletion with Confirmation

To avoid accidental deletions, use the -Confirm parameter:

```
Remove-Item -Path "C:\SensitiveData\*" -Recurse -Confirm
```

This prompts for confirmation before each deletion.

Tips and Best Practices

1. Always Test with -WhatIf

Before running destructive commands like Remove-Item, use -WhatIf to simulate the command:

```
Remove-Item -Path "C:\Data\*" -Recurse -WhatIf
```

This shows what would happen without actually deleting anything.

2. Logging Actions

Consider logging your file operations for audit trails:

```
$log = "C:\Logs\file_ops.log"
"$(Get-Date): Copying Files..." | Out-File -Append $log
Copy-Item "C:\Source\*" "C:\Destination" -Recurse
"$(Get-Date): Copy Completed." | Out-File -Append $log
```

3. Error Handling

Use Try/Catch blocks to handle errors gracefully:

```
try {
    Remove-Item -Path "C:\ImportantData\*" -Recurse -Force
} catch {
    Write-Host "Error occurred: $_"
}
```

4. Creating Backups

Always backup critical files before delete or move operations:

```
Copy-Item "C:\Critical\*" "D:\Backup\Critical" -Recurse
```

5. Automating with Scripts

You can combine all these operations into reusable scripts. For example, a cleanup script:

```
# CleanupScript.ps1
$source = "C:\Downloads"
$destination = "D:\Archives\Downloads"

# Copy files
Copy-Item -Path $source -Destination $destination -Recurse -Force

# Log the move
"Moved files from $source to $destination on $(Get-Date)" |
```

```
Out-File -Append "C:\Logs\cleanup.log"

# Delete originals
Remove-Item -Path $source\* -Recurse -Force
```

Conclusion

Mastering the commands for copying, moving, renaming, and deleting files in PowerShell is essential for any scripter or system administrator. These commands form the backbone of automation tasks, from nightly backups and system maintenance to user data management and deployment processes.

When used with care—and enhanced with safety features like -WhatIf, logging, and backups—these tools can save you significant time and reduce the risk of human error. As you continue learning PowerShell, you'll find that combining these basic cmdlets with loops, conditionals, and custom logic opens up even more powerful workflows and automation possibilities.

RECURSIVE SEARCHES AND FILTERS

PowerShell is a powerful scripting language and automation framework that shines when it comes to managing file systems, processes, and data structures. One of the most valuable techniques in PowerShell is the use of **recursive searches and filters**, particularly when dealing with large file systems or complex hierarchical data. In this section, we'll take a deep dive into how recursion works in PowerShell, how to implement it effectively, and how to apply filtering techniques to retrieve exactly the information you need.

What Is a Recursive Search?

A **recursive search** is a search that not only looks at the top-level items in a directory or data structure but also delves into all subdirectories or nested objects, continuing the process until there are no more items to inspect. Recursion is a technique where a function calls itself to repeat a process.

In the context of PowerShell, recursive searches are frequently used when navigating file systems, searching through nested folders, or querying hierarchical data like Active Directory structures or nested XML/JSON objects.

Basic Example: Searching Files Recursively

```
Get-ChildItem -Path "C:\Users\Paul\Documents" -Recurse
```

This command lists all files and directories within C:\Users\Paul\Documents and all its subfolders.

Understanding Get-ChildItem and the -Recurse Parameter

The Get-ChildItem cmdlet (also known by its alias gci or dir) is used to retrieve the items and child items in one or more specified locations. Adding the -Recurse parameter tells PowerShell to include all subfolders in the search.

```
Get-ChildItem -Path "C:\Scripts" -Recurse -File
```

Here, -File is used to ensure that only files (not directories) are returned.

Including Hidden and System Files

By default, hidden and system files are excluded. To include them:

```
Get-ChildItem -Path "C:\" -Recurse -Force
```

The -Force parameter includes hidden and system files.

Filtering Recursively

PowerShell allows for filtering at multiple stages:

1. **Provider-level filtering**: Done at the file system level.
2. **Where-Object filtering**: Done in PowerShell after items are retrieved.

Using the -Filter Parameter

```
Get-ChildItem -Path "C:\Projects" -Recurse -Filter "*.ps1"
```

This searches for all .ps1 (PowerShell script) files in the directory and subdirectories. The -Filter parameter is generally more efficient than

Where-Object because it is applied by the provider (like the file system) before the data is sent to PowerShell.

Using Where-Object for Advanced Filters

```
Get-ChildItem -Path "C:\Logs" -Recurse | Where-Object {
$_.LastWriteTime -gt (Get-Date).AddDays(-7) }
```

This returns all files modified in the last 7 days.

You can also combine filters:

```
Get-ChildItem -Path "C:\Logs" -Recurse -File | Where-Object
{ $_.Extension -eq ".log" -and $_.Length -gt 1MB }
```

This finds all .log files over 1MB in size.

Building Custom Recursive Functions

Although -Recurse is convenient, sometimes you need more control. That's when writing a **custom recursive function** becomes valuable.

Example: Recursive File Search by Extension

```
function Get-FilesByExtension {
    param (
        [string]$Path,
        [string]$Extension
    )

    $items = Get-ChildItem -Path $Path

    foreach ($item in $items) {
        if ($item.PSIsContainer) {
            Get-FilesByExtension -Path $item.FullName -
Extension $Extension
        } elseif ($item.Extension -eq $Extension) {
            $item
        }
    }
}

Get-FilesByExtension -Path "C:\Data" -Extension ".csv"
```

This manually navigates each directory, giving you the opportunity to insert custom logic at each step.

Use Cases and Real-World Examples

Cleaning Up Old Files

```
Get-ChildItem -Path "C:\Temp" -Recurse -File | Where-Object
{ $_.LastWriteTime -lt (Get-Date).AddDays(-30) } | Remove-
Item -Force
```

This finds and deletes files not modified in the last 30 days.

Finding Duplicate Files by Name

```
Get-ChildItem -Path "C:\Media" -Recurse -File | Group-Object
-Property Name | Where-Object { $_.Count -gt 1 }
```

This groups files by name and shows only those with duplicates.

Exporting a Report of Large Files

```
Get-ChildItem -Path "C:\" -Recurse -File | Where-Object {
$_.Length -gt 100MB } | Select-Object FullName, Length |
Export-Csv -Path "C:\large_files.csv" -NoTypeInformation
```

Useful for space audits or migration planning.

Recursive Search in Structured Data

Recursive techniques are also useful when navigating structured data like JSON or XML.

Recursively Searching JSON

```
$json = Get-Content -Path "C:\config.json" | ConvertFrom-
Json

function Search-Json {
    param(
        $Node
    )

    foreach ($key in $Node.PSObject.Properties.Name) {
        $value = $Node.$key
```

```
        if ($value -is
[System.Management.Automation.PSObject]) {
            Search-Json $value
        } else {
            Write-Output "$key: $value"
        }
    }
}

Search-Json -Node $json
```

Recursively Parsing XML

```
[xml]$xml = Get-Content -Path "C:\data.xml"

function Traverse-Xml {
    param($node)

    foreach ($child in $node.ChildNodes) {
        Write-Output $child.Name
        Traverse-Xml $child
    }
}

Traverse-Xml $xml.DocumentElement
```

Tips for Effective Recursive Searches

- **Limit depth when necessary** using parameters like -Depth (PowerShell 7+).
- **Test without -Recurse first** to avoid performance issues or runaway scripts.
- **Combine filters wisely** to reduce data volume early in the pipeline.
- **Use Try/Catch blocks** when deleting or modifying data.

Example with Depth Control

```
Get-ChildItem -Path "C:\Projects" -Recurse -Depth 2 -File
```

This limits the recursion to only two levels deep (PowerShell 7+ feature).

Conclusion

Recursive searches and filters are cornerstone techniques in PowerShell that allow for powerful automation and insight into data and file systems. Whether you're scanning for configuration files, generating system reports, or cleaning up old data, recursion—combined with efficient filtering—gives you the precision and flexibility needed to perform complex tasks quickly and reliably. Mastering these techniques not only expands your scripting capabilities but also makes you significantly more effective in automating administrative tasks and managing data at scale.

CREATING REPORTS

PowerShell is not just a tool for automation and configuration—it's also a powerful reporting engine that can turn raw data into meaningful insights. Whether you're an IT administrator needing to audit Active Directory accounts or a DevOps engineer monitoring service uptime, PowerShell's versatility makes it ideal for generating reports. In this section, we'll explore how to create, format, and export reports using PowerShell.

Why Reports Matter

Reports help users and organizations understand the current state of their systems. From listing outdated software to summarizing disk space usage, reports offer critical visibility. PowerShell allows users to collect data, filter it, organize it, and output it in a human-readable format or machine-readable file such as CSV, HTML, or JSON.

Basic Report Creation

Let's begin with a basic example—gathering disk space information for all logical drives on a computer:

```
Get-PSDrive -PSProvider FileSystem | Select-Object Name,
```

```
Used, Free | Format-Table -AutoSize
```

This command pulls all drives using the FileSystem provider and displays their name, used space, and free space in a table format. This is a rudimentary form of reporting, but it's a great starting point.

Enhancing Output with Select-Object and Format Cmdlets

You can tailor the output further using Select-Object to include or exclude properties and Format-Table or Format-List for display options. For example:

```
Get-Process | Select-Object Name, CPU, Id | Format-Table -AutoSize
```

This snippet displays running processes with specific attributes, making it easier to digest.

Filtering and Sorting for Clarity

Reports should only include relevant data. Use Where-Object to filter and Sort-Object to order the information:

```
Get-Service | Where-Object {$_.Status -eq 'Running'} | Sort-Object DisplayName | Select-Object DisplayName, Status
```

This command filters to show only running services and sorts them alphabetically.

Exporting Data to CSV

CSV (Comma-Separated Values) files are widely supported and can be opened in Excel or other spreadsheet tools. To export data:

```
Get-LocalUser | Select-Object Name, Enabled, LastLogon | Export-Csv -Path "C:\Reports\LocalUsers.csv" -NoTypeInformation
```

The -NoTypeInformation switch removes the metadata line, making the file cleaner.

Exporting Data to HTML

For more visually appealing reports that can be shared or embedded, HTML output is ideal:

```
Get-EventLog -LogName System -Newest 50 | ConvertTo-Html -
Property TimeGenerated, EntryType, Source, Message -Title
"System Event Log" | Out-File "C:\Reports\SystemEvents.html"
```

This will create a web-ready HTML report of the latest 50 system log entries.

Exporting to JSON

JSON is useful for integration with APIs and modern web applications. Here's how to export data to JSON:

```
Get-Service | Select-Object Name, Status | ConvertTo-Json |
Out-File "C:\Reports\Services.json"
```

Scheduling Reports with Task Scheduler

PowerShell scripts can be scheduled to run automatically using Windows Task Scheduler. To do this:

1. Save your PowerShell script with a .ps1 extension.
2. Open Task Scheduler and create a new task.
3. Set the trigger (e.g., daily at 8 AM).
4. In the Actions tab, use powershell.exe as the program and pass your script as an argument:

```
powershell.exe -ExecutionPolicy Bypass -File "C:
\Scripts\GenerateReport.ps1"
```

This allows automated report generation and delivery.

Emailing Reports

Reports are more useful when shared. You can automate email delivery with PowerShell's Send-MailMessage cmdlet:

```
Send-MailMessage -From "admin@domain.com" -To
"recipient@domain.com" -Subject "Daily Report" -Body "Find
the attached report." -SmtpServer "smtp.domain.com" -
Attachments "C:\Reports\LocalUsers.csv"
```

Make sure your SMTP server allows sending and that credentials (if needed) are securely handled.

Formatting and Styling HTML Reports

The default HTML report generated by ConvertTo-Html is basic. You can enhance it with custom CSS. Here's an example:

```
$style = @"
<style>
    table {border-collapse: collapse; width: 100%;}
    th, td {border: 1px solid black; padding: 8px; text-
align: left;}
    th {background-color: #f2f2f2;}
</style>
"@
```

```
Get-Process | Select-Object Name, CPU, Id | ConvertTo-Html -
Head $style -Title "Process Report" | Out-File "C:
\Reports\Processes.html"
```

This generates a styled HTML report that's more presentable for stakeholders.

Using Functions to Standardize Reports

To make your reporting scripts reusable and maintainable, encapsulate them in functions:

```
function Get-UserLoginReport {
    $users = Get-LocalUser | Select-Object Name, Enabled,
LastLogon
    $users | Export-Csv -Path "C:
\Reports\UserLoginReport.csv" -NoTypeInformation
}
```

```
Get-UserLoginReport
```

This approach modularizes the code, making it easier to update and reuse.

Logging and Error Handling

Robust scripts should log activity and handle errors gracefully:

```
try {
    Get-LocalUser | Export-Csv -Path "C:
\Reports\LocalUsers.csv" -NoTypeInformation
    Write-Output "Report generated successfully."
} catch {
    Write-Error "Failed to generate report: $_"
}
```

This ensures you are aware when something goes wrong and can act accordingly.

Best Practices for Report Creation

1. **Keep it Simple**: Avoid overloading the report with too much data.
2. **Be Consistent**: Use standard file names and directory structures.
3. **Secure Sensitive Data**: Don't include passwords or confidential data in reports.
4. **Automate**: Schedule recurring reports to save time.
5. **Validate**: Always check the output manually when creating a new script.

Conclusion

Creating reports in PowerShell is an essential skill that can make your scripts more informative and actionable. Whether you're exporting to CSV for data manipulation, HTML for visualization, or JSON for integration, PowerShell provides the tools to generate professional and consistent reports. By mastering these reporting techniques, you not only add value to your scripting toolbox but also empower your team and organization with insights that drive decisions.

Working with Text Files and CSVs

READING/WRITING FILES

PowerShell provides robust tools for handling files, making it easy to read from and write to files for automation, logging, data manipulation, and more. In this section, we will explore how to read and write files using PowerShell, covering common use cases, techniques, and best practices.

Why File I/O Matters in PowerShell

File input and output (I/O) operations are central to many scripts. Whether you're automating backups, processing logs, or saving results from a command, knowing how to efficiently read from and write to files can save time and make your scripts far more powerful. PowerShell supports multiple methods to work with files, including:

- `Get-Content`
- `Set-Content`
- `Add-Content`
- `Out-File`
- StreamReader/StreamWriter classes from .NET

Each of these tools has unique strengths and is suited to different scenarios.

Writing Files

Using Set-Content

Set-Content writes data to a file, overwriting existing content by default:

```
"Hello, world!" | Set-Content -Path "C:\Logs\output.txt"
```

To write multiple lines:

```
$lines = @("Line 1", "Line 2", "Line 3")
$lines | Set-Content -Path "C:\Logs\output.txt"
```

Using Add-Content

Add-Content appends data to a file without overwriting existing contents:

```
"This line is appended." | Add-Content -Path "C:
\Logs\output.txt"
```

This is useful for logging operations where maintaining a historical record is important.

Using Out-File

Out-File is another way to send output to a file. It's especially useful for capturing command output.

```
Get-Process | Out-File -FilePath "C:\Logs\processes.txt"
```

You can also control width and encoding:

```
Get-Process | Out-File -FilePath "C:\Logs\processes.txt" -
Width 200 -Encoding UTF8
```

Reading and Writing with .NET Stream Classes

For advanced file handling, .NET classes offer more control. System.IO.StreamReader and System.IO.StreamWriter are two commonly used classes.

Reading with StreamReader

```
$reader = [System.IO.StreamReader]::new("C:
\Logs\example.txt")

while (($line = $reader.ReadLine()) -ne $null) {
    Write-Host $line
}

$reader.Close()
```

Writing with StreamWriter

```
$writer = [System.IO.StreamWriter]::new("C:
\Logs\example.txt", $false)
$writer.WriteLine("First line")
```

```
$writer.WriteLine("Second line")
$writer.Close()
```

The second parameter in StreamWriter constructor ($false) indicates whether to append ($true) or overwrite ($false).

File Existence and Safety Checks

Before performing read/write operations, it's wise to verify file existence to avoid errors:

```
if (Test-Path -Path "C:\Logs\example.txt") {
    Get-Content "C:\Logs\example.txt"
} else {
    Write-Host "File not found."
}
```

To create a new file if it doesn't exist:

```
if (-not (Test-Path "C:\Logs\newfile.txt")) {
    New-Item -ItemType File -Path "C:\Logs\newfile.txt"
}
```

Reading Files

Using Get-Content

The most straightforward way to read text from a file is with Get-Content. This cmdlet reads a file line-by-line and returns each line as a string object.

```
Get-Content -Path "C:\Logs\example.txt"
```

This command reads the file and outputs its contents to the console. To store the contents in a variable for further processing:

```
$lines = Get-Content -Path "C:\Logs\example.txt"
```

Now, $lines is an array of strings, one per line in the file.

Reading Specific Lines

To read just the first or last few lines:

```
# First 5 lines
Get-Content -Path "C:\Logs\example.txt" -TotalCount 5
```

```
# Last 5 lines
Get-Content -Path "C:\Logs\example.txt" | Select-Object -
Last 5
```

Reading Files With Encoding

When dealing with special characters or non-ASCII text, specifying encoding is important:

```
Get-Content -Path "C:\Logs\unicode.txt" -Encoding UTF8
```

Supported encodings include: ASCII, UTF8, Unicode, UTF7, UTF32, and Default.

Using Here-Strings for Multi-Line Content

Here-Strings allow you to write multi-line strings easily, which is helpful when generating configuration files or documentation.

```
@"
This is line 1
This is line 2
"@ | Set-Content -Path "C:\Logs\multiline.txt"
```

Handling Large Files

When working with large files, streaming line-by-line is better than loading the entire file into memory:

```
$reader = [System.IO.StreamReader]::new("C:
\Logs\bigfile.txt")
while (($line = $reader.ReadLine()) -ne $null) {
    # Process line
}
$reader.Close()
```

Alternatively, use the -ReadCount parameter with Get-Content:

```
Get-Content -Path "C:\Logs\bigfile.txt" -ReadCount 100 |
ForEach-Object {
    # Process 100 lines at a time
}
```

Logging with Timestamps

A common task is appending log entries with timestamps:

```
$timestamp = Get-Date -Format "yyyy-MM-dd HH:mm:ss"
"$timestamp - Task completed successfully" | Add-Content "C:
\Logs\app.log"
```

This technique is helpful in debugging and monitoring script performance.

Combining Read and Write Operations

You can read a file, modify its contents, and write it back like this:

```
$content = Get-Content "C:\Logs\data.txt"
$modified = $content | ForEach-Object { $_.ToUpper() }
$modified | Set-Content "C:\Logs\data.txt"
```

This example converts each line to uppercase and writes it back to the same file.

Best Practices

- **Use full paths** to avoid ambiguity.
- **Escape special characters** if your file path includes symbols (e.g., \, []).
- **Handle encoding** when reading/writing non-ASCII characters.
- **Use try/catch blocks** for error handling in production scripts.
- **Clean up resources** like StreamReader and StreamWriter using .Close() or try/finally.
- **Backup original files** before overwriting critical data.

Conclusion

Reading and writing files is a core capability of PowerShell and is essential for tasks ranging from automation to reporting. By mastering Get-Content, Set-Content, Add-Content, and other related cmdlets, along with .NET-based file operations, you can efficiently manage data in any script.

Whether you're appending log entries, processing massive log files, or generating configuration files dynamically, PowerShell provides the flexibility and power to handle it all. With the knowledge from this section, you'll be well-equipped to build more sophisticated scripts that interact with the filesystem in practical and meaningful ways.

CSV MANIPULATION WITH IMPORT-CSV / EXPORT-CSV

Comma-separated values (CSV) files are a cornerstone of data exchange between systems, making them one of the most commonly used file formats in scripting and automation workflows. PowerShell, with its powerful object-oriented structure, provides two robust cmdlets for working with CSV files: Import-Csv and Export-Csv. This chapter will delve into how to read, modify, and write CSV files effectively in PowerShell, providing practical examples and best practices for manipulating structured data.

Understanding CSV Files in PowerShell

A CSV file is essentially a text file where each line represents a row of data, and each value in the row is separated by a comma. The first line usually contains headers, which are used as property names in PowerShell.

PowerShell takes full advantage of these headers to convert CSV data into custom objects, making it incredibly easy to work with structured data. The two primary cmdlets used are:

- Import-Csv: Reads a CSV file and converts each row into a custom PowerShell object.
- Export-Csv: Converts PowerShell objects into a CSV format and writes them to a file.

Using Import-Csv

The Import-Csv cmdlet is straightforward but powerful. It reads a

CSV file and creates an array of objects, with each object representing a row.

Basic Usage

```
$users = Import-Csv -Path "C:\Data\users.csv"
```

This command imports the contents of users.csv into the $users variable. If the CSV has headers like Name, Email, and Role, you can access those fields like this:

```
foreach ($user in $users) {
    Write-Output "User: $($user.Name), Email: $
($user.Email), Role: $($user.Role)"
}
```

Working with Delimiters

Although commas are standard, some CSV files use different delimiters like semicolons or tabs. You can specify the delimiter with the -Delimiter parameter:

```
$products = Import-Csv -Path "products.csv" -Delimiter ';'
```

Filtering and Searching Data

You can easily filter imported CSV data using Where-Object:

```
$admins = $users | Where-Object { $_.Role -eq "Admin" }
```

Modifying CSV Data

Once the data is in memory as objects, you can modify it just like any other PowerShell object.

Updating Values

To change the email domain of every user:

```
foreach ($user in $users) {
    $user.Email = $user.Email -replace "@old-domain.com",
"@new-domain.com"
}
```

Adding New Properties

You can add new calculated properties to each object:

```
foreach ($user in $users) {
    $user.Username = $user.Email.Split('@')[0]
}
```

Removing Rows

To remove users who are no longer active:

```
$activeUsers = $users | Where-Object { $_.Status -eq
"Active" }
```

Using Export-Csv

After modifying or generating data, you'll likely want to export it back to a CSV file. The Export-Csv cmdlet allows you to do this easily.

Basic Export

```
$users | Export-Csv -Path "C:\Data\updated_users.csv" -
NoTypeInformation
```

The -NoTypeInformation flag prevents PowerShell from adding a type definition comment at the top of the file.

Appending Data to an Existing File

To add rows to an existing CSV:

```
$newUsers | Export-Csv -Path "C:\Data\users.csv" -Append -
NoTypeInformation
```

Note: Ensure the structure of the new objects matches the existing CSV, or PowerShell may produce unexpected results.

Custom Headers and Column Order

To change the order or names of columns:

```
$users | Select-Object Name, Username, Email | Export-Csv -
Path "C:\Data\cleaned_users.csv" -NoTypeInformation
```

Practical Example: Managing User Accounts

Let's walk through a practical example of using CSV manipulation to manage user accounts in a system.

Scenario:

You receive a CSV file new_users.csv from HR with columns: FirstName, LastName, Email. Your task is to:

- Generate usernames.
- Assign a default role.
- Save the updated data into a new file.

Script:

```
$newUsers = Import-Csv -Path "C:\Data\new_users.csv"
```

```
foreach ($user in $newUsers) {
    $user.Username = ($user.FirstName.Substring(0,1) +
$user.LastName).ToLower()
    $user.Role = "Employee"
}


$newUsers | Export-Csv -Path "C:\Data\processed_users.csv" -
NoTypeInformation
```

Error Handling and Validation

When working with external data, it's essential to handle errors and validate input.

Handling Missing Files

```
if (Test-Path "C:\Data\input.csv") {
    $data = Import-Csv -Path "C:\Data\input.csv"
} else {
    Write-Error "File not found."
}
```

Validating Required Columns

```
$requiredColumns = @("Name", "Email")
$headers = (Import-Csv -Path "C:\Data\file.csv" | Select-
Object -First 1 | Get-Member -MemberType NoteProperty).Name


foreach ($column in $requiredColumns) {
    if (-not ($headers -contains $column)) {
        throw "Missing required column: $column"
    }
}
```

Best Practices

1. Always Use -NoTypeInformation

This avoids adding the #TYPE line in your CSV, which can confuse users or other programs reading the file.

2. Avoid Manual Parsing

Don't parse CSV files manually using Get-Content and Split().

PowerShell's native cmdlets handle this more reliably.

3. Normalize Data Before Export

Ensure consistent formatting (e.g., lowercase emails, trimmed whitespace) to make your data clean and reliable.

4. Use Select-Object to Reorder Columns

If the output needs to be in a specific format, explicitly reorder the columns before export.

5. Validate Data Integrity

Check for null or unexpected values in key columns to prevent logic errors or bad exports.

Summary

CSV manipulation is a vital skill for any PowerShell scripter. By mastering Import-Csv and Export-Csv, you can seamlessly move data between systems, clean and transform datasets, and generate reliable outputs for reports or integrations. These cmdlets harness PowerShell's object-oriented design, allowing for elegant, readable scripts that perform complex operations with minimal code.

In the next chapter, we'll build on this knowledge by exploring how to integrate CSV workflows into larger automation pipelines and scheduled tasks, ensuring your data operations are both repeatable and robust.

REAL-WORLD EXAMPLE: AUTOMATING USER IMPORTS

Automating user imports is one of the most practical and valuable uses of PowerShell in enterprise environments. Organizations frequently need to onboard large numbers of users from CSV files or HR systems into Active Directory (AD), Microsoft 365, or other identity platforms. Manual data entry for this task is not only time-consuming but also prone to errors. In this section, we'll walk through a real-world scenario where PowerShell scripting dramatically simplifies and streamlines the user import process.

The Scenario

Imagine you work in the IT department of a mid-sized company. Your HR department sends you a CSV file every Monday morning with the details of new hires. This CSV includes fields like First Name, Last Name, Department, Job Title, and Email. Your job is to take this CSV and use it to create new user accounts in Active Directory, set up their home directories, assign them to security groups based on department, and send a confirmation email to the IT helpdesk.

Doing all of this manually would take hours each week, especially if the number of hires increases. With PowerShell, we can automate the entire process.

Preparing the CSV File

Here is a sample of what the CSV file might look like:

```
FirstName,LastName,Department,JobTitle,Email
John,Doe,Accounting,Accountant,john.doe@company.com
Jane,Smith,Engineering,Software
Engineer,jane.smith@company.com
```

Step 1: Reading the CSV File

The first step in our script is to read in the CSV file and convert it into a set of PowerShell objects:

```
$users = Import-Csv -Path "C:\HR\NewHires.csv"
```

This simple line of code loads the CSV into memory, where each row becomes an object with properties matching the column headers.

Step 2: Creating User Accounts

Next, we loop through each user object and create a new AD account. We'll use the New-ADUser cmdlet:

```
foreach ($user in $users) {
    $username = ($user.FirstName.Substring(0,1) +
$user.LastName).ToLower()
    $password = ConvertTo-SecureString "TempP@ssword123" -
AsPlainText -Force
```

```
    New-ADUser -Name "$($user.FirstName) $($user.LastName)"
\
                -GivenName $user.FirstName \
                -Surname $user.LastName \
                -SamAccountName $username \
                -UserPrincipalName "$username@company.com" \
                -Department $user.Department \
                -Title $user.JobTitle \
                -EmailAddress $user.Email \
                -AccountPassword $password \
                -Enabled $true
}
```

This code constructs a simple username by combining the first letter of the first name with the last name, sets a temporary password, and then creates the user with the relevant attributes.

Step 3: Creating Home Directories

Often, users need dedicated home directories for file storage. Here's how we can automate that:

```
foreach ($user in $users) {
    $homeDir = "\\fileserver\users\$($user.FirstName).$
($user.LastName)"
    New-Item -Path $homeDir -ItemType Directory
    # Set permissions
    $acl = Get-Acl $homeDir
    $permission = "DOMAIN\$($user.FirstName).$
($user.LastName)","Modify","ContainerInherit,ObjectInherit",
"None","Allow"
    $accessRule = New-Object
System.Security.AccessControl.FileSystemAccessRule
$permission
    $acl.AddAccessRule($accessRule)
    Set-Acl $homeDir $acl
}
```

This code snippet creates a directory and assigns user-specific NTFS permissions to it. Be sure to replace DOMAIN with your actual domain name.

Step 4: Adding Users to Security Groups

Assigning users to groups can control access to resources like shared drives, email lists, and applications.

```
foreach ($user in $users) {
    switch ($user.Department) {
        "Accounting" { Add-ADGroupMember -Identity
"AccountingUsers" -Members $user.SamAccountName }
        "Engineering" { Add-ADGroupMember -Identity
"EngineeringUsers" -Members $user.SamAccountName }
    }
}
```

This uses a switch statement to assign users to department-specific security groups.

Step 5: Sending Confirmation Email

Lastly, let's notify the IT helpdesk that the accounts have been created. We'll use the Send-MailMessage cmdlet:

```
$body = "The following users have been created:`n"

foreach ($user in $users) {
    $body += "$($user.FirstName) $($user.LastName) - $
($user.Email)`n"
}

Send-MailMessage -From "noreply@company.com" \
                 -To "helpdesk@company.com" \
                 -Subject "New AD Users Created" \
                 -Body $body \
                 -SmtpServer "smtp.company.com"
```

This will compile a simple list of new users and send it to the helpdesk for reference or further action.

Putting It All Together

You can wrap this entire process into a single script and even schedule it using Task Scheduler or as part of a CI/CD pipeline if you're managing user onboarding through a DevOps workflow. Here's a

simplified version:

```
$users = Import-Csv -Path "C:\HR\NewHires.csv"

foreach ($user in $users) {
    # Generate Username and Secure Password
    $username = ($user.FirstName.Substring(0,1) +
$user.LastName).ToLower()
    $password = ConvertTo-SecureString "TempP@ssword123" -
AsPlainText -Force

    # Create AD User
    New-ADUser -Name "$($user.FirstName) $($user.LastName)"
\
                -GivenName $user.FirstName \
                -Surname $user.LastName \
                -SamAccountName $username \
                -UserPrincipalName "$username@company.com" \
                -Department $user.Department \
                -Title $user.JobTitle \
                -EmailAddress $user.Email \
                -AccountPassword $password \
                -Enabled $true

    # Create Home Directory
    $homeDir = "\\fileserver\users\$($user.FirstName).$
($user.LastName)"
    New-Item -Path $homeDir -ItemType Directory
    $acl = Get-Acl $homeDir
    $permission = "DOMAIN\
$username","Modify","ContainerInherit,ObjectInherit","None",
"Allow"
    $accessRule = New-Object
System.Security.AccessControl.FileSystemAccessRule
$permission
    $acl.AddAccessRule($accessRule)
    Set-Acl $homeDir $acl

    # Add to Group
    switch ($user.Department) {
        "Accounting" { Add-ADGroupMember -Identity
"AccountingUsers" -Members $username }
        "Engineering" { Add-ADGroupMember -Identity
"EngineeringUsers" -Members $username }
```

```
        }

        # Log output
        Write-Host "User $username created successfully."
}


# Send notification
$body = "The following users have been created:`n" + ($users
| ForEach-Object { "$($_.FirstName) $($_.LastName) - $
($_.Email)`n" })

Send-MailMessage -From "noreply@company.com" -To
"helpdesk@company.com" -Subject "New AD Users Created" -Body
$body -SmtpServer "smtp.company.com"
```

Conclusion

Automating user imports with PowerShell transforms a tedious, error-prone process into a seamless, reliable operation. With just a few hundred lines of code, you can ensure consistent user provisioning, reduce onboarding time, and free up IT resources for more strategic work. Once you've built and tested this script, it can be adapted to various input sources or extended to work with platforms beyond Active Directory, such as Azure AD or Google Workspace. The flexibility and power of PowerShell make it an ideal tool for these kinds of real-world administrative tasks.

Registry and Environment Variables

NAVIGATING THE REGISTRY PROVIDER

PowerShell providers act as data access engines, allowing users to access different types of data stores in a similar way to how they access the file system. One such provider is the **Registry Provider**, which allows users to browse, read, and manipulate the Windows registry as if it were a standard file system. Understanding how to work with the Registry Provider can unlock powerful scripting capabilities, especially for system administrators seeking to automate system configuration and maintenance.

Introduction to the Windows Registry

The Windows registry is a hierarchical database that stores configuration settings and options for the operating system and installed applications. It contains critical information such as:

- User preferences
- Hardware configurations
- Software settings
- System policies

Accessing and modifying the registry should be done with caution, as incorrect changes can lead to system instability or even failure.

Accessing the Registry in PowerShell

PowerShell exposes the registry through the **Registry Provider**, enabling access using familiar cmdlets such as Get-Item, Set-Item, Remove-Item, and others. The registry is mounted into PowerShell as two drives:

- HKLM: – Represents HKEY_LOCAL_MACHINE

- HKCU: – Represents HKEY_CURRENT_USER

These drives can be navigated like folders in a file system.

Example:

```
Set-Location HKLM:\Software
Get-ChildItem
```

This command navigates to the HKEY_LOCAL_MACHINE\Software key and lists all subkeys.

Navigating the Registry Hierarchy

You can use the same navigational commands in the registry as you would in the file system:

- Get-ChildItem (alias: dir, ls): Lists subkeys and values
- Set-Location (alias: cd): Changes the current registry location
- Get-Location (alias: pwd): Shows the current location

Example:

```
cd HKCU:\Software
ls
```

You can also use tab-completion to assist with path discovery.

Reading Registry Values

To read the contents of a specific key or value:

```
Get-ItemProperty -Path "HKCU:
\Software\Microsoft\Windows\CurrentVersion\Explorer"
```

This will display all values under the specified key.

If you want to access a specific value:

```
(Get-ItemProperty -Path "HKCU:\Software\MyApp").SettingName
```

This assumes that SettingName is a value under the MyApp key.

Creating and Modifying Registry Keys and Values

Creating a Key

```
New-Item -Path "HKCU:\Software\MyApp"
```

This command creates a new key under the Software key in HKEY_CURRENT_USER.

Adding or Modifying a Value

```
New-ItemProperty -Path "HKCU:\Software\MyApp" -Name
"SettingName" -Value "Enabled" -PropertyType String
```

Use Set-ItemProperty to change an existing value:

```
Set-ItemProperty -Path "HKCU:\Software\MyApp" -Name
"SettingName" -Value "Disabled"
```

Deleting Keys and Values

To remove a registry key:

```
Remove-Item -Path "HKCU:\Software\MyApp" -Recurse
```

Use the -Recurse flag to ensure all subkeys are deleted.

To delete a value:

```
Remove-ItemProperty -Path "HKCU:\Software\MyApp" -Name
"SettingName"
```

Working with Registry Permissions

While PowerShell enables registry manipulation, permissions may restrict what you can do. If you get access denied errors, consider running PowerShell with elevated permissions (as Administrator).

Use Get-Acl and Set-Acl to view and modify Access Control Lists (ACLs) for registry keys.

Example:

```
$acl = Get-Acl "HKLM:\Software\MyApp"
$acl
```

This shows the current permissions for the key. Modifying ACLs is more advanced and generally not recommended unless necessary.

Exporting and Importing Registry Keys

PowerShell can't directly export or import .reg files like regedit, but you can invoke the legacy reg.exe utility:

Export:

```
reg export "HKCU\Software\MyApp" "C:\Backup\MyApp.reg"
```

Import:

```
reg import "C:\Backup\MyApp.reg"
```

Scripting Examples

Script: Backup a Registry Key

```
param(
    [string]$Key = "HKCU:\Software\MyApp",
    [string]$BackupFile = "C:\Backup\MyApp.reg"
)
reg export $Key $BackupFile /y
```

Script: Enforce a Registry Setting

```
$key = "HKCU:\Software\MyApp"
if (-not (Test-Path $key)) {
    New-Item -Path $key
}
Set-ItemProperty -Path $key -Name "SettingName" -Value
"Enabled"
```

This script ensures the key exists and then applies a specific setting.

Best Practices

- **Always backup before modifying:** A mistake in the registry can corrupt the OS.
- **Use clear variable names:** Especially when scripting changes.
- **Comment your scripts:** Explain why registry keys are being modified.
- **Run in test environments:** Validate changes in a virtual machine or isolated system.
- **Consider Group Policy:** For enterprise environments, Group Policy is often a safer way to enforce registry-based settings.

Conclusion

The PowerShell Registry Provider bridges the gap between raw registry editing tools and script automation. By treating the registry like a file system, PowerShell makes registry manipulation accessible and scriptable. With great power comes great responsibility, so always validate and backup before deploying registry changes, particularly across multiple systems.

Understanding how to navigate and script against the registry opens up a powerful set of tools for system configuration, software deployment, user environment customization, and much more. Mastery of the Registry Provider equips administrators with the precision and automation capabilities essential for modern IT operations.

MODIFYING KEYS AND VALUES SAFELY

In PowerShell scripting, manipulating data stored in hash tables (dictionaries) and other key-value structures is a common task. Whether you're updating configuration settings, parsing JSON data, or transforming input from a CSV, modifying keys and values safely is essential. This section covers best practices, safe techniques, and real-world examples to help you perform these tasks confidently.

Understanding Hash Tables in PowerShell

A hash table in PowerShell is a collection of key-value pairs. Keys are unique identifiers, and values are associated data. Hash tables provide quick lookups and efficient storage for dynamic data sets.

Creating a Hash Table:

```
$person = @{
    FirstName = "John"
    LastName  = "Doe"
    Age       = 30
}
```

You can access values using their keys:
```
Write-Output $person['FirstName']
```

Or:
```
Write-Output $person.FirstName
```

Safely Modifying Values

Modifying values is straightforward, but you must ensure the key exists and the data type is appropriate.

Basic Value Update

```
$person['Age'] = 31
```

Using .ContainsKey() to Check for Existence

Before modifying a key's value, check if it exists:

```
if ($person.ContainsKey('Age')) {
    $person['Age'] = 32
} else {
    Write-Warning "Key 'Age' does not exist."
}
```

This prevents runtime errors and ensures safe code execution.

Enforcing Data Types

PowerShell is loosely typed, but enforcing data types is a good practice:

```
if ($person['Age'] -is [int]) {
    $person['Age'] += 1
} else {
    Write-Warning "Age is not an integer."
}
```

Safely Adding and Removing Keys

Adding a new key-value pair is easy:

```
$person['Occupation'] = 'Engineer'
```

However, be cautious when overwriting existing keys. Use .ContainsKey():

```
if (-not $person.ContainsKey('Occupation')) {
    $person['Occupation'] = 'Engineer'
} else {
    Write-Warning "Key 'Occupation' already exists."
}
```

Removing Keys

Removing a key that doesn't exist will throw an error:

```
if ($person.ContainsKey('Occupation')) {
    $person.Remove('Occupation')
```

```
} else {
    Write-Warning "Cannot remove non-existent key
'Occupation'."
}
```

Replacing Keys Safely

PowerShell doesn't allow renaming keys directly. You need to remove the old key and add a new one:

```
if ($person.ContainsKey('FirstName')) {
    $person['GivenName'] = $person['FirstName']
    $person.Remove('FirstName')
}
```

To maintain atomicity, wrap in a script block or function.

Looping Through Keys and Values Safely

When modifying a hash table during iteration, avoid changing the size (adding/removing keys) directly in the loop. Instead, collect changes and apply them afterward.

Example – Changing Key Names

```
$updates = @{
    'FirstName' = 'GivenName'
    'LastName'  = 'Surname'
}

foreach ($oldKey in $updates.Keys) {
    if ($person.ContainsKey($oldKey)) {
        $newKey = $updates[$oldKey]
        $person[$newKey] = $person[$oldKey]
        $person.Remove($oldKey)
    }
}
```

Example – Modifying Values in a Loop

```
foreach ($key in $person.Keys) {
    if ($key -eq 'Age' -and $person[$key] -is [int]) {
        $person[$key]++
    }
}
```

Use the .Keys snapshot, as modifying the hash table itself during iteration may result in unpredictable behavior.

Immutable Data Patterns

In complex scripts or multithreaded environments, it's safer to use immutable patterns—where you create a new hash table rather than modifying the original.

Example – Creating a Modified Copy

```
$newPerson = @{}
foreach ($key in $person.Keys) {
    $value = $person[$key]
    if ($key -eq 'Age' -and $value -is [int]) {
        $newPerson[$key] = $value + 1
    } else {
        $newPerson[$key] = $value
    }
}
```

This prevents side effects and supports debugging and testing.

Defensive Coding Techniques

Always use defensive coding techniques:

1. **Validate input types**:

```
if ($input -isnot [hashtable]) {
    throw "Expected a hashtable."
}
```

2. **Handle nulls and empties**:

```
if ($person['FirstName']) {
    # Proceed
} else {
    Write-Warning "FirstName is null or empty."
}
```

3. **Try-Catch for Risky Operations**:

```
try {
    $person.Remove('UnknownKey')
} catch {
```

```
    Write-Error $_.Exception.Message
}
```

4. **Use $PSCmdlet.ThrowTerminatingError()** in advanced **functions** when needed.

Real-World Scenarios

Updating Configuration Values

```
$config = Get-Content config.json | ConvertFrom-Json
if ($config.ContainsKey('LogLevel')) {
    $config['LogLevel'] = 'Verbose'
}
$config | ConvertTo-Json | Set-Content config.json
```

Merging Two Hash Tables

```
$defaults = @{ LogLevel = 'Info'; Timeout = 30 }
$custom   = @{ Timeout = 60 }

$merged = $defaults.Clone()
foreach ($key in $custom.Keys) {
    $merged[$key] = $custom[$key]
}
```

Summary

Modifying keys and values in PowerShell hash tables is powerful but must be done carefully. Key takeaways include:
- Always check for key existence.
- Validate data types before modification.
- Avoid modifying collections while iterating through them.
- Use immutable patterns when safety and traceability are paramount.
- Implement defensive coding practices to avoid runtime errors and hard-to-debug issues.

Following these guidelines ensures your scripts are more robust, maintainable, and less error-prone. In the next section, we'll explore converting data structures and transforming hash tables into JSON,

CSV, and other formats.

ACCESSING AND SETTING ENVIRONMENT VARIABLES

Environment variables are fundamental components of the Windows operating system and are heavily utilized in PowerShell scripting. These variables provide a way to influence the behavior of processes on a computer. PowerShell provides built-in access to these variables and allows you to retrieve and modify them easily. This section will guide you through the concepts, practical uses, and best practices when accessing and setting environment variables in PowerShell.

What Are Environment Variables?

Environment variables are key-value pairs that are used to pass configuration information to applications. These values can define user-specific settings, system paths, locale settings, and much more. For example:

- PATH: Specifies directories where executable programs are located.
- TEMP and TMP: Define the directories for temporary files.
- USERNAME: Stores the current logged-in user's name.

Environment variables are grouped by their scope:

- **System Environment Variables**: Available to all users on the system.
- **User Environment Variables**: Available only to the currently logged-in user.
- **Process Environment Variables**: Limited to the scope of the current process (session-based).

Accessing Environment Variables in PowerShell

PowerShell treats environment variables as members of the Env: drive. This makes it intuitive to retrieve and list environment variables using familiar PowerShell cmdlets.

Viewing All Environment Variables

To list all available environment variables:
```
Get-ChildItem Env:
```

This command displays all environment variables available to the current PowerShell session.

Retrieving a Specific Environment Variable

You can access a specific variable using the syntax:
```
$env:VARIABLE_NAME
```

For example:
```
$env:USERNAME
$env:PATH
```

This will return the values of the USERNAME and PATH variables, respectively.

Setting Environment Variables in PowerShell

PowerShell allows you to set environment variables using the $env: prefix. However, the persistence of the changes depends on the scope.

Setting Process-Level Environment Variables

These changes last only for the duration of the PowerShell session:
```
$env:MY_VAR = "Hello World"
echo $env:MY_VAR  # Output: Hello World
```

Once you close the session, MY_VAR will no longer be available.

Setting User or System Environment Variables Permanently

To persist changes across sessions, you must update the Windows Registry.

Setting a User Environment Variable
```
[Environment]::SetEnvironmentVariable("MY_VAR", "Hello User", "User")
```

Setting a System Environment Variable

Note: You must run PowerShell as Administrator to change system-level variables.
```
[Environment]::SetEnvironmentVariable("MY_VAR", "Hello System", "Machine")
```

Practical Examples

Append to the PATH Variable

Appending to the existing PATH variable is a common use case:

```
$oldPath = [Environment]::GetEnvironmentVariable("PATH",
"User")
$newPath = "$oldPath;C:\MyTools"
[Environment]::SetEnvironmentVariable("PATH", $newPath,
"User")
```

This adds C:\MyTools to the user's path permanently.

Using Environment Variables in Scripts

You can use environment variables to make your scripts more dynamic and user-independent:

```
$logPath = "$env:TEMP\script.log"
Start-Transcript -Path $logPath
```

This script will always store logs in the temporary directory of the current user.

Viewing Environment Variable Scope

To understand where an environment variable is stored (process, user, or system), use:

```
[Environment]::GetEnvironmentVariable("MY_VAR", "Process")
[Environment]::GetEnvironmentVariable("MY_VAR", "User")
[Environment]::GetEnvironmentVariable("MY_VAR", "Machine")
```

Each call checks a different scope. If you find a value at more than one level, the order of precedence is:

1. Process
2. User
3. Machine

Removing Environment Variables

To delete an environment variable, set its value to $null:

```
[Environment]::SetEnvironmentVariable("MY_VAR", $null,
"User")
```

For temporary variables:

```
Remove-Item Env:MY_VAR
```

Environment Variables in Scripts and Profiles

Using in Scripts

When automating with PowerShell scripts, setting environment variables at the start of your script can help with configuration:

```
$env:CONFIG_PATH = "C:\Config\app.config"
```

Using in Profile Scripts

You can define environment variables in your profile for consistent access across sessions:

```
# Add to your profile (e.g., $PROFILE)
$env:EDITOR = "notepad++"
```

After saving this to your profile, EDITOR will always be set when you open PowerShell.

Environment Variables and Security

Environment variables can contain sensitive data such as API keys or passwords. Be cautious:

- Never hard-code sensitive values directly in shared scripts.
- Use secure storage mechanisms for secrets, such as the Windows Credential Manager or Azure Key Vault.
- Limit variable scope to reduce exposure.
  Example of a less secure practice:

```
$env:API_KEY = "12345-abcdef"
```

Better practice:

```
$secureApiKey = Get-StoredCredential -Target "MyApiKey"
```

Troubleshooting Environment Variables

If you're experiencing issues with environment variables:

- **Changes not taking effect?** Restart the session or system.
- **Not recognized in other applications?** Confirm you've set them

at the right scope.
- **Double-check spelling and paths.** Even minor typos can break scripts.

Use tools like SystemPropertiesAdvanced.exe or the GUI Environment Variables Editor in Windows for visual inspection.

Best Practices

- Use process-level variables for temporary needs.
- Use user-level for persistent, user-specific configuration.
- Use system-level only when necessary, and always back up the registry.
- Avoid using environment variables for critical secrets.
- Document your environment variables, especially in production scripts.

Summary

PowerShell makes it easy to access and modify environment variables through the Env: drive and the [Environment] .NET class. Understanding how these variables work and how to manage them properly allows you to write more portable, reusable, and secure scripts.

Whether you're automating tasks, customizing your environment, or building cross-user applications, mastering environment variables is an essential skill for any PowerShell scripter.

In the next section, we'll look at **Working with the Windows Registry**, which builds directly on the concepts introduced here.

Managing Processes and Services

GET-PROCESS, STOP-PROCESS, START-SERVICE, ETC.

PowerShell provides a powerful and consistent set of cmdlets to manage processes and services on Windows and other supported operating systems. Among the most commonly used are Get-Process, Stop-Process, Start-Service, and their counterparts. In this section, we will explore these cmdlets in detail, including how to use them effectively in real-world scenarios.

Managing Processes with PowerShell

Get-Process

Get-Process is used to retrieve information about the processes that are currently running on a computer. This cmdlet returns a collection of objects that represent each running process, including details such as process name, ID, memory usage, and CPU time.

Syntax:

```
Get-Process [-Name] <string[]> [-ComputerName <string[]>
```

Example 1: List all processes

```
Get-Process
```

This command returns all currently running processes on the local machine.

Example 2: Get a specific process by name

```
Get-Process -Name notepad
```

This will return all processes named "notepad".

Example 3: Filter by memory usage

```
Get-Process | Where-Object { $_.WorkingSet -gt 100MB }
```

This returns processes that are using more than 100MB of memory.

Stop-Process

Stop-Process is used to terminate running processes. This can be useful for closing applications that are not responding or for scripting application restarts.

Syntax:
```
Stop-Process [-Id] <int[]> [-Force]
Stop-Process [-Name] <string[]> [-Force]
```
Example 1: Stop a process by name
```
Stop-Process -Name notepad
```
This command stops all instances of Notepad.

Example 2: Stop a process by ID
```
Stop-Process -Id 1234
```
Use this when you know the process ID and want to terminate it precisely.

Example 3: Force stop a process
```
Stop-Process -Name chrome -Force
```
The -Force parameter ensures the process is terminated even if it is not responding.

Warning: Be careful with Stop-Process as it does not prompt for confirmation and can cause data loss if used on applications with unsaved work.

Managing Services with PowerShell

Services are background applications that typically run without user interaction. PowerShell provides cmdlets to start, stop, suspend, and restart services.

Get-Service

This cmdlet retrieves the status of services on a local or remote machine.

Syntax:
```
Get-Service [[-Name] <string[]>] [-ComputerName <string[]>]
```
Example 1: Get all services
```
Get-Service
```
This lists all services and their statuses.

Example 2: Get a specific service
```
Get-Service -Name wuauserv
```
This retrieves the Windows Update service status.

Example 3: List only running services
```
Get-Service | Where-Object { $_.Status -eq 'Running' }
```
Start-Service

Starts one or more stopped services.

Syntax:

```
Start-Service [-Name] <string[]>
```

Example:

```
Start-Service -Name wuauserv
```

This starts the Windows Update service.

Stop-Service

Stops one or more running services.

Syntax:

```
Stop-Service [-Name] <string[]> [-Force]
```

Example:

```
Stop-Service -Name wuauserv
```

This stops the Windows Update service.

Example with force:

```
Stop-Service -Name spooler -Force
```

Use -Force to override user confirmation.

Restart-Service

Restarts one or more services.

Syntax:

```
Restart-Service [-Name] <string[]> [-Force]
```

Example:

```
Restart-Service -Name wuauserv
```

This is useful when you need to reinitialize a service after changes.

Set-Service

Changes the properties of a service, such as its startup type.

Syntax:

```
Set-Service [-Name] <string> [-StartupType <string>]
```

Example:

```
Set-Service -Name wuauserv -StartupType Disabled
```

This disables the Windows Update service from starting automatically.

Combining Cmdlets

PowerShell's pipeline and scripting capabilities allow you to create powerful combinations of these cmdlets. Here are a few examples:

Example 1: Stop all running services that match a pattern

```
Get-Service | Where-Object { $_.DisplayName -like '*Update*'
-and $_.Status -eq 'Running' } | Stop-Service
```

Example 2: Restart all services dependent on a specific one

```
$dependencies = Get-Service -Name wuauserv | Select-Object -
ExpandProperty DependentServices
$dependencies | Restart-Service
```

Example 3: Kill high-memory processes

```
Get-Process | Where-Object { $_.WorkingSet -gt 500MB } |
Stop-Process -Force
```

Using These Cmdlets in Scripts

You can use these commands in automated scripts for system maintenance, software deployment, troubleshooting, or performance monitoring. For example:

```
# Restart a service and log the action
$serviceName = 'wuauserv'
Restart-Service -Name $serviceName
"[$(Get-Date)] Restarted service: $serviceName" | Out-File -
FilePath C:\Logs\ServiceRestart.log -Append
```

This script restarts the Windows Update service and logs the action with a timestamp.

Permissions Considerations

Most process and service cmdlets require administrative privileges. If you're running these commands in a standard user PowerShell session, you may encounter access denied errors.

To run PowerShell as administrator:

1. Search for PowerShell in the Start menu.
2. Right-click and select **Run as administrator**.

Conclusion

Cmdlets like Get-Process, Stop-Process, Start-Service, Stop-Service, and Restart-Service are foundational for managing systems with

PowerShell. Mastering these allows you to perform a wide range of administrative tasks efficiently and effectively. With just a few lines of code, you can retrieve vital system information, control resource usage, and ensure that essential services are running as needed. Whether you're managing a single PC or hundreds of remote machines, these tools empower you to automate and streamline system operations.

SERVICE MONITORING SCRIPTS

Monitoring Windows services is one of the most essential tasks for a system administrator. Services often power critical applications, and if they fail silently, it can lead to major disruptions. In this section, we will explore how to create PowerShell scripts that help monitor the status of services, alert on failures, and even attempt automatic restarts. These scripts can be scheduled to run at intervals or integrated into larger system monitoring frameworks.

Why Monitor Services?

Windows services run in the background to perform system and application-level functions. If a service stops unexpectedly, it could lead to degraded performance or a complete outage of critical applications. By proactively monitoring services, you can:

- Ensure high availability of applications
- Detect failures before users do
- Automate recovery actions
- Integrate with alerting systems (email, Slack, Teams)

Core Cmdlets for Service Monitoring

Before diving into script examples, here are the primary PowerShell cmdlets used for managing and monitoring services:

- Get-Service: Retrieves the status of services.
- Start-Service: Starts a stopped service.
- Stop-Service: Stops a running service.

- Restart-Service: Restarts a service.
- Set-Service: Modifies service properties (startup type, status, etc.).

Example 1: Basic Service Status Checker

This script checks the status of a specified service and outputs its status.

```
$serviceName = "wuauserv"  # Windows Update Service
$service = Get-Service -Name $serviceName

Write-Output "Service '$serviceName' is currently: $
($service.Status)"
```

This simple script is useful for ad-hoc checks or integrating into batch scripts.

Example 2: Logging Service Status to a File

To track service status over time, log the output to a file with timestamps:

```
$serviceName = "wuauserv"
$logPath = "C:\Logs\ServiceStatus.log"
$timestamp = Get-Date -Format "yyyy-MM-dd HH:mm:ss"

$service = Get-Service -Name $serviceName

$logEntry = "$timestamp - $serviceName is $
($service.Status)"
Add-Content -Path $logPath -Value $logEntry
```

Example 3: Restarting a Stopped Service

For services that must always be running, create a script that attempts to restart them if they are not.

```
$criticalServices = @("wuauserv", "Spooler", "BITS")

foreach ($serviceName in $criticalServices) {
    $service = Get-Service -Name $serviceName
```

```
    if ($service.Status -ne 'Running') {
        Write-Output "$serviceName is not running.
Attempting restart."
        Restart-Service -Name $serviceName -Force
        Start-Sleep -Seconds 5
        $newStatus = (Get-Service -Name $serviceName).Status
        Write-Output "$serviceName status after restart:
$newStatus"
    }
    else {
        Write-Output "$serviceName is running normally."
    }
}
```

Example 4: Email Alert on Service Failure

To receive email alerts when a service is down, use the Send-MailMessage cmdlet.

```
$serviceName = "wuauserv"
$service = Get-Service -Name $serviceName

if ($service.Status -ne 'Running') {
    $subject = "Alert: $serviceName is not running"
    $body = "$serviceName was found to be in a $
($service.Status) state on $(hostname)."
    $smtpServer = "smtp.yourdomain.com"
    $to = "admin@yourdomain.com"
    $from = "monitor@yourdomain.com"

    Send-MailMessage -To $to -From $from -Subject $subject -
Body $body -SmtpServer $smtpServer
    Write-Output "Alert email sent."
}
else {
    Write-Output "$serviceName is running."
}
```

Example 5: Monitoring Multiple Services on Multiple Machines

If you're in a domain environment or have remote PowerShell access set up, you can monitor services on multiple machines:

```
$computers = @("Server1", "Server2", "Server3")
$servicesToCheck = @("wuauserv", "Spooler")

foreach ($computer in $computers) {
    foreach ($service in $servicesToCheck) {
        try {
            $svc = Get-Service -ComputerName $computer -Name
$service -ErrorAction Stop
            Write-Output "$computer - $service status: $
($svc.Status)"
        } catch {
            Write-Output "$computer - $service could not be
checked: $_"
        }
    }
}
```

Scheduling Service Monitoring Scripts

You can automate these scripts using Task Scheduler:
1. Open Task Scheduler
2. Create a Basic Task
3. Choose a trigger (e.g., every 5 minutes)
4. Select "Start a program"
5. Use powershell.exe as the program and pass the script path as the argument:

powershell.exe -File "C:\Scripts\MonitorServices.ps1"

This ensures the script runs at your chosen intervals without manual execution.

Integrating with Monitoring Platforms

Many system administrators combine PowerShell scripts with third-party monitoring tools like Nagios, Zabbix, or PRTG. By writing custom checks in PowerShell and returning standardized output, you can plug into these systems easily. For example, outputting OK,

WARNING, or CRITICAL allows monitoring agents to parse results and react accordingly.

Best Practices

- **Use logging**: Always keep logs to troubleshoot service issues.
- **Handle exceptions**: Wrap commands in try-catch blocks to avoid silent failures.
- **Parameterize scripts**: Make your scripts reusable by accepting parameters.
- **Use credential management**: Avoid hardcoding credentials; use secure string or credential vaults.
- **Limit permissions**: Run scripts with the least privilege necessary.

Conclusion

Service monitoring scripts are a foundational component of proactive IT management. PowerShell offers powerful capabilities to create flexible, robust, and intelligent scripts for ensuring service uptime. By combining scheduled execution, logging, automated remediation, and alerting, you can significantly reduce downtime and improve service reliability. As your scripting skills grow, you can integrate these checks into broader operational workflows, increasing the efficiency and responsiveness of your IT environment.

Event Logs and System Info

READING WINDOWS EVENT LOGS

Windows Event Logs are one of the most essential tools in the toolkit of any system administrator, cybersecurity analyst, or PowerShell scripter. They provide a chronological record of system, security, and application-level events that can help identify system errors, security breaches, performance bottlenecks, and more. As a PowerShell user, knowing how to navigate and manipulate these logs can greatly enhance your ability to monitor, audit, and automate administrative tasks. In this chapter, we'll explore what Windows Event Logs are, how to access and interpret them, and how to use PowerShell to work with them effectively.

What Are Windows Event Logs?

Windows Event Logs are structured records of significant occurrences in the operating system and applications. These logs are written by various system components, including the operating system kernel, drivers, services, and user-mode applications. Each log entry, called an event, contains crucial metadata such as:

- **Date and time of the event**
- **Event ID**
- **Event level (Information, Warning, Error, Critical)**
- **Source (the application or service that logged the event)**
- **User and computer involved**
- **Event description**

Event logs are stored in binary .evtx files, typically located in the C:\Windows\System32\winevt\Logs\ directory.

Main Types of Logs

1. **Application Log**: Events logged by applications or programs. For example, a database error or an application crash.
2. **System Log**: Events logged by Windows system components, such as driver failures or system services.
3. **Security Log**: Contains audit events like login attempts, file access, and changes to user privileges.
4. **Setup Log**: Events related to application setup and installations.
5. **Forwarded Events**: Events collected from remote computers.

Accessing Event Logs with Event Viewer

Before diving into PowerShell, let's touch on the traditional GUI tool: Event Viewer.

1. Press Win + R, type eventvwr, and hit Enter.
2. The Event Viewer interface organizes logs into folders:
- **Windows Logs** (Application, Security, System, etc.)
- **Applications and Services Logs**
3. You can filter, search, and export logs using the built-in GUI tools.

Although Event Viewer is useful for quick checks, it becomes cumbersome for repeated tasks or bulk analysis. That's where PowerShell shines.

Using PowerShell to Read Event Logs

PowerShell provides multiple cmdlets to interact with event logs. The two main cmdlet families are:
- Get-EventLog – For older classic logs
- Get-WinEvent – For modern event logs and XML-based logs

Using Get-EventLog

This cmdlet is simpler but only works with the classic logs (Application, System, Security).

```
# Get the 10 most recent entries from the System log
Get-EventLog -LogName System -Newest 10
```

177

```
# Filter by event level (e.g., Errors only)
Get-EventLog -LogName System -EntryType Error -Newest 5

# Filter by date
Get-EventLog -LogName Application | Where-Object {
$_.TimeGenerated -gt (Get-Date).AddDays(-1) }
```

Using Get-WinEvent

This cmdlet is more powerful and supports querying any log, including custom and forwarded logs.

```
# List all available logs
Get-WinEvent -ListLog *

# Read the Application log
Get-WinEvent -LogName Application -MaxEvents 5

# Filter by date range
$Start = (Get-Date).AddDays(-1)
$End = Get-Date
Get-WinEvent -FilterHashtable @{LogName='System';
StartTime=$Start; EndTime=$End}
```

Understanding Event Properties

Each event returned by Get-EventLog or Get-WinEvent contains properties that give you detailed insights:

- **Message**: The human-readable description of the event
- **TimeCreated**: When the event occurred
- **Id**: The event ID, useful for filtering specific types of events
- **LevelDisplayName**: Shows if the event is an Error, Warning, or Information
- **ProviderName**: The source that generated the event
- **UserId**: The account associated with the event
  Example:

```
$event = Get-WinEvent -LogName System -MaxEvents 1
$event | Select-Object Id, TimeCreated, LevelDisplayName,
Message
```

Filtering Event Logs

PowerShell lets you perform complex filtering, which is vital for automation and monitoring.

Filtering by Event ID

```
# Find all event ID 1000 errors in the Application log
Get-WinEvent -FilterHashtable @{LogName='Application';
Id=1000}
```

Filtering by Provider Name

```
# Events generated by the 'Microsoft-Windows-Kernel-Power'
source
Get-WinEvent -FilterHashtable @{ProviderName='Microsoft-
Windows-Kernel-Power'}
```

Filtering by Keywords or Message Text

While you can't filter message text directly in the FilterHashtable, you can use Where-Object:

```
Get-WinEvent -LogName System | Where-Object { $_.Message -
like '*shutdown*' }
```

Exporting and Saving Logs

PowerShell enables you to save filtered logs for analysis or archiving:

```
# Export to CSV
Get-WinEvent -LogName System -MaxEvents 100 | Select-Object
TimeCreated, Id, Message | Export-Csv -Path "system_log.csv"
-NoTypeInformation

# Export to XML
Get-WinEvent -LogName Application -MaxEvents 10 | Export-
Clixml -Path "app_log.xml"
```

Creating Custom Event Monitors

You can create scripts that monitor specific types of events and trigger actions. Example:

```
# Monitor for failed logon attempts
```

```
$events = Get-WinEvent -FilterHashtable
@{LogName='Security'; Id=4625; StartTime=(Get-
Date).AddMinutes(-30)}
foreach ($e in $events) {
    Write-Output "Failed logon detected: $($e.TimeCreated) -
$($e.Message)"
}
```

Automation Ideas for PowerShell Scripting

- **Daily Security Audits**: Generate reports on failed logins, privilege changes, or system reboots.
- **Alerting**: Combine with email cmdlets to send notifications for critical errors.
- **Log Rotation and Archiving**: Automatically backup logs older than X days.
- **Scheduled Log Checks**: Run scripts via Task Scheduler to check for abnormal activity.

Conclusion

Mastering Windows Event Logs gives you visibility into the heartbeat of the system. PowerShell provides a rich interface to query, filter, and manipulate these logs efficiently. With a little creativity, you can automate monitoring, build auditing systems, and ensure you're always one step ahead of potential issues. Whether you're troubleshooting a mysterious crash or building a security compliance script, Event Logs will always be one of your most trusted allies in PowerShell scripting.

In the next section, we'll explore how to create PowerShell scripts that automatically respond to specific event log entries—enabling proactive system management and real-time responses.

GATHERING SYSTEM DIAGNOSTICS

System diagnostics are critical for understanding, maintaining, and troubleshooting computers and servers in a Windows environment.

Whether you're a beginner learning PowerShell or an experienced administrator looking to automate repetitive tasks, mastering the collection of diagnostic data is a fundamental skill. This section will guide you through gathering essential system diagnostics using PowerShell, providing practical scripts, explanations, and best practices.

Why Diagnostics Matter

Diagnostics provide insight into the health and performance of a computer system. With system diagnostics, administrators can:
- Monitor resource usage
- Identify hardware or software failures
- Detect abnormal behaviors
- Ensure compliance and security baselines
- Provide historical data for comparison

In many organizations, this data is collected proactively to prevent outages or diagnose issues before they become critical.

Key System Diagnostic Areas

Here are the primary categories of diagnostics that are useful in most environments:
1. **CPU and Memory Usage**
2. **Disk Usage and Performance**
3. **Network Configuration and Activity**
4. **Running Processes and Services**
5. **System Event Logs**
6. **Operating System and Installed Software Information**

We'll tackle each one of these with PowerShell examples and guidance.

Gathering CPU and Memory Usage

PowerShell provides several cmdlets and WMI (Windows Management Instrumentation) classes for retrieving real-time performance metrics.

```
Get-CimInstance Win32_Processor | Select-Object Name,
LoadPercentage
Get-CimInstance Win32_OperatingSystem | Select-Object
TotalVisibleMemorySize, FreePhysicalMemory
```

These commands fetch:
- CPU load percentage per processor
- Total and free physical memory (in kilobytes)

    You can convert the memory values to megabytes:

```
$os = Get-CimInstance Win32_OperatingSystem
"Total Memory: $([math]::round($os.TotalVisibleMemorySize /
1KB, 2)) MB"
"Free Memory: $([math]::round($os.FreePhysicalMemory / 1KB,
2)) MB"
```

For real-time monitoring, consider using Get-Counter:

```
Get-Counter '\Processor(_Total)\% Processor Time'
Get-Counter '\Memory\Available MBytes'
```

Disk Usage and Performance

Check current usage of all drives:

```
Get-CimInstance Win32_LogicalDisk -Filter "DriveType=3" | \
Select-Object DeviceID,
@{Name="Size(GB)";Expression={"{0:N2}" -f ($_.Size / 1GB)}},
\
@{Name="FreeSpace(GB)";Expression={"{0:N2}" -f ($_.FreeSpace
/ 1GB)}}
```

    To assess disk performance:

```
Get-Counter '\PhysicalDisk(_Total)\Avg. Disk Queue Length'
```

    A high disk queue length might indicate disk I/O bottlenecks.

Network Configuration and Activity

To retrieve adapter configuration:

```
Get-NetIPConfiguration | Select-Object InterfaceAlias,
IPv4Address, DNSServer
```

    To see active network connections:

```
Get-NetTCPConnection | Group-Object State | Select-Object
Name, Count
```
To collect bandwidth and error metrics:
```
Get-Counter '\Network Interface(*)\Bytes Total/sec'
Get-Counter '\Network Interface(*)\Packets Received Errors'
```

Running Processes and Services

See top memory-using processes:
```
Get-Process | Sort-Object WorkingSet -Descending | Select-
Object -First 10 Name, ID, CPU, WorkingSet
```
Check all running services:
```
Get-Service | Where-Object {$_.Status -eq 'Running'} | Sort-
Object DisplayName
```
Find services set to start automatically but are not running:
```
Get-Service | Where-Object {$_.StartType -eq 'Automatic' -
and $_.Status -ne 'Running'}
```

System Event Logs

Windows logs events in several categories such as System, Application, and Security.

Retrieve the last 20 system events:
```
Get-EventLog -LogName System -Newest 20
```
Filter logs for critical errors:
```
Get-EventLog -LogName System -EntryType Error -After (Get-
Date).AddDays(-7)
```
Export event logs for further analysis:
```
Get-EventLog -LogName Application -After (Get-
Date).AddDays(-1) | Export-Csv "C:\logs\AppEvents.csv" -
NoTypeInformation
```

OS and Installed Software Info

Gather basic OS information:
```
Get-CimInstance Win32_OperatingSystem | Select-Object
Caption, Version, BuildNumber, OSArchitecture
```

Get installed programs:

```
Get-ItemProperty HKLM:
\Software\Wow6432Node\Microsoft\Windows\CurrentVersion\Unins
tall\* | \
Select-Object DisplayName, DisplayVersion, Publisher,
InstallDate
```

Note: Installed software can also reside in other registry paths depending on system architecture.

Creating a Diagnostic Report Script

You can combine these into a single script to output a snapshot of system diagnostics:

```
$report = @{}

$cpu = Get-CimInstance Win32_Processor
$mem = Get-CimInstance Win32_OperatingSystem
$disk = Get-CimInstance Win32_LogicalDisk -Filter
"DriveType=3"
$net = Get-NetIPConfiguration
$proc = Get-Process | Sort-Object CPU -Descending | Select-
Object -First 5
$serv = Get-Service | Where-Object {$_.Status -eq 'Running'}
$logs = Get-EventLog -LogName System -EntryType Error -
Newest 5
$os = Get-CimInstance Win32_OperatingSystem

$report['CPU Load %'] = $cpu.LoadPercentage
$report['Total Memory (MB)'] =
[math]::Round($mem.TotalVisibleMemorySize / 1KB, 2)
$report['Free Memory (MB)'] =
[math]::Round($mem.FreePhysicalMemory / 1KB, 2)
$report['Disk Info'] = $disk | Select-Object DeviceID,
@{Name="Size(GB)";Expression={"{0:N2}" -f ($_.Size / 1GB)}},
\
@{Name="FreeSpace(GB)";Expression={"{0:N2}" -f ($_.FreeSpace
/ 1GB)}}
$report['IP Addresses'] = $net | ForEach-Object {
$_.IPv4Address.IPAddress }
$report['Top Processes'] = $proc | Select-Object Name, CPU
$report['Running Services'] = $serv.DisplayName
$report['Recent System Errors'] = $logs | Select-Object
```

```
TimeGenerated, Message
$report['OS Info'] = $os.Caption + " " + $os.Version

$report | Format-List
```

This script collects key data and stores it in a hash table, which is then printed out in an easy-to-read format.

You could also export this data to a text file:

```
$report | Out-File -FilePath "C:\logs\SystemDiagnostics.txt"
```

Best Practices

- **Run with elevated permissions**: Some diagnostics require administrator rights.
- **Schedule periodic collection**: Use Task Scheduler to run PowerShell scripts regularly.
- **Log and archive data**: Save output to a central location for future comparison.
- **Automate and alert**: Combine diagnostics with email or notification tools for proactive alerts.

Conclusion

Gathering system diagnostics with PowerShell is both powerful and accessible, even for beginners. By understanding the essential categories—CPU, memory, disk, network, processes, services, logs, and OS data—you can build robust scripts that help monitor and maintain healthy systems. Start small, build reusable scripts, and automate as your skills grow. Diagnostics are the heartbeat of system administration—learn to listen well.

Local User and Group Management

CREATING USERS, MANAGING GROUPS

Managing user accounts and groups is a fundamental task for any system administrator, but doing so manually through graphical interfaces can quickly become inefficient, especially in environments where consistency, speed, and automation are critical. PowerShell offers a powerful, scriptable solution to streamline these administrative tasks, allowing you to create, modify, and manage local users and groups with precision and repeatability. In this chapter, we will explore how to leverage PowerShell's built-in cmdlets to efficiently handle local account management. Whether you're setting up a single workstation or configuring multiple machines in a standardized way, mastering these techniques will not only save time but also reduce human error and enhance security through automation. By the end of this chapter, you'll be equipped with the knowledge to create, manage, and automate local user and group configurations, transforming routine account management into a seamless part of your administrative workflow.

Creating New Users

Creating Local Users

The New-LocalUser cmdlet is used to create a user on a standalone Windows computer:

```
New-LocalUser -Name "jsmith" -Password (Read-Host -
AsSecureString "Enter password") -FullName "John Smith" -
Description "Local test user"
```

You can then add the user to a local group:

```
Add-LocalGroupMember -Group "Administrators" -Member
"jsmith"
```

Bulk User Creation

PowerShell excels at bulk operations. To create multiple users, use a CSV file:

users.csv

```
FirstName,LastName,Username,Password
Alice,Smith,asmith,D3f@u1tP@ssw0rd
Bob,Jones,bjones,D3f@u1tP@ssw0rd
```

Script to import CSV and create users:

```
# Path to CSV file
$csvPath = "C:\Path\To\users.csv"


# Import the CSV file
$users = Import-Csv -Path $csvPath


# Loop through each user in the CSV
foreach ($user in $users) {
    $username    = $user.Username
    $password    = ConvertTo-SecureString $user.Password -
AsPlainText -Force
    $fullname    = "$($user.FirstName) $($user.LastName)"
    $description = "Local user account for $fullname"


    # Check if user already exists
    if (Get-LocalUser -Name $username -ErrorAction
SilentlyContinue) {
        Write-Host "User '$username' already exists.
Skipping..." -ForegroundColor Yellow
    } else {
        # Create the local user
        try {
            New-LocalUser -Name $username `
                          -Password $password `
                          -FullName $fullname `
                          -Description $description


            # Optionally, add to a group (e.g., 'Users' or
'Administrators')
            Add-LocalGroupMember -Group "Users" -Member
$username
```

```
        Write-Host "User '$username' created
successfully." -ForegroundColor Green
        }
        catch {
            Write-Host "Failed to create user '$username'.
Error: $_" -ForegroundColor Red
        }
    }
}
```

This technique allows for rapid onboarding or migration scenarios.

Creating and Managing Groups

Managing Local Groups with PowerShell

Groups help simplify system management by allowing permissions to be assigned collectively to multiple users. Instead of configuring permissions for individual accounts, local groups enable administrators to efficiently manage access and roles on a per-group basis. PowerShell provides straightforward cmdlets to create and manage **local groups**, making automation and bulk management tasks seamless.

Creating Local Groups

To create a **local group** on a Windows machine using PowerShell, use the New-LocalGroup cmdlet:

```
New-LocalGroup -Name "LocalAdmins" -Description "Custom
local admin group"
```

This command creates a local group named LocalAdmins with a description. Unlike Active Directory, local groups do **not** require specifying scopes like Global or categories like Security or Distribution. Local groups are simpler and confined to the machine where they are created.

Adding Users to Local Groups

To add users to a **local group**, use the Add-LocalGroupMember cmdlet.

- **Add a single user to a local group:**

```
Add-LocalGroupMember -Group "LocalAdmins" -Member "jdoe"
```

- **Add multiple users to a local group:**

```
$Users = "jdoe","asmith","bjones"
```

```
Add-LocalGroupMember -Group "LocalAdmins" -Member $Users
```

This approach allows you to efficiently assign multiple local user accounts to a group in one command.

Removing Users from Local Groups

To remove users from a **local group**, use the Remove-LocalGroupMember cmdlet.

- **Remove a single user from a local group:**

```
Remove-LocalGroupMember -Group "LocalAdmins" -Member "jdoe"
```

If you want to suppress confirmation prompts, add -Confirm:$false:

```
Remove-LocalGroupMember -Group "LocalAdmins" -Member "jdoe"
-Confirm:$false
```

- **Remove multiple users:**

```
$Users = "jdoe","asmith","bjones"
Remove-LocalGroupMember -Group "LocalAdmins" -Member $Users
-Confirm:$false
```

Summary of Key Cmdlets for Local Group Management

Task	Cmdlet Example
Create Local Group	New-LocalGrou

p-Name" GroupName" -Description" Description" Add-

Add User(s) to Group

LocalGroupMember -Group "GroupName" -Member "Usern

Remove User(s)

ame"Remove-LocalGroupMember-Group"GroupName"-M

View Group Members

ember"Username"Get-LocalGroupMember-Group"Grou

This streamlined approach enables administrators to manage local groups effectively, ensuring consistent permission management across standalone or workgroup-based Windows systems.

Listing Users and Groups

Querying Local Users and Groups with PowerShell

While Active Directory provides robust cmdlets for querying users and groups in a domain environment, managing standalone or workgroup machines requires using PowerShell's local account cmdlets. Below is how you can perform similar queries for **local groups** and **local users**.

Get a List of Users in a Local Group

To list all members of a local group, use the Get-LocalGroupMember cmdlet:

```
Get-LocalGroupMember -Group "LocalAdmins"
```

This command returns all users and groups that are members of the LocalAdmins group.

Get All Local Groups a User Belongs To

PowerShell doesn't provide a direct cmdlet to list all groups a local user belongs to, but you can achieve this by filtering through all local groups:

```
$User = "jdoe"
Get-LocalGroup | ForEach-Object {
    if (Get-LocalGroupMember -Group $_.Name | Where-Object {
$_.Name -eq $User }) {
        $_.Name
    }
}
```

This script loops through each local group and checks if the user is a member, outputting the group names where the user belongs.

List All Local Users

To list all local user accounts on a machine, use the Get-LocalUser cmdlet:

```
Get-LocalUser
```

This will display all local user accounts, including their status (Enabled/Disabled) and other basic properties.

If you want to filter for only enabled users:

```
Get-LocalUser | Where-Object { $_.Enabled -eq $true }
```

Summary of Key Cmdlets for Querying Local Users and Groups

Task	Cmdlet Example
List users in a group	Get-LocalGroupMember-Grou

List all local users

List enabled local users

Find groups a user belongs to

p
"
GroupName"
Get-LocalUser
Get-LocalUser
Looopth

rough Get-LocalGroup and check membership

These tools provide a lightweight yet powerful way to manage and audit local accounts, ensuring effective user and group governance on standalone Windows systems.

Modifying Users and Groups

Modifying Local Users and Groups with PowerShell

Unlike Active Directory, where user and group objects have extensive attributes, local accounts on Windows systems have a simpler set of properties. PowerShell provides cmdlets to modify key aspects of local users and groups, allowing administrators to adjust configurations efficiently.

Change Local User Properties

To modify properties of a local user, use the Set-LocalUser cmdlet. While local users don't have attributes like Title or Department, you can update properties such as the **Full Name**, **Description**, and **Password**.

- **Example: Change Full Name and Description**

```
Set-LocalUser -Name "jdoe" -FullName "John Doe" -Description
"HR Manager - Human Resources Department"
```

- **Example: Update Password**

```
$NewPassword = ConvertTo-SecureString "N3wP@ssw0rd" -
AsPlainText -Force
Set-LocalUser -Name "jdoe" -Password $NewPassword
```

Rename a Local Group

To rename a local group, use the Rename-LocalGroup cmdlet:

```
Rename-LocalGroup -Name "LocalAdmins" -NewName "IT Admins"
```

- This command renames the LocalAdmins group to IT Admins.

Note: If you attempt to rename built-in groups (like "Administrators"), you may encounter restrictions depending on system policies.

Summary of Key Cmdlets for Modifying Local Users and Groups

Task	Cmdlet Example
Change user properties	Set

-LocalUserName "jdoe" -FullName "John Doe" -Descri

Update user password

p
t
i
o
n
"
H
R
M
a
n
a
g
e
r
"
S
e
t
-
L
o
c
a
l
U
s
e
r
-
N
a
m
e
"
j
d
o
e
"
-
P
a
s
s
w

Rename a local group

ord$NewPasswordRename-LocalGroup -Name "OldGroup

" - N e w N a m e " N e w G r o u p "

PowerShell's local account management cmdlets offer a streamlined way to modify user and group configurations without relying on manual GUI operations. These tools are especially useful for scripting changes across multiple systems in workgroup or standalone environments.

Deleting Users and Groups

Removing Local Users and Groups with PowerShell

In standalone or workgroup environments, managing the lifecycle of user accounts and groups includes the safe removal of obsolete or unnecessary accounts. PowerShell provides simple cmdlets to delete local users and groups, streamlining account cleanup and improving system security.

Deleting a Local User

To delete a local user account, use the Remove-LocalUser cmdlet:

```
Remove-LocalUser -Name "jdoe"
```

- To suppress confirmation prompts, add the -Confirm:$false parameter:

```
Remove-LocalUser -Name "jdoe" -Confirm:$false
```

This command permanently deletes the local user jdoe.

Deleting a Local Group

To delete a local group, use the Remove-LocalGroup cmdlet:

```
Remove-LocalGroup -Name "HR Department"
```

- To bypass confirmation prompts:

```
Remove-LocalGroup -Name "HR Department" -Confirm:$false
```

This removes the specified local group from the system.

Summary of Key Cmdlets for Removing Local Users and Groups

Task	Cmdlet Example
Delete a local user	Remove-LocalUser -Name "Username"

Delete a local group

ame" -Confirm:$false Remove-LocalGroup -Name" Grou

```
pName" -Confirm:$false
```

These cmdlets make it easy to manage and clean up local accounts, ensuring that only authorized users and groups remain on your systems. Always verify the accounts scheduled for removal to prevent accidental deletion of critical users or groups.

For enhanced safety, consider scripting a backup or export of user and group information before performing bulk deletions.

Best Practices

Effective user and group management with PowerShell goes beyond simply running commands—it requires thoughtful practices to ensure security, reliability, and maintainability. Below are key best practices to follow when scripting administrative tasks for local or Active Directory environments.

Use Secure Strings for Passwords

Always handle passwords securely by using **Secure Strings**. Avoid storing plain text passwords in scripts or files to reduce the risk of credential exposure.

```
$Password = ConvertTo-SecureString "P@ssw0rd123" -
AsPlainText -Force
```

For more secure approaches, consider reading encrypted passwords from a file or prompting for input.

Use CSV Files for Bulk Operations

When managing multiple users or groups, leverage **CSV files** to streamline bulk operations. This ensures consistency, simplifies management, and makes your scripts reusable.

```
Import-Csv -Path "C:\users.csv" | ForEach-Object {
    # Process each user
}
```

CSV-driven automation reduces manual errors and provides clear documentation of intended changes.

Log Changes for Auditing and Rollback

Implement logging in your scripts to track changes. This is essential for auditing, troubleshooting, and rolling back unintended modifications.

```
"[$(Get-Date)] Created user $($_.Username)" | Out-File -
FilePath "C:\Logs\UserCreation.log" -Append
```

Maintaining logs provides accountability and a historical record of administrative actions.

Test in a Lab Before Deploying to Production

Always **test scripts in a lab environment** before applying them to production systems. This helps identify potential issues, unintended consequences, and ensures scripts behave as expected.

Testing safeguards production stability and minimizes risk.

Use -WhatIf on Destructive Cmdlets

When using cmdlets that can delete or modify critical data—such as Remove-LocalUser, Remove-LocalGroupMember, or Remove-ADUser—always start with the -WhatIf parameter.

```
Remove-LocalUser -Name "testuser" -WhatIf
```

The -WhatIf flag simulates the action without making changes, allowing you to verify the impact before execution.

Summary of Best Practices

Practice	D es cr ip ti o

Secure Passwords

Use SecureStrings or encryption for handling credentials

Bulk Operations

Use CSV files

to automate repetitive tasks Record changes for auditing and roll b

Logging

	ac
	k
	p
	ur
	p
	os
	es
Lab Testing	V
	a l
	i d
	a t
	e
	s c
	r i
	pt
	s
	in
	a
	sa
	f e
	en
	v i
	r o
	n
	m
	en
	t
	be
	f o
	r e
	pr
	o
	d
	uc
	t i
	o
	n
	de

Safe Execution

ployment Use - What If to prevent accidental destructive actions

By adhering to these best practices, administrators can ensure their PowerShell automation is secure, efficient, and reliable, reducing operational risks while enhancing control over user and group management tasks.

Real-World Example: Onboarding Script

Consolidated Script for Local User Creation and Group Assignment

```
# Define user details
$FirstName = "Emily"
$LastName  = "Clark"
$Username  = "eclark"
$Password  = ConvertTo-SecureString "P@ssw0rd123" -
AsPlainText -Force
$Groups    = @("HRTeam", "VPNUsers")  # Local group names

# Create the local user
New-LocalUser -Name $Username `
              -Password $Password `
              -FullName "$FirstName $LastName" `
              -Description "User account for $FirstName
$LastName"

# Assign user to specified local groups
foreach ($Group in $Groups) {
    Add-LocalGroupMember -Group $Group -Member $Username
}

Write-Host "User $Username created and added to groups
successfully." -ForegroundColor Green
```

Key Differences from Active Directory Version
- **No OU or Directory Path**: Local users don't reside in Organizational Units (OUs). They are created directly on the machine.
- **No UserPrincipalName**: Local accounts don't use UPNs or domain-based logins.
- **Group Names**: Ensure that the local groups (e.g., HRTeam, VPNUsers) already exist. You can create them using New-LocalGroup if needed.

Example: Creating Required Local Groups First
If the groups don't exist, you can add this before the user creation:

```
$Groups = @("HRTeam", "VPNUsers")

foreach ($Group in $Groups) {
    if (-not (Get-LocalGroup -Name $Group -ErrorAction
```

```
SilentlyContinue)) {
        New-LocalGroup -Name $Group -Description "Auto-
created group: $Group"
    }
}
```

Summary

This script automates local user creation and ensures proper group membership assignment, streamlining administrative tasks on standalone Windows systems. It's ideal for lab setups, workgroup environments, or automated provisioning scripts.

For production use, consider enhancing it with:

- Error handling
- Logging
- Password security improvements
- Checks for existing users before creation

Conclusion

Mastering PowerShell for user and group management gives administrators a major advantage. From handling everyday tasks to orchestrating large-scale directory updates, scripting allows you to achieve consistency, scalability, and security. The more you practice these commands and adapt them to your organization's needs, the more efficient and powerful your IT workflows will become.

In the next chapter, we'll explore **automated provisioning and de-provisioning** workflows using PowerShell jobs and scheduled tasks to fully automate lifecycle management.

PASSWORD RESETS AND USER AUDITS

PowerShell scripting is a powerful and essential tool for system administrators, particularly when it comes to managing users in Active Directory (AD). Two of the most common and critical tasks for IT professionals are resetting passwords and auditing user accounts. These tasks are necessary for maintaining security, ensuring compliance, and simplifying user management.

This chapter will walk you through the processes of automating password resets and conducting thorough user audits using PowerShell. You'll learn not only how to perform these tasks but also how to build reusable scripts that enhance efficiency and consistency across your organization.

Understanding the Importance of Password Resets and Audits

Why Automate Password Resets?

Password resets are one of the most frequent help desk requests in any organization. Automating this process with PowerShell can significantly reduce the workload on IT staff, increase response time, and ensure a more consistent approach to password policies.

Why Perform User Audits?

User audits help IT administrators verify that only authorized users have access to the network. They are essential for:

- Compliance with regulatory standards
- Identifying inactive or orphaned accounts
- Detecting unauthorized access
- Cleaning up old or unused accounts

By automating these audits, organizations can maintain security hygiene and adhere to internal policies more easily.

Automating Password Resets with PowerShell

Password Reset Scripts for Local Windows Accounts with PowerShell

Managing local account passwords is a common administrative task, and PowerShell provides efficient ways to handle both individual and bulk password resets on Windows machines. Below are examples of how to adapt traditional Active Directory password reset scripts for **local Windows accounts**.

Basic Password Reset Script (Local Account)

Here's a simple script to reset a **local user's password**:

```
$Username = Read-Host "Enter the username"
$NewPassword = Read-Host "Enter the new password" -
AsSecureString
```

```
Set-LocalUser -Name $Username -Password $NewPassword

Write-Host "Password for $Username has been reset."
```

This script prompts the administrator for a username and a new password, then applies the change using Set-LocalUser. Note that, unlike Active Directory, local accounts **do not** have a ChangePasswordAtLogon flag.

Bulk Password Resets for Local Accounts

You can reset passwords for multiple local users from a CSV file. The CSV should contain a column named Username.

```
$Users = Import-Csv "C:\Scripts\users.csv"

foreach ($User in $Users) {
    $SecurePassword = ConvertTo-SecureString "P@ssw0rd123" -
AsPlainText -Force
    Set-LocalUser -Name $User.Username -Password
$SecurePassword
    Write-Host "Password reset for $($User.Username)"
}
```

This script assigns a default password (P@ssw0rd123) to each user listed in the CSV file. Since local accounts don't support enforcing password changes at next login via PowerShell, you would need to configure local security policies separately if required.

Best Practices for Local Password Resets

- **Audit Logging:** Always log password changes for accountability and auditing purposes.
- **Randomized Passwords:** Use unique, randomized passwords for each account and communicate them securely.
- **Script Security:** Restrict access to scripts that perform password changes to prevent unauthorized use.
- **Secure Credential Storage:** Use secure methods like **DPAPI**, **HashiCorp Vault**, or **Azure Key Vault** for storing administrative credentials and sensitive data.
- **Avoid Hardcoding Passwords:** Where possible, avoid embedding plaintext passwords directly into scripts.

By following these practices, administrators can maintain a higher level of security and control when managing local account passwords across Windows systems.

Conducting User Audits with PowerShell

Auditing Local Windows Accounts with PowerShell

User audits can be customized based on what you want to track. Below are several key types of audits tailored for **local Windows accounts**.

Finding Inactive Local Users

PowerShell does not track detailed login history for local accounts like Active Directory does, but you can check for disabled accounts or manually maintained logs. However, here's how to find **disabled** local users:

```
Get-LocalUser | Where-Object { $_.Enabled -eq $false } |
Select-Object Name, Enabled |
Export-Csv "C:\Reports\DisabledLocalUsers.csv" -
NoTypeInformation
```

This exports a list of disabled local user accounts.

Identifying Users Without Passwords

Accounts without passwords can be a security risk:

```
Get-LocalUser | Where-Object { $_.PasswordRequired -eq
$false } |
Select-Object Name |
Export-Csv "C:\Reports\NoPasswordUsers.csv" -
NoTypeInformation
```

These accounts should be reviewed to ensure they comply with security policies.

Finding Locked-Out Local Users

Windows does not natively expose lockout status for local accounts via PowerShell. However, if account lockout policies are enforced, you can identify **disabled** accounts as a proxy:

```
Get-LocalUser | Where-Object { $_.Enabled -eq $false } |
Select-Object Name |
Export-Csv "C:\Reports\LockedOutOrDisabledUsers.csv" -
NoTypeInformation
```

This helps administrators identify accounts that are no longer active.

Listing Accounts with Passwords That Never Expire

For local accounts, you can check which accounts have the PasswordExpires property set to $false:

```
Get-LocalUser | Where-Object { $_.PasswordExpires -eq $false
} |
Select-Object Name |
Export-Csv "C:\Reports\NeverExpireLocalAccounts.csv" -
NoTypeInformation
```

Accounts with non-expiring passwords pose a security risk and should be reviewed regularly.

Users in Critical Local Groups

Auditing membership of critical local groups like Administrators ensures only authorized users have elevated privileges:

```
Get-LocalGroupMember -Group "Administrators" |
Select-Object Name, ObjectClass |
Export-Csv "C:\Reports\LocalAdministrators.csv" -
NoTypeInformation
```

Regular reviews of local group memberships help maintain proper security boundaries.

These PowerShell audits provide visibility into local user accounts and group memberships, supporting better security and account management on standalone or workgroup machines.

Building a Unified Audit Script

Consolidated Local User Audit with PowerShell

Instead of running each audit separately, you can combine multiple checks into one script and output the results to separate CSV files or a single Excel workbook using the ImportExcel module.

First, install the ImportExcel module if you haven't already:

```
Install-Module -Name ImportExcel -Scope CurrentUser
```

Set the path for your report:

```
$reportPath = "C:\Reports\Local_User_Audit_Report.xlsx"
```

Audit Checks for Local Windows Accounts

Inactive Users (No Logon in Last 90 Days)

Note: Local accounts don't track LastLogonDate like AD, but you can check enabled accounts and infer usage based on password age or other criteria if available.

```
Get-LocalUser |
    Where-Object { $_.Enabled -eq $true -and
$_.PasswordLastSet -lt (Get-Date).AddDays(-90) } |
    Export-Excel -Path $reportPath -WorksheetName
'InactiveUsers' -AutoSize
```

Accounts That Have Never Logged On

Local accounts don't store explicit logon history natively, but you can flag accounts with a PasswordLastSet value of $null (if applicable):

```
Get-LocalUser |
    Where-Object { !$_.PasswordLastSet } |
    Export-Excel -Path $reportPath -WorksheetName
'NoLogonDate' -AutoSize
```

Disabled Accounts (Instead of Locked Out Users)

Local accounts don't lock out in the same way as AD. Instead, check for disabled accounts:

```
Get-LocalUser |
    Where-Object { $_.Enabled -eq $false } |
    Export-Excel -Path $reportPath -WorksheetName
'DisabledAccounts' -AutoSize
```

Accounts with Non-Expiring Passwords

Local accounts can have passwords set to never expire, but detecting this requires using net user parsing:

```
Get-LocalUser | ForEach-Object {
    $user = $_.Name
    $passwordInfo = net user $user |
        Select-String "Password never expires"

    if ($passwordInfo -match "Yes") {
        [PSCustomObject]@{
            User = $user
```

```
          PasswordNeverExpires = 'Yes'
      }
    }
} | Export-Excel -Path $reportPath -WorksheetName
'NeverExpire' -AutoSize
```

Local Administrators Group Membership

Instead of Domain Admins, check members of the local Administrators group:

```
Get-LocalGroupMember -Group "Administrators" |
    Export-Excel -Path $reportPath -WorksheetName
'LocalAdmins' -AutoSize
```

Completion Message

```
Write-Host "Local user audit completed. Reports generated at
$reportPath"
```

This script provides a consolidated audit of local Windows accounts, exporting key security-related information to an Excel workbook for easy review and reporting.

Conclusion

Password resets and user audits are fundamental components of a secure IT environment. By leveraging PowerShell scripting, administrators can automate repetitive tasks, reduce human error, and improve response times.

This chapter has provided practical scripts for individual and bulk password resets, as well as a wide range of audit checks that can be tailored to your organization's needs. These scripts can serve as building blocks for more comprehensive automation strategies in your environment.

In the next chapter, we'll explore logging, error handling, and notifications to ensure your scripts are not only functional but also maintainable and resilient in production environments.

Introduction to Active Directory (AD)

AD CMDLETS, OU STRUCTURE

Understanding Active Directory (AD) cmdlets and how they interact with Organizational Units (OUs) is essential for any PowerShell scripter working in a Windows Server environment. In this section, we'll explore how AD cmdlets work, the significance of OU structure in Active Directory, and best practices for managing and scripting with both.

Introduction to AD Cmdlets

Active Directory cmdlets are part of the ActiveDirectory module, which comes with the Remote Server Administration Tools (RSAT) on client systems and is built into Windows Server. These cmdlets allow administrators to automate nearly all aspects of Active Directory management, including users, groups, computers, and OUs.

Before using AD cmdlets, ensure the module is imported:

```
Import-Module ActiveDirectory
```

You can verify the module and list all available cmdlets with:

```
Get-Command -Module ActiveDirectory
```

What is an Organizational Unit (OU)?

An Organizational Unit is a container within Active Directory used to organize users, groups, computers, and other OUs. OUs are primarily used to:

- Delegate administrative control
- Apply Group Policy settings
- Organize resources logically

Think of OUs like folders in a file system. They help structure your AD in a meaningful way that aligns with your organization's departments, geographical locations, or functions.

Common AD Cmdlets for OU Management

Here are some frequently used AD cmdlets that interact with OUs:

Get-ADOrganizationalUnit

Retrieves information about one or more OUs.

```
Get-ADOrganizationalUnit -Filter *
```

This command returns all OUs in the domain.

New-ADOrganizationalUnit

Creates a new OU.

```
New-ADOrganizationalUnit -Name "HR" -Path
"DC=example,DC=com"
```

Set-ADOrganizationalUnit

Modifies an existing OU.

```
Set-ADOrganizationalUnit -Identity "OU=HR,DC=example,DC=com"
-ProtectedFromAccidentalDeletion $false
```

Remove-ADOrganizationalUnit

Deletes an OU.

```
Remove-ADOrganizationalUnit -Identity
"OU=HR,DC=example,DC=com"
```

Note: Always use caution when removing OUs, especially if they contain objects.

Structuring OUs Effectively

An effective OU structure reflects your organization's operational and administrative needs. Poor OU design can lead to administrative confusion, improper policy application, and increased troubleshooting time.

Best Practices for OU Design

1. **Keep it Simple:** Avoid overly complex hierarchies.
2. **Function over Form:** Design around administrative delegation and policy application, not just visual hierarchy.
3. **Avoid User and Computer Mixes:** Separate users and computers into different OUs for better Group Policy targeting.
4. **Use Naming Conventions:** Consistent naming helps scripts and

documentation.

5. **Delegate Carefully:** Use OUs to assign administrative rights without giving global control.

Example OU Structure

A basic structure might look like:

```
DC=example,DC=com
|
+--OU=Users
|    +--OU=HR
|    +--OU=IT
|    +--OU=Sales
|
+--OU=Computers
|    +--OU=Desktops
|    +--OU=Laptops
|    +--OU=Servers
|
+--OU=Groups
```

This structure allows clear segmentation and policy application.

Using Cmdlets with OU Filters

AD cmdlets frequently use the -SearchBase and -SearchScope parameters to narrow results to a specific OU or subtree.

Example: Get all users in the IT OU

```
Get-ADUser -Filter * -SearchBase
"OU=IT,OU=Users,DC=example,DC=com"
```

This command retrieves all users located specifically within the IT sub-OU.

Example: Move a computer to another OU

```
Move-ADObject -Identity
"CN=PC001,OU=Desktops,OU=Computers,DC=example,DC=com" -
TargetPath "OU=Laptops,OU=Computers,DC=example,DC=com"
```

Scripting for OU Creation

Creating OUs with scripts can be very useful during new domain setups or onboarding new departments.

Script Example: Create Departmental OUs

```
$departments = @("HR", "IT", "Finance", "Marketing")
foreach ($dept in $departments) {
    New-ADOrganizationalUnit -Name $dept -Path
"OU=Users,DC=example,DC=com"
}
```

This script creates four OUs under the Users OU.

Protecting OUs from Deletion

By default, most OUs created using the GUI are protected from accidental deletion. This can also be done using PowerShell:

```
Set-ADOrganizationalUnit -Identity
"OU=IT,OU=Users,DC=example,DC=com" -
ProtectedFromAccidentalDeletion $true
```

This setting is crucial for high-importance OUs.

Bulk OU Reporting

You can extract and export OU information for documentation or auditing.

Export OU list to CSV

```
Get-ADOrganizationalUnit -Filter * | Select-Object Name,
DistinguishedName | Export-Csv -Path "C:
\Reports\OU_List.csv" -NoTypeInformation
```

This generates a CSV of all OUs with their names and distinguished paths.

Troubleshooting OU Scripts

Common Errors
- **"Access Denied"**: You lack the required permissions.
- **"Object Already Exists"**: The OU name already exists at that level.
- **"Invalid DistinguishedName"**: Ensure the path format is correct.

Debugging Tips
- Use -Verbose for detailed output.
- Wrap commands in try {} catch {} for error handling.

```
    try {
            New-ADOrganizationalUnit  -Name  "TestOU"  -Path
"DC=example,DC=com" -Verbose
    } catch {
      Write-Error "Failed to create OU: $_"
    }
```

Summary

AD cmdlets provide a robust framework for interacting with Active Directory, and when combined with a well-planned OU structure, they empower administrators to manage environments efficiently and with precision. Proper OU design ensures scalability, simplified policy management, and delegation control. Mastering OU-based scripting in PowerShell is a foundational skill for any Windows administrator.

In the next section, we will dive deeper into managing users and groups within these OUs, focusing on automation and advanced filtering.

Creating/Managing AD Users/Groups

Active Directory (AD) is a foundational component in most Windows-based enterprise environments. It provides centralized management of users, groups, computers, and other resources within a network. In this chapter, we focus on how to use PowerShell to create and manage Active Directory users and groups. These tasks are fundamental for system administrators and invaluable for automating user provisioning and access control.

Prerequisites

Before beginning, ensure the following prerequisites are met:
1. **Active Directory Module**: You need the Active Directory module for Windows PowerShell installed. It's included with the Remote Server Administration Tools (RSAT).
2. **Permissions**: You must have appropriate permissions to create and manage users and groups in AD.
3. **PowerShell Version**: PowerShell 5.1 or later is recommended for full functionality and compatibility.

```
Import-Module ActiveDirectory
```

This command imports the Active Directory module into your session.

Creating AD Users

Creating users in Active Directory can be done manually via GUI or efficiently through PowerShell for bulk operations or automation.

Basic User Creation

To create a single user:

```
New-ADUser -Name "John Doe" -GivenName "John" -Surname "Doe"
-SamAccountName "jdoe" -UserPrincipalName
"jdoe@yourdomain.com" -Path "OU=Users,DC=yourdomain,DC=com"
-AccountPassword (ConvertTo-SecureString "P@ssw0rd123" -
AsPlainText -Force) -Enabled $true
```

Bulk User Creation from CSV

For larger environments, creating users in bulk from a CSV file is more efficient.

CSV format:

```
FirstName,LastName,Username,Password
Jane,Doe,jdoe,P@ssword123
Tom,Smith,tsmith,P@ssword456
```

PowerShell Script:

```
$users = Import-Csv -Path "C:\scripts\new_users.csv"

foreach ($user in $users) {
    $name = "$($user.FirstName) $($user.LastName)"
    $sam = $user.Username
    $upn = "$sam@yourdomain.com"
    $password = ConvertTo-SecureString $user.Password -
AsPlainText -Force

    New-ADUser -Name $name -GivenName $user.FirstName -
Surname $user.LastName -SamAccountName $sam -
UserPrincipalName $upn -Path "OU=Users,DC=yourdomain,DC=com"
-AccountPassword $password -Enabled $true
}
```

Modifying AD Users

User accounts may require updates, such as name changes, password resets, or enabling/disabling access.

Modifying User Attributes

```
Set-ADUser -Identity jdoe -Title "IT Support Specialist" -
Department "IT"
```

Enabling/Disabling Accounts

```
Disable-ADAccount -Identity jdoe
Enable-ADAccount -Identity jdoe
```

Resetting Passwords

```
Set-ADAccountPassword -Identity jdoe -NewPassword
(ConvertTo-SecureString "NewP@ssw0rd" -AsPlainText -Force)
```

Creating AD Groups

Groups simplify access management by grouping users with common access needs.

Types of Groups
- **Security Groups**: Used to assign permissions to resources.
- **Distribution Groups**: Used for email distribution lists.

Creating a New Group
```
New-ADGroup -Name "IT Dept" -GroupScope Global -Path
"OU=Groups,DC=yourdomain,DC=com" -GroupCategory Security
```

Modifying Group Properties
```
Set-ADGroup -Identity "IT Dept" -Description "Group for IT
Department Members"
```

Managing Group Membership

Adding Members
```
Add-ADGroupMember -Identity "IT Dept" -Members jdoe, tsmith
```

Removing Members
```
Remove-ADGroupMember -Identity "IT Dept" -Members jdoe -
Confirm:$false
```

Listing Group Members
```
Get-ADGroupMember -Identity "IT Dept"
```

Advanced User and Group Management

Searching for Users
```
Get-ADUser -Filter {Name -like "*Doe*"} -Properties * |
Select-Object Name, Department, Title
```

Finding Inactive Accounts
```
Search-ADAccount -AccountInactive -UsersOnly | Select-Object
Name, LastLogonDate
```

Moving Users Between OUs
```
Move-ADObject -Identity "CN=John
Doe,OU=Users,DC=yourdomain,DC=com" -TargetPath
"OU=Inactive,DC=yourdomain,DC=com"
```

Auditing and Reporting

Generating reports on users and groups helps maintain compliance

and security.
Exporting User List
```
Get-ADUser -Filter * -Property DisplayName, EmailAddress | \
Select-Object DisplayName, EmailAddress | \
Export-Csv -Path "C:\Reports\AllUsers.csv" -
NoTypeInformation
```

Exporting Group Membership
```
Get-ADGroupMember -Identity "IT Dept" | \
Select-Object Name, SamAccountName | \
Export-Csv -Path "C:\Reports\IT_Dept_Members.csv" -
NoTypeInformation
```

Conclusion

PowerShell provides a powerful, flexible way to manage Active Directory users and groups. Whether creating individual users or automating large-scale changes, mastering these commands greatly enhances an admin's efficiency. With structured scripting and reporting, you can ensure consistent, secure, and scalable AD management.

As you become comfortable with these basics, explore more advanced topics like group policy automation, dynamic group membership using scripts, and integrating PowerShell with third-party identity platforms. These skills are not only valuable in enterprise settings but also critical for roles in cloud and hybrid environments.

AD Scripting Examples

BULK USER CREATION

Active Directory (AD) is a foundational component in most Windows-based enterprise environments. It provides centralized management of users, groups, computers, and other resources within a network. In this chapter, we focus on how to use PowerShell to create and manage Active Directory users and groups. These tasks are fundamental for system administrators and invaluable for automating user provisioning and access control.

Prerequisites

Before beginning, ensure the following prerequisites are met:
1. **Active Directory Module**: You need the Active Directory module for Windows PowerShell installed. It's included with the Remote Server Administration Tools (RSAT).
2. **Permissions**: You must have appropriate permissions to create and manage users and groups in AD.
3. **PowerShell Version**: PowerShell 5.1 or later is recommended for full functionality and compatibility.

```
Import-Module ActiveDirectory
```
This command imports the Active Directory module into your session.

Creating AD Users

Creating users in Active Directory can be done manually via GUI or efficiently through PowerShell for bulk operations or automation.

Basic User Creation

To create a single user:

```
New-ADUser -Name "John Doe" -GivenName "John" -Surname "Doe"
```

```
-SamAccountName "jdoe" -UserPrincipalName
"jdoe@yourdomain.com" -Path "OU=Users,DC=yourdomain,DC=com"
-AccountPassword (ConvertTo-SecureString "P@ssw0rd123" -
AsPlainText -Force) -Enabled $true
```

Bulk User Creation from CSV

For larger environments, creating users in bulk from a CSV file is more efficient.

CSV format:

```
FirstName,LastName,Username,Password
Jane,Doe,jdoe,P@ssword123
Tom,Smith,tsmith,P@ssword456
```

PowerShell Script:

```
$users = Import-Csv -Path "C:\scripts\new_users.csv"

foreach ($user in $users) {
    $name = "$($user.FirstName) $($user.LastName)"
    $sam = $user.Username
    $upn = "$sam@yourdomain.com"
    $password = ConvertTo-SecureString $user.Password -
AsPlainText -Force

    New-ADUser -Name $name -GivenName $user.FirstName -
Surname $user.LastName -SamAccountName $sam -
UserPrincipalName $upn -Path "OU=Users,DC=yourdomain,DC=com"
-AccountPassword $password -Enabled $true
}
```

Modifying AD Users

User accounts may require updates, such as name changes, password resets, or enabling/disabling access.

Modifying User Attributes

```
Set-ADUser -Identity jdoe -Title "IT Support Specialist" -
Department "IT"
```

Enabling/Disabling Accounts

```
Disable-ADAccount -Identity jdoe
Enable-ADAccount -Identity jdoe
```

Resetting Passwords

```
Set-ADAccountPassword -Identity jdoe -NewPassword
(ConvertTo-SecureString "NewP@ssw0rd" -AsPlainText -Force)
```

Creating AD Groups

Groups simplify access management by grouping users with common access needs.

Types of Groups

- **Security Groups**: Used to assign permissions to resources.
- **Distribution Groups**: Used for email distribution lists.

Creating a New Group

```
New-ADGroup -Name "IT Dept" -GroupScope Global -Path
"OU=Groups,DC=yourdomain,DC=com" -GroupCategory Security
```

Modifying Group Properties

```
Set-ADGroup -Identity "IT Dept" -Description "Group for IT
Department Members"
```

Managing Group Membership

Adding Members

```
Add-ADGroupMember -Identity "IT Dept" -Members jdoe, tsmith
```

Removing Members

```
Remove-ADGroupMember -Identity "IT Dept" -Members jdoe -
Confirm:$false
```

Listing Group Members

```
Get-ADGroupMember -Identity "IT Dept"
```

Advanced User and Group Management

Searching for Users

```
Get-ADUser -Filter {Name -like "*Doe*"} -Properties * |
Select-Object Name, Department, Title
```

Finding Inactive Accounts

```
Search-ADAccount -AccountInactive -UsersOnly | Select-Object
Name, LastLogonDate
```

Moving Users Between OUs

```
Move-ADObject -Identity "CN=John
Doe,OU=Users,DC=yourdomain,DC=com" -TargetPath
"OU=Inactive,DC=yourdomain,DC=com"
```

Auditing and Reporting

Generating reports on users and groups helps maintain compliance and security.

Exporting User List

```
Get-ADUser -Filter * -Property DisplayName, EmailAddress | \
Select-Object DisplayName, EmailAddress | \
Export-Csv -Path "C:\Reports\AllUsers.csv" -
NoTypeInformation
```

Exporting Group Membership

```
Get-ADGroupMember -Identity "IT Dept" | \
Select-Object Name, SamAccountName | \
Export-Csv -Path "C:\Reports\IT_Dept_Members.csv" -
NoTypeInformation
```

Conclusion

PowerShell provides a powerful, flexible way to manage Active Directory users and groups. Whether creating individual users or automating large-scale changes, mastering these commands greatly enhances an admin's efficiency. With structured scripting and reporting, you can ensure consistent, secure, and scalable AD management.

As you become comfortable with these basics, explore more advanced topics like group policy automation, dynamic group membership using scripts, and integrating PowerShell with third-party identity platforms. These skills are not only valuable in enterprise settings but also critical for roles in cloud and hybrid environments.

GROUP MEMBERSHIP AUDITS

Auditing group memberships is a crucial task in the management and security of any Windows-based IT environment. It allows administrators to ensure that users have appropriate access rights and that no unnecessary or unauthorized privileges exist. PowerShell provides a powerful, scriptable way to perform these audits efficiently. In this section, we'll explore how to use PowerShell to perform comprehensive group membership audits, discuss real-world scenarios where this is useful, and break down scripts and cmdlets commonly used in this context.

Why Group Membership Audits Matter

Active Directory (AD) groups are often used to manage permissions across file shares, applications, and other resources. Over time, group memberships can become bloated or outdated due to organizational changes, employee turnover, or oversight. This can lead to:

- **Security risks** – Users retaining access to sensitive resources they no longer need.
- **Compliance issues** – Failing to meet audit requirements for frameworks like HIPAA, SOX, or GDPR.
- **Operational inefficiencies** – Unnecessary group memberships can complicate troubleshooting and permissions management.

Regular auditing helps maintain the principle of least privilege, ensuring users only have the access they need to perform their roles.

Understanding Group Types

Before diving into audits, it's important to understand the types of groups in AD:

- **Security Groups**: Used to assign permissions to resources.
- **Distribution Groups**: Used for email distribution lists; not security-related.

For the purpose of audits, we typically focus on **security groups**, especially those tied to administrative roles or access control lists (ACLs).

Auditing a Single Group Membership

To check the members of a single group, use the Get-ADGroupMember cmdlet. This requires the **Active Directory module for Windows PowerShell**.

```
Get-ADGroupMember -Identity "Domain Admins"
```

This command returns the direct members of the specified group. However, it does **not** resolve nested groups. For deeper audits, you need to recursively expand memberships.

Recursive Group Membership Lookup

To get all members, including those in nested groups:

```
function Get-NestedGroupMembers {
    param (
        [string]$GroupName
    )
    $members = Get-ADGroupMember -Identity $GroupName
    foreach ($member in $members) {
        if ($member.objectClass -eq 'group') {
            Get-NestedGroupMembers -GroupName
$member.SamAccountName
        } else {
            $member
        }
    }
}


Get-NestedGroupMembers -GroupName "Domain Admins"
```

This recursive function ensures you capture the full list of all users who ultimately have access through a group hierarchy.

Exporting Group Membership to CSV

For auditing purposes, it's often helpful to export the results:

```
Get-ADGroupMember -Identity "HR Access" |
Select-Object Name, SamAccountName, objectClass |
Export-Csv -Path "C:\Audits\HR_Group_Members.csv" -NoTypeInformation
```

This makes it easy to review and share audit results with stakeholders or compliance teams.

Auditing All Groups in a Domain

Sometimes you need a domain-wide audit. The script below gathers the members of all security groups and writes them to individual CSV files:

```
$groups = Get-ADGroup -Filter * | Where-Object {
$_.GroupCategory -eq "Security" }
foreach ($group in $groups) {
    $members = Get-ADGroupMember -Identity
$group.SamAccountName -ErrorAction SilentlyContinue
    $members | Select-Object Name, SamAccountName,
objectClass |
    Export-Csv -Path "C:\Audits\$
($group.SamAccountName)_Members.csv" -NoTypeInformation
}
```

This approach works well for periodic audits and storing historical membership snapshots.

Advanced Filtering and Reporting

You might need to filter results by user type or identify inactive users in groups. Here's how to refine your output:

Find Only Users in a Group

```
Get-ADGroupMember -Identity "Finance Team" | Where-Object {
$_.objectClass -eq "user" }
```

Find Users Who Haven't Logged In Recently

```
$group = Get-ADGroupMember -Identity "Finance Team" | Where-
Object { $_.objectClass -eq "user" }
foreach ($user in $group) {
    $userDetails = Get-ADUser -Identity $user.SamAccountName
-Properties LastLogonDate
    if ($userDetails.LastLogonDate -lt (Get-
Date).AddDays(-90)) {
        Write-Output "$($userDetails.Name) last logged in on
```

```
$($userDetails.LastLogonDate)"
    }
}
```

This helps identify stale accounts that may no longer need access.

Real-World Use Case: Quarterly Access Reviews

Let's say your organization conducts quarterly reviews of users with elevated access. Here's how PowerShell helps streamline the process:

1. **Identify high-privilege groups** – Domain Admins, Server Admins, Helpdesk, etc.
2. **Export current membership**
3. **Cross-reference with HR or department leads** for validation
4. **Document changes** and update AD accordingly

You can even schedule the script with Task Scheduler or a central automation tool like System Center Orchestrator or Azure Automation.

Logging and Notifications

Consider adding logging and email notifications to your scripts:

```
$timestamp = Get-Date -Format "yyyyMMdd-HHmmss"
$logfile = "C:\Audits\MembershipAudit_$timestamp.txt"

try {
    $groups = Get-ADGroup -Filter *
    foreach ($group in $groups) {
        $members = Get-ADGroupMember -Identity
$group.SamAccountName -ErrorAction SilentlyContinue
        Add-Content -Path $logfile -Value "Group: $
($group.Name) - Members: $($members.Count)"
    }
    Send-MailMessage -To "itsecurity@domain.com" -From
"auditbot@domain.com" -Subject "Group Audit Completed" -Body
"Audit finished at $timestamp." -SmtpServer
"mail.domain.com"
} catch {
    Add-Content -Path $logfile -Value "Error: $
($_.Exception.Message)"
```

}

Integrating with Change Management

If your organization follows strict change control, your audit script can include:
- Ticket number for each requested change
- Justification fields
- Export formats compatible with ticketing systems like Jira or ServiceNow

Tips for Effective Auditing

- **Label your scripts clearly** and maintain version history.
- **Use tags or comments** to define the purpose of each section.
- **Schedule audits regularly**, such as monthly or quarterly.
- **Validate results with department leads** to avoid disruptions.
- **Archive reports securely** for compliance and historical tracking.

Conclusion

Group membership audits are essential for maintaining a secure and compliant Active Directory environment. PowerShell offers a flexible and powerful way to automate these audits, generate reports, and flag potential risks. Whether you're preparing for a compliance audit, cleaning up legacy permissions, or just keeping your environment tidy, these PowerShell tools and techniques will save time and reduce risk. By integrating these scripts into a regular review process and automating wherever possible, you can ensure your access controls remain tight, transparent, and traceable.

LAST LOGIN REPORT

Keeping track of user activity is a vital part of system administration.

One key metric for assessing whether user accounts are still active or have gone stale is the *last login time*. PowerShell offers a powerful and flexible way to generate reports detailing the last time each user logged into the network or system. In this section, we'll walk through how to create a robust Last Login Report using PowerShell, including how to extract the relevant data, filter it based on your criteria, and export it for use in other tools such as Excel.

Why Monitor Last Logins?

Inactive user accounts are a potential security risk. They are often overlooked and may retain elevated privileges, making them a prime target for attackers. Regularly auditing these accounts helps ensure:

- Security hygiene by identifying stale accounts.
- License optimization in environments like Office 365 or Microsoft 365.
- Compliance with policies or regulations requiring regular access reviews.
- Cleanup of Active Directory by disabling or removing unused accounts.

Tools Required

To build a Last Login Report in PowerShell, you'll need:

1. **Windows PowerShell or PowerShell Core**
2. **Active Directory module** (part of RSAT or installed via Install-WindowsFeature -Name RSAT-AD-PowerShell)
3. Appropriate **permissions** to query Active Directory

Understanding LastLogon vs. LastLogonDate

There are several attributes associated with user logon activity in Active Directory:

- lastLogon: Non-replicated. Stored per domain controller.
- lastLogonTimestamp: Replicated, but can be up to 14 days out of date.

- lastLogonDate: A friendly representation of lastLogonTimestamp.

If precision is not critical and you're okay with a delay of up to 14 days, lastLogonDate is easier to use and doesn't require querying every domain controller.

Basic Script for Last Login Report

Here's a foundational script to gather the last login data from Active Directory:

```
Import-Module ActiveDirectory

$users = Get-ADUser -Filter * -Properties DisplayName,
LastLogonDate |
    Select-Object Name, DisplayName, LastLogonDate |
    Sort-Object LastLogonDate -Descending

$users | Export-Csv -Path "C:\Reports\LastLoginReport.csv" -
NoTypeInformation
```

Explanation:
- Get-ADUser -Filter *: Retrieves all user accounts.
- -Properties LastLogonDate: Ensures we fetch the last logon timestamp.
- Select-Object: Narrows the output to only the fields we care about.
- Sort-Object: Sorts the list by login date.
- Export-Csv: Outputs the results to a CSV file for further use.

Enhancing the Report

Filtering Out Service or Disabled Accounts

Many environments have service accounts or intentionally disabled users. Let's filter them:

```
$users = Get-ADUser -Filter {Enabled -eq $true -and
```

```
PasswordNeverExpires -eq $false} -Properties DisplayName,
LastLogonDate |
    Where-Object { $_.LastLogonDate -ne $null } |
    Select-Object Name, DisplayName, LastLogonDate |
    Sort-Object LastLogonDate -Descending
```

Identifying Inactive Accounts (e.g., 90 Days of Inactivity)

```
$cutoff = (Get-Date).AddDays(-90)

$inactiveUsers = Get-ADUser -Filter * -Properties
LastLogonDate |
    Where-Object { $_.LastLogonDate -lt $cutoff -and
$_.Enabled -eq $true } |
    Select-Object Name, SamAccountName, LastLogonDate

$inactiveUsers | Export-Csv "C:
\Reports\InactiveUsers90Days.csv" -NoTypeInformation
```

Customizing Output

You can customize the CSV or terminal output to include more columns such as:
- Department
- EmailAddress
- SamAccountName
- WhenCreated

```
$report = Get-ADUser -Filter * -Properties DisplayName,
LastLogonDate, Department, EmailAddress, WhenCreated |
    Select-Object DisplayName, Department, EmailAddress,
LastLogonDate, WhenCreated

$report | Export-Csv -Path "C:
\Reports\ExtendedLastLogin.csv" -NoTypeInformation
```

Cross-Domain Controller Reporting (Advanced)

If you need highly accurate last logon data, query all domain controllers. Here's a simplified example:

```
$DomainControllers = Get-ADDomainController -Filter *
$users = Get-ADUser -Filter * -Properties SamAccountName
```

```
foreach ($user in $users) {
    $logons = foreach ($dc in $DomainControllers) {
        Get-ADUser $user.SamAccountName -Server $dc.HostName
-Properties LastLogon |
            Select-Object
@{Name='DC';Expression={$dc.HostName}},
@{Name='LastLogon';Expression={$_.LastLogon}}
    }
    $latest = ($logons | Sort-Object LastLogon -Descending |
Select-Object -First 1)
    Write-Output "$($user.SamAccountName),$($latest.DC),$
($latest.LastLogon)"
}
```

Note: This method is time-consuming and is typically used in scripts that run overnight.

Scheduling Regular Reports

To automate report generation:
1. Save your PowerShell script as a .ps1 file.
2. Open Task Scheduler.
3. Create a new task:
- Set a trigger (e.g., weekly on Mondays at 6 AM).
- Set the action to run PowerShell with the script path.
- Make sure you set the "Run whether user is logged in or not" option.

Security Best Practices

- Run scripts with **least privilege**.
- Encrypt report files if they contain sensitive data.
- Secure access to the exported reports folder.
- Audit the logs for script execution (especially if running scheduled tasks).

Conclusion

Creating a Last Login Report with PowerShell empowers you to audit user activity efficiently and proactively manage your Active Directory environment. Whether you're cleaning up old accounts, optimizing license usage, or improving your security posture, this script is an indispensable tool in a system administrator's toolkit. With just a few lines of PowerShell, you can gain valuable insight into your domain's user behavior and maintain a healthier, more secure IT infrastructure.

Remote Management and Remoting

INVOKE-COMMAND, ENTER-PSSESSION

PowerShell is a powerful automation tool that shines in both local and remote environments. As environments grow and the need for automation across multiple machines increases, understanding how to execute commands remotely becomes essential. This is where Invoke-Command and Enter-PSSession come into play. These two cmdlets form the backbone of PowerShell remoting, allowing administrators to manage multiple systems seamlessly and securely.

Introduction to PowerShell Remoting

PowerShell remoting enables you to run commands on remote computers as if you were executing them locally. It uses Windows Remote Management (WinRM), a service that enables secure communication between systems. This can be especially helpful for system administrators managing multiple servers, or anyone looking to automate routine tasks across a network of machines.

To use remoting, WinRM must be enabled and properly configured on the remote machines. On Windows systems, this can be achieved by running the following command in an elevated PowerShell session:

```
Enable-PSRemoting -Force
```

This command configures the necessary firewall rules, starts the WinRM service, and sets it to start automatically.

Invoke-Command Overview

The Invoke-Command cmdlet allows you to execute commands or scripts on one or more remote computers simultaneously. It is designed for non-interactive tasks, such as pushing out configuration changes, gathering information, or automating routine maintenance.

Syntax and Usage

The basic syntax of Invoke-Command is:

```
Invoke-Command -ComputerName <ComputerName> -ScriptBlock {
<command> }
```

For example, to get the list of processes running on a remote machine:

```
Invoke-Command -ComputerName Server01 -ScriptBlock { Get-
Process }
```

You can also run scripts stored locally by using the -FilePath parameter:

```
Invoke-Command -ComputerName Server01 -FilePath "C:
\Scripts\Maintenance.ps1"
```

To run a command on multiple machines at once:

```
Invoke-Command -ComputerName Server01, Server02, Server03 -
ScriptBlock { Get-Service }
```

Passing Variables to Remote Sessions

When using Invoke-Command, local variables are not automatically available inside the remote script block. If you want to use them, you need to pass them explicitly using the -ArgumentList parameter.

```
$serviceName = "W32Time"
Invoke-Command -ComputerName Server01 -ScriptBlock {
    param($name)
    Get-Service -Name $name
} -ArgumentList $serviceName
```

This makes sure the value of $serviceName is available to the remote block as $name.

Using Credentials

To connect with alternate credentials, use the -Credential parameter:

```
$cred = Get-Credential
Invoke-Command -ComputerName Server01 -ScriptBlock { Get-
Date } -Credential $cred
```

This is especially useful when your current user account doesn't have permission on the remote system.

Enter-PSSession Overview

Unlike Invoke-Command, which is non-interactive and runs commands in batch, Enter-PSSession is interactive. It starts a remote PowerShell session where you can run commands one at a time as though you were directly connected to that machine.

Syntax and Usage

The basic syntax is:

```
Enter-PSSession -ComputerName <ComputerName>
```

After running this, your prompt will change to reflect the remote session, indicating that the commands you now type are being executed on the remote machine.

For example:

```
Enter-PSSession -ComputerName Server01
```

You might see a prompt like this:

```
[Server01]: PS C:\Users\Administrator>
```

Now, any commands you run apply to Server01 until you exit the session.

To exit the session, simply type:

```
Exit-PSSession
```

Using Alternate Credentials

As with Invoke-Command, you can use the -Credential parameter:

```
Enter-PSSession -ComputerName Server01 -Credential (Get-Credential)
```

Connecting via Session Objects

You can also create a session using New-PSSession and then enter it:

```
$session = New-PSSession -ComputerName Server01
Enter-PSSession -Session $session
```

This gives you more control over managing your remote sessions, including reusing sessions across multiple cmdlets.

Security Considerations

PowerShell remoting is secure by default. It uses Kerberos or NTLM for authentication and can encrypt traffic using HTTPS. However, several best practices should be followed:

- Always use HTTPS for remote communication over untrusted networks.
- Use least privilege accounts where possible.
- Consider using Just Enough Administration (JEA) for fine-grained access control.
- Enable auditing and logging on remote sessions for traceability.
  To configure HTTPS for WinRM:
1. Create or obtain a certificate for the remote host.
2. Bind the certificate to WinRM:

```
winrm create winrm/config/Listener?Address=*+Transport=HTTPS
@{Hostname="<hostname>",
CertificateThumbprint="<thumbprint>"}
```

Adjust firewall rules to allow traffic on port 5986.

Session Management and Cleanup

When working with multiple sessions, especially with Invoke-Command or New-PSSession, it's important to clean up after yourself.

```
$sessions = New-PSSession -ComputerName Server01, Server02
Invoke-Command -Session $sessions -ScriptBlock { Get-
EventLog -LogName System -Newest 5 }
Remove-PSSession -Session $sessions
```

This ensures system resources are freed and security is maintained.

Common Pitfalls and Troubleshooting

WinRM Not Enabled

Make sure remoting is enabled using:
```
Enable-PSRemoting -Force
```

Firewall Blocking Ports

Ensure TCP port 5985 (HTTP) or 5986 (HTTPS) is open on the remote machine.

DNS or Network Issues

If -ComputerName fails, confirm DNS resolution and network connectivity. You can use:
```
Test-Connection -ComputerName Server01
```

Authentication Failures

If you see access denied errors, ensure you are using the correct credentials or that the machine is part of the same domain (for Kerberos). For workgroup computers, consider using HTTPS and specifying credentials explicitly.

PowerShell Versions

Ensure the remote computer has a compatible version of PowerShell installed. PowerShell remoting works best when versions are consistent between systems.

Use Cases

Centralized Management

Run a script across all servers to gather metrics, restart services, or deploy changes:
```
Invoke-Command -ComputerName (Get-Content servers.txt) -
ScriptBlock { Restart-Service -Name "Spooler" }
```

Troubleshooting

Use Enter-PSSession to quickly connect and diagnose an issue:
```
Enter-PSSession -ComputerName WebServer01
Get-EventLog -LogName Application -Newest 10
Exit-PSSession
```

Automation Pipelines

Use Invoke-Command inside scheduled jobs or CI/CD pipelines to automate environment changes:

```
Invoke-Command -ComputerName BuildServer -ScriptBlock { &"C:
\Deploy\DeployApp.ps1" }
```

Conclusion

PowerShell's Invoke-Command and Enter-PSSession cmdlets are essential tools for any administrator or power user managing remote systems. Invoke-Command excels at running commands in bulk across many machines, while Enter-PSSession is perfect for one-on-one interaction with a remote host. Mastering these cmdlets unlocks a higher level of automation, efficiency, and control in your infrastructure management toolkit.

In the chapters that follow, we'll build on this foundation to show how remote execution integrates with module deployment, scheduled tasks, configuration management, and more. The more fluent you become with remote PowerShell, the more powerful and flexible your scripts will be.

REMOTE EXECUTION SCENARIOS

Remote execution is one of PowerShell's most powerful and flexible capabilities. In enterprise environments, system administrators often need to manage servers, deploy configurations, run diagnostics, or apply fixes across multiple machines. Instead of logging into each system manually, PowerShell allows remote execution of commands and scripts, saving time and ensuring consistency.

This section will explore various remote execution scenarios using PowerShell. We'll cover core concepts, enabling remoting, security considerations, and real-world examples to help beginners understand and master remote execution in PowerShell.

Understanding PowerShell Remoting

PowerShell Remoting is built on Windows Remote Management (WinRM), which is a web services-based protocol. It allows administrators to run PowerShell commands on remote computers using the Invoke-Command cmdlet or to enter a persistent session using Enter-PSSession.

Key concepts:

- **WinRM:** The foundation of remoting. It must be enabled and configured on both local and remote machines.
- **Sessions:** Persistent or one-time connections to a remote system.
- **Commands and Scripts:** Can be executed remotely as if they were run locally.

Enabling PowerShell Remoting

To begin using remoting, it needs to be enabled on the target computer. For Windows Server editions, it is enabled by default. On client editions (like Windows 10/11), you may need to enable it manually.

```
Enable-PSRemoting -Force
```

This command:

- Starts the WinRM service.
- Sets the service to start automatically.
- Creates a listener for incoming requests.
- Enables the required firewall exceptions.

Ensure that the remote machine has network connectivity and is on the same domain or has appropriate trusted host configurations for workgroup setups.

Using Invoke-Command for Remote Tasks

Invoke-Command is the most common way to execute commands on one or many remote computers.

Single Computer Example

```
Invoke-Command -ComputerName Server01 -ScriptBlock { Get-Process }
```

This runs Get-Process on Server01 and returns the results to your local session.

Multiple Computers Example

```
Invoke-Command -ComputerName Server01, Server02, Server03 -
```

```
ScriptBlock { Get-Service -Name wuauserv }
```

This checks the Windows Update service status on all three servers.

Using Credentials

If the target machines require alternate credentials:

```
$cred = Get-Credential
Invoke-Command -ComputerName Server01 -Credential $cred -
ScriptBlock { Get-EventLog -LogName System -Newest 5 }
```

Creating Persistent Sessions with New-PSSession

Sessions are useful when you want to run multiple commands against a single remote machine without re-authenticating or re-establishing a connection each time.

```
$session = New-PSSession -ComputerName Server01
Invoke-Command -Session $session -ScriptBlock { Get-Date }
Remove-PSSession $session
```

Entering an Interactive Remote Session

Enter-PSSession allows you to interactively work on a remote system as if you were on a local PowerShell prompt:

```
Enter-PSSession -ComputerName Server01
```

Your prompt will change to indicate the remote session:

```
[Server01]: PS C:\Users\Admin>
```

To exit, simply type:

```
Exit-PSSession
```

Common Remote Execution Scenarios

Restarting a Service Across Servers

```
$servers = @("Server01", "Server02")
Invoke-Command -ComputerName $servers -ScriptBlock {
    Restart-Service -Name Spooler
}
```

Checking Disk Space on All Domain Controllers

```
$dcList = Get-ADComputer -Filter 'OperatingSystem -like
"*Server*"' | Select-Object -ExpandProperty Name
Invoke-Command -ComputerName $dcList -ScriptBlock {
```

```
    Get-PSDrive -PSProvider FileSystem | Select-Object Name,
Free, Used
}
```

Installing Software

Assuming the software is accessible via a network share:

```
Invoke-Command -ComputerName Server01 -ScriptBlock {
    Start-Process "\\fileshare\installers\7zip.exe" -
ArgumentList "/S" -Wait
}
```

d. Gathering System Info for Audit

```
$servers = Get-Content .\servers.txt
Invoke-Command -ComputerName $servers -ScriptBlock {
    Get-ComputerInfo | Select-Object CsName, WindowsVersion,
OsArchitecture
} | Export-Csv .\AuditReport.csv -NoTypeInformation
```

Remote File Execution

You may need to run a script stored locally on a remote machine:

Option 1: Use -FilePath with Invoke-Command

```
Invoke-Command -ComputerName Server01 -FilePath .
\Scripts\UpdateDriver.ps1
```

Option 2: Copy Script to Remote Machine First

```
Copy-Item .\Scripts\UpdateDriver.ps1 -Destination "\
\Server01\C$\Temp"
Invoke-Command -ComputerName Server01 -ScriptBlock {
    &"C:\Temp\UpdateDriver.ps1"
}
```

Remote Execution in Workgroup Environments

If computers are not in the same domain, use TrustedHosts and HTTPS where possible.

Add a Trusted Host

```
Set-Item WSMan:\localhost\Client\TrustedHosts -Value
"Server01"
```

Use Alternate Credentials

```
$cred = Get-Credential
Invoke-Command -ComputerName Server01 -Credential $cred -
ScriptBlock { hostname }
```

Security Considerations

PowerShell Remoting is powerful, but with that power comes responsibility:

- **Use HTTPS endpoints** where possible to encrypt traffic.
- **Avoid plaintext credentials**; use Get-Credential or secure string techniques.
- **Implement JEA (Just Enough Administration)** for delegated tasks.
- **Monitor and audit** remote session activity.

Troubleshooting Remoting Issues

WinRM Not Configured

Make sure remoting is enabled and the WinRM service is running:
```
Enable-PSRemoting -Force
```

Firewall Blocking Port

Default remoting uses TCP port 5985 (HTTP) or 5986 (HTTPS). Check firewall settings:
```
New-NetFirewallRule -Name "PowerShellRemoting" -DisplayName
"PowerShell Remoting" -Enabled True -Direction Inbound -
Protocol TCP -LocalPort 5985 -Action Allow
```

Authentication Failures

Ensure correct credentials are used, and that you're allowed to connect (Remote Management Users group).

Conclusion

PowerShell remoting transforms system administration by enabling centralized, remote control of servers and workstations. Whether you're managing a handful of systems or hundreds, remote execution is an essential tool in your scripting toolkit. With proper security, configuration, and practice, it becomes an irreplaceable part of daily IT operations.

Scheduled Tasks and Automation

CREATING, UPDATING, AND MONITORING SCHEDULED TASKS

Automating routine tasks is one of the most powerful capabilities of PowerShell, and one of the most effective ways to do this is through the use of **Scheduled Tasks**. These allow you to run scripts or commands at specific times, during system startup or login, or based on certain triggers. This chapter will walk you through how to create, update, and monitor scheduled tasks using PowerShell, giving you the power to manage them efficiently and programmatically.

Why Use Scheduled Tasks?

Scheduled Tasks help automate repetitive or time-sensitive tasks without manual intervention. Common use cases include:
- Running daily or weekly maintenance scripts
- Automating backups
- Scheduling report generation
- Executing updates or clean-up routines outside business hours

With PowerShell, you can manage these tasks across many machines, ensuring consistency and efficiency.

Prerequisites

To manage scheduled tasks in PowerShell, you need to run your scripts or commands with **administrator privileges**. Also, ensure you have the **ScheduledTasks** module available, which is included by default in Windows 8/2012 and newer.

To verify:
```
Get-Command -Module ScheduledTasks
```

Creating a Basic Scheduled Task

To create a new task, you need three components:
1. **Action** - What the task will do
2. **Trigger** - When the task will execute
3. **Principal** - Who will execute the task

Step-by-Step Example

1. Define the Action

```
$Action = New-ScheduledTaskAction -Execute 'PowerShell.exe'
-Argument '-File "C:\Scripts\DailyReport.ps1"'
```

2. Define the Trigger

```
$Trigger = New-ScheduledTaskTrigger -Daily -At 9am
```

3. Define the Principal

```
$Principal = New-ScheduledTaskPrincipal -UserId "SYSTEM" -
LogonType ServiceAccount -RunLevel Highest
```

4. Register the Task

```
Register-ScheduledTask -TaskName "DailyReport" -Action
$Action -Trigger $Trigger -Principal $Principal -Description
"Runs daily report script at 9am."
```

Advanced Scheduling Options

PowerShell allows you to configure tasks in much more detail. Some examples:

Weekly Trigger

```
$Trigger = New-ScheduledTaskTrigger -Weekly -DaysOfWeek
Monday,Wednesday,Friday -At 8am
```

At System Startup

```
$Trigger = New-ScheduledTaskTrigger -AtStartup
```

On User Logon

```
$Trigger = New-ScheduledTaskTrigger -AtLogOn
```

You can even use multiple triggers for a single task by combining them in an array.

```
$Triggers = @(
    New-ScheduledTaskTrigger -AtLogOn,
    New-ScheduledTaskTrigger -Daily -At 2am
)
```

Updating an Existing Scheduled Task

If you need to update a task—perhaps to change its time or script path —you can do so using Set-ScheduledTask and Unregister-ScheduledTask (if re-creating from scratch).

Update Example: Change Trigger Time

```
$NewTrigger = New-ScheduledTaskTrigger -Daily -At 10am
$Task = Get-ScheduledTask -TaskName "DailyReport"
Set-ScheduledTask -TaskName "DailyReport" -Trigger
$NewTrigger
```

Note: Set-ScheduledTask cannot modify all properties directly. Sometimes it is easier to unregister and re-register the task.

Unregister and Recreate

```
Unregister-ScheduledTask -TaskName "DailyReport" -Confirm:
$false
Register-ScheduledTask -TaskName "DailyReport" -Action
$Action -Trigger $NewTrigger -Principal $Principal
```

Monitoring Scheduled Tasks

Monitoring involves checking the status, history, or last run result of a task. This is crucial for ensuring that tasks are actually executing as expected.

List All Tasks

```
Get-ScheduledTask | Select-Object TaskName, State
```

Get Detailed Info on a Specific Task

```
Get-ScheduledTaskInfo -TaskName "DailyReport"
```

This returns:

- LastRunTime
- NextRunTime
- LastTaskResult

Checking Execution History

PowerShell doesn't provide native support for task history (due to it being stored in Event Viewer), but you can access logs via the Event Viewer:

```
Get-WinEvent -LogName Microsoft-Windows-TaskScheduler/
Operational |
    Where-Object { $_.Message -like '*DailyReport*' }
```

This will return all logged events related to the task name "DailyReport".

Error Handling and Logging

A good practice is to wrap your scheduled script in a try-catch block and include logging.

Logging Template

```
$logPath = "C:\Logs\DailyReport.log"
try {
    # Your actual script logic
    "[$(Get-Date)] Script started." | Out-File -FilePath
$logPath -Append

    # Simulate some work
    Start-Sleep -Seconds 3

    "[$(Get-Date)] Script completed successfully." | Out-
File -FilePath $logPath -Append
}
catch {
    "[$(Get-Date)] ERROR: $_" | Out-File -FilePath $logPath
-Append
}
```

This way, even if the task fails, you have a trace of what happened.

Tips for Managing Multiple Scheduled Tasks

- **Name tasks consistently**, using prefixes like Daily_, Weekly_, Startup_, etc.
- **Store task definitions in version-controlled files**.
- **Tag tasks** using the Description field to identify their purpose.
- **Centralize log files** for easier monitoring.

Bulk Deployment Across Systems

You can deploy tasks to multiple systems using PowerShell Remoting:

```
Invoke-Command -ComputerName Server01,Server02 -ScriptBlock
{
```

```
    $Action = New-ScheduledTaskAction -Execute
'PowerShell.exe' -Argument '-File "C:\Scripts\Maintain.ps1"'
    $Trigger = New-ScheduledTaskTrigger -Daily -At 1am
    $Principal = New-ScheduledTaskPrincipal -UserId "SYSTEM"
-LogonType ServiceAccount -RunLevel Highest


    Register-ScheduledTask -TaskName "Maintenance" -Action
$Action -Trigger $Trigger -Principal $Principal
}
```

Ensure WinRM is enabled and authorized on remote machines for this to work.

Common Pitfalls

- **Permissions**: Scheduled tasks may not run correctly under accounts without sufficient rights.
- **Paths**: Always use full paths to scripts and ensure they exist.
- **Environment Variables**: Tasks run in a different session; avoid relying on user-specific paths like %USERPROFILE%.
- **Interactive Tasks**: Avoid relying on GUI interactions—they won't display when running in the background.

Summary

PowerShell provides a robust interface for creating, updating, and monitoring scheduled tasks. Whether you're managing a single workstation or hundreds of servers, learning to leverage this capability empowers you to automate and control your environment more effectively. With proper structure, logging, and error handling, scheduled tasks become reliable tools in your PowerShell toolbox.

Mastering this topic gives you a strong foundation in system automation, taking you one step closer to becoming a PowerShell pro.

AUTOMATING WITH TASK SCHEDULER AND START-SCHEDULEDTASK

One of the most powerful ways to make your PowerShell scripts work for you is by automating their execution. In this chapter, we will explore how to use Task Scheduler in Windows to run PowerShell scripts automatically. You will learn how to create tasks manually through the Task Scheduler GUI, how to use PowerShell to automate task creation, and how to trigger existing tasks using Start-ScheduledTask. By the end, you will understand how to turn your scripts into hands-off, recurring tools that operate on a schedule you define.

Why Automate with Task Scheduler?

Automation allows you to run your PowerShell scripts without manual intervention. Some typical use cases include:

- Running daily or weekly reports.
- Executing cleanup scripts during off-hours.
- Performing system maintenance or updates.
- Monitoring log files or system events.

Task Scheduler is a built-in tool in Windows that can be harnessed easily with PowerShell, making it ideal for beginner and intermediate scripters looking to elevate their productivity.

Creating a Task Manually in Task Scheduler

Before diving into scripting, let's look at how to create a scheduled task manually. This will help you understand what goes on under the hood.

Steps to Create a Scheduled Task:

1. Open **Task Scheduler** by typing it in the Start Menu.
2. Click **Create Basic Task**.
3. Name your task (e.g., "Daily AD User Report") and optionally provide a description.
4. Choose the trigger (e.g., Daily, Weekly, At log on).

5. Set the start time and recurrence.

6. Choose **Start a program** as the action.

7. In the **Program/script** field, enter powershell.exe.

8. In the **Add arguments (optional)** field, enter your script path like:

```
-ExecutionPolicy Bypass -File "C:\Scripts\MyScript.ps1"
```

9. Complete the wizard and click **Finish**.

Now your script will run according to the defined schedule.

Creating Scheduled Tasks with PowerShell

While the GUI is great for one-off tasks, real power comes from using PowerShell itself to create tasks. Here's how to create a scheduled task using PowerShell.

Step-by-Step Breakdown:

1. Define the Action

The action defines what will be run:

```
$action = New-ScheduledTaskAction -Execute "PowerShell.exe"
-Argument "-NoProfile -ExecutionPolicy Bypass -File C:
\Scripts\MyScript.ps1"
```

2. Define the Trigger

This defines when the task will run:

```
$trigger = New-ScheduledTaskTrigger -Daily -At 3am
```

3. Define the Principal

This defines under which user context the task will run:

```
$principal = New-ScheduledTaskPrincipal -UserId "NT
AUTHORITY\SYSTEM" -LogonType ServiceAccount -RunLevel
Highest
```

4. Register the Task

Finally, register the task with Task Scheduler:

```
Register-ScheduledTask -TaskName "DailyReport" -Action
$action -Trigger $trigger -Principal $principal
```

Your script is now registered and will run daily at 3 AM using the SYSTEM account.

Using Start-ScheduledTask

Once a task is created, you may want to trigger it manually. The Start-ScheduledTask cmdlet allows you to do just that.

Basic Syntax:

```
Start-ScheduledTask -TaskName "DailyReport"
```

You can also specify the task path if it resides in a folder:

```
Start-ScheduledTask -TaskPath "\MyTasks\" -TaskName
"DailyReport"
```

This is helpful for testing your task or re-running it after fixing a script error.

Monitoring Scheduled Tasks

You can check the status of your tasks using Get-ScheduledTask:

```
Get-ScheduledTask -TaskName "DailyReport"
```

To see detailed information including last run time and next scheduled time:

```
Get-ScheduledTaskInfo -TaskName "DailyReport"
```

You can also disable or enable tasks:

```
Disable-ScheduledTask -TaskName "DailyReport"
Enable-ScheduledTask -TaskName "DailyReport"
```

Common Pitfalls and How to Avoid Them

Execution Policy

PowerShell scripts may be blocked by the system's execution policy. Always include:

```
-ExecutionPolicy Bypass
```

in your arguments to avoid issues.

Permissions

Tasks running under certain accounts (like SYSTEM) may not have access to user-specific paths. Always test your scripts in the same user context they will run in.

Quoting Paths

Paths with spaces must be enclosed in quotes. Use escaped quotes in the script:

```
-File "\"C:\My Scripts\script.ps1\""
```

Real-World Example: Log Cleanup Script

Suppose you have a script that deletes log files older than 30 days. Here's how to automate it:

Script (CleanLogs.ps1):

```
$logPath = "C:\Logs"
$daysOld = 30

Get-ChildItem -Path $logPath -Recurse -File | Where-Object {
    $_.LastWriteTime -lt (Get-Date).AddDays(-$daysOld)
} | Remove-Item -Force
```

Scheduled Task Code:

```
$action = New-ScheduledTaskAction -Execute "PowerShell.exe"
-Argument "-NoProfile -ExecutionPolicy Bypass -File C:
\Scripts\CleanLogs.ps1"
$trigger = New-ScheduledTaskTrigger -Daily -At 2am
$principal = New-ScheduledTaskPrincipal -UserId "NT
AUTHORITY\SYSTEM" -LogonType ServiceAccount -RunLevel
Highest
Register-ScheduledTask -TaskName "CleanLogsDaily" -Action
$action -Trigger $trigger -Principal $principal
```

Test Manually:

```
Start-ScheduledTask -TaskName "CleanLogsDaily"
```

Summary

Automating your scripts with Task Scheduler and Start-ScheduledTask allows you to free up time, reduce errors, and ensure your scripts run consistently. Whether you're creating simple cleanup routines or complex reports, scheduling them ensures they happen like clockwork.

In this chapter, you've learned:

- How to create a scheduled task manually and via PowerShell.
- How to define actions, triggers, and principals.
- How to trigger tasks manually with Start-ScheduledTask.
- How to monitor and troubleshoot scheduled tasks.

With this knowledge, you're well-equipped to build a truly

automated system using PowerShell as the engine and Task Scheduler as the timer.

In the next section, we will explore how to create more robust automation with error handling, logging, and email notifications for failed or successful runs.

Windows Updates and Software Inventory

QUERYING INSTALLED SOFTWARE

As a system administrator or PowerShell enthusiast, one of the most common tasks you will encounter is the need to audit, track, or troubleshoot installed software on Windows machines. Whether you're managing a single workstation or a fleet of enterprise machines, PowerShell provides a powerful toolkit to query and analyze the software installed across your environment.

This section explores the various methods available for querying installed software using PowerShell. We will cover techniques that leverage native Windows tools, registry queries, and modern cmdlets that provide robust and readable results.

Why Query Installed Software?

Before diving into the technical details, it's important to understand the use cases for querying installed software:

- **Auditing and compliance** – Ensure all required software is installed and prohibited software is absent.
- **Troubleshooting** – Identify software versions or presence that may cause compatibility issues.
- **Inventory management** – Maintain a current list of applications for licensing and asset tracking.
- **Automation** – Create scripts that check and report on required software for onboarding or patching purposes.

With these goals in mind, let's explore how PowerShell makes it easy to collect and analyze this data.

Method 1: Using Get-WmiObject

One of the traditional ways to query installed software is through

Windows Management Instrumentation (WMI):

```
Get-WmiObject -Class Win32_Product
```

Pros:
- Built into all versions of PowerShell.
- Returns detailed software properties such as name, version, vendor, and install date.

Cons:
- **Performance hit**: This cmdlet triggers a reconfiguration for each installed MSI-based product, which can be time-consuming and disruptive.
- Only detects software installed with Windows Installer (MSI).

Because of its potential side effects, avoid using Win32_Product in production scripts. There are safer alternatives.

Method 2: Reading From the Registry

Most Windows software writes installation details to specific locations in the Windows Registry. You can query these keys directly using PowerShell:

```
# 64-bit applications
$registryPath64 = 'HKLM:
\Software\Microsoft\Windows\CurrentVersion\Uninstall'

# 32-bit applications on 64-bit OS
$registryPath32 = 'HKLM:
\Software\Wow6432Node\Microsoft\Windows\CurrentVersion\Unins
tall'

Get-ChildItem $registryPath64, $registryPath32 | ForEach-
Object {
    Get-ItemProperty $_.PSPath
} | Select-Object DisplayName, DisplayVersion, Publisher,
InstallDate
```

Pros:
- No side effects (unlike Win32_Product).

- Detects both MSI and non-MSI software.

Cons:

- Requires parsing multiple registry paths for comprehensive results.
- The data format and completeness may vary between applications.

Method 3: Using Get-Package and Get-PackageProvider

Modern PowerShell versions (5.0 and above) include cmdlets that integrate with package management providers:

```
Get-Package
```

This returns all packages installed by supported package managers (like MSI, Chocolatey, NuGet).

Example Output:

Name	Version	Source	ProviderName
Git	2.30.1	Programs	msi
Notepad++	7.9.5	Programs	msi

Pros:

- Easy to use and script.
- Aggregates packages from different providers.

Cons:

- Only includes packages installed via recognized providers.
- May not reflect all traditional desktop apps.

Method 4: Custom Functions for Software Inventory

You can wrap the registry queries into a reusable function to simplify inventory tasks across multiple systems:

```
function Get-InstalledSoftware {
```

```
[CmdletBinding()]
param (
    [switch]$Include32Bit
)


$paths = @('HKLM:
\Software\Microsoft\Windows\CurrentVersion\Uninstall')
    if ($Include32Bit) {
        $paths += 'HKLM:
\Software\Wow6432Node\Microsoft\Windows\CurrentVersion\Unins
tall'
    }

    foreach ($path in $paths) {
        Get-ChildItem -Path $path | ForEach-Object {
            $app = Get-ItemProperty $_.PSPath
            [PSCustomObject]@{
                Name        = $app.DisplayName
                Version     = $app.DisplayVersion
                Publisher   = $app.Publisher
                InstallDate = $app.InstallDate
            }
        }
    }
}


# Usage
Get-InstalledSoftware -Include32Bit | Format-Table -AutoSize
```

This allows you to easily reuse and export results to CSV:

```
Get-InstalledSoftware -Include32Bit | Export-Csv -Path "C:
\Reports\SoftwareInventory.csv" -NoTypeInformation
```


Querying Remote Systems

PowerShell's ability to run commands on remote systems via WinRM
makes it easy to collect software data across your network:

```
Invoke-Command -ComputerName "Server01" -ScriptBlock {
    Get-ItemProperty 'HKLM:
\Software\Microsoft\Windows\CurrentVersion\Uninstall\*' |
    Select-Object DisplayName, DisplayVersion, Publisher,
InstallDate
}
```

For larger environments, loop through a list of computers:

```
$computers = Get-Content "C:\computers.txt"
foreach ($computer in $computers) {
    Invoke-Command -ComputerName $computer -ScriptBlock {
        Get-ItemProperty 'HKLM:
\Software\Microsoft\Windows\CurrentVersion\Uninstall\*' |
        Select-Object DisplayName, DisplayVersion, Publisher
    } | Export-Csv -Append -Path "C:
\Reports\SoftwareInventory_All.csv" -NoTypeInformation
```

Filtering and Searching Installed Software

Once you have the data, filtering is easy with PowerShell's built-in object filtering:

```
Get-InstalledSoftware -Include32Bit | Where-Object {
$_.Publisher -like "*Microsoft*" }
```

Or search for a specific application:

```
Get-InstalledSoftware -Include32Bit | Where-Object { $_.Name
-like "*Chrome*" }
```

Cross-Platform Alternatives

While this book focuses on Windows PowerShell, it's worth noting that cross-platform solutions like PowerShell 7.x and tools like winget (Windows Package Manager) also support application querying and can be integrated into your scripts:

```
winget list
```

This command shows all apps recognized by the Windows Package Manager.

Summary

Querying installed software is a foundational PowerShell skill with a wide range of practical applications—from inventory management to automation and compliance. While there are multiple ways to get this

data, each method comes with its own advantages and limitations:
- Use **registry-based queries** for safety and accuracy.
- Avoid **Win32_Product** in production environments.
- Leverage **Get-Package** and **Get-PackageProvider** for modern package managers.
- Create reusable functions to streamline reporting and inventory.

By mastering these techniques, you'll be better equipped to monitor, manage, and automate software-related tasks on Windows systems at scale.

In the next section, we'll explore how to **uninstall software remotely using PowerShell**, further enhancing your automation capabilities.

CHECKING FOR AND INSTALLING WINDOWS UPDATES

In enterprise IT environments, ensuring that systems are up-to-date with the latest Windows updates is essential for security, performance, and compatibility. PowerShell offers administrators a powerful, scriptable way to manage Windows updates across multiple machines. This section will guide you through checking for, downloading, and installing updates using PowerShell, making it easier to automate patch management and reduce administrative overhead.

Why Use PowerShell for Windows Updates?

While Windows Update can be managed through the GUI (Settings > Update & Security), using PowerShell provides several advantages:
- **Automation**: Schedule regular update checks and installations.
- **Remote Management**: Update remote systems without logging in.
- **Scripting**: Integrate into broader system management or configuration scripts.
- **Logging and Reporting**: Generate update reports across devices.

Understanding the Windows Update PowerShell Environment

Windows does not include native PowerShell cmdlets for managing updates. Instead, administrators rely on third-party modules such as **PSWindowsUpdate**. This community module interfaces with the Windows Update Agent, offering a comprehensive suite of commands.

Installing the PSWindowsUpdate Module

To begin, open PowerShell **as Administrator** and install the module from the PowerShell Gallery:

```
Install-Module -Name PSWindowsUpdate -Force
```

If prompted about an untrusted repository, type Y to proceed.

After installation, import the module:

```
Import-Module PSWindowsUpdate
```

To ensure the module is installed and imported correctly, use:

```
Get-Command -Module PSWindowsUpdate
```

This will list all available cmdlets provided by the module.

Checking for Available Updates

To list all available updates on the local computer:

```
Get-WindowsUpdate
```

This command queries Microsoft Update servers (or WSUS, if configured) and lists all applicable updates. Each update entry includes a KB article number, update title, and category.

To display updates in a more readable format:

```
Get-WindowsUpdate | Format-Table -AutoSize
```

You can also filter updates by category:

```
Get-WindowsUpdate -Category 'Security Updates'
```

Downloading and Installing Updates

To download and install all available updates:

```
Install-WindowsUpdate -AcceptAll -AutoReboot
```

- -AcceptAll: Accepts all found updates.
- -AutoReboot: Automatically restarts the computer if required.

If you want to control the reboot manually:

```
Install-WindowsUpdate -AcceptAll -IgnoreReboot
```

This will install the updates but skip automatic rebooting.

Installing Specific Updates

To install a specific update using its KB number:

```
Get-WindowsUpdate -KBArticleID 'KB5034204' | Install-
WindowsUpdate -AcceptAll
```

This allows for more precise update management, especially useful in critical production environments.

Running Windows Updates on Remote Computers

To manage updates on remote systems, use the -ComputerName parameter with credential delegation:

```
Invoke-WUJob -ComputerName "Server01" -Script { Install-
WindowsUpdate -AcceptAll -AutoReboot } -Confirm:$false
```

You can manage updates on multiple systems:

```
$computers = @("Server01", "Server02", "Server03")
Invoke-WUJob -ComputerName $computers -Script { Install-
WindowsUpdate -AcceptAll -AutoReboot } -Confirm:$false
```

This is particularly effective for orchestrating updates across fleets of devices, especially when paired with Active Directory.

Scheduling Update Scripts

You can create scheduled tasks to automate update checks and installations. Here's how to schedule an update every Sunday at 2 AM:

```
$action = New-ScheduledTaskAction -Execute "PowerShell.exe"
-Argument "-NoProfile -WindowStyle Hidden -Command
\"Install-WindowsUpdate -AcceptAll -AutoReboot\""

$trigger = New-ScheduledTaskTrigger -Weekly -DaysOfWeek
Sunday -At 2am
Register-ScheduledTask -TaskName "WeeklyWindowsUpdate" -
Action $action -Trigger $trigger -RunLevel Highest -User
"SYSTEM"
```

This ensures that updates are installed regularly without requiring manual intervention.

Logging Update Activity

Logging is essential for compliance and troubleshooting. You can log update activity to a text file using redirection:

```
Install-WindowsUpdate -AcceptAll -IgnoreReboot | Out-File -
FilePath "C:\Logs\WindowsUpdateLog.txt" -Append
```

Or you can use Start-Transcript and Stop-Transcript:

```
Start-Transcript -Path "C:\Logs\WUTranscript.txt"
Install-WindowsUpdate -AcceptAll -IgnoreReboot
Stop-Transcript
```

Real-World Example: Update Script with Error Handling

Here is a complete script for updating a server with error handling, logging, and notifications:

```
Start-Transcript -Path "C:\Logs\UpdateLog.txt" -Append
try {
    Write-Output "Checking for Windows Updates..."
    $updates = Get-WindowsUpdate

    if ($updates) {
        Write-Output "Installing updates..."
        Install-WindowsUpdate -AcceptAll -IgnoreReboot
        Write-Output "Updates installed successfully."
    } else {
        Write-Output "No updates available."
    }
} catch {
    Write-Error "An error occurred: $_"
} finally {
    Stop-Transcript
}
```

This script provides a solid foundation for scheduled or manual patch operations in an automated and traceable manner.

Troubleshooting Common Issues

- **Missing PSWindowsUpdate Module**: Make sure you're running PowerShell as Administrator and your system is connected to the internet.

- **Windows Update Service Not Running**: Ensure the wuauserv service is running:

```
Get-Service -Name wuauserv
```

Start the service if needed:

```
Start-Service -Name wuauserv
```

- **Group Policy or WSUS Conflicts**: Updates may not appear if a Group Policy object or WSUS configuration restricts updates.

Conclusion

PowerShell scripting provides administrators with a powerful, repeatable, and scalable method to manage Windows updates. Whether maintaining a single PC or hundreds of servers, automating updates with PowerShell can dramatically reduce manual effort, ensure system security, and keep infrastructure in a healthy state.

By incorporating logging, error handling, and scheduling into your scripts, you can build a comprehensive update strategy tailored to your organization's needs. In the next section, we'll explore how to audit system configuration baselines using PowerShell, ensuring that post-update environments remain compliant with your policies.

Working with APIs and REST

INVOKE-RESTMETHOD AND INVOKE-WEBREQUEST

PowerShell is not just a scripting language for system administrators; it's also a powerful tool for interacting with web services and APIs. Two of the most versatile cmdlets in this realm are Invoke-RestMethod and Invoke-WebRequest. These cmdlets allow you to send HTTP and HTTPS requests to RESTful web services and retrieve data in various formats.

This section of the book will explore the syntax, functionality, and real-world applications of both cmdlets. We'll look at how to send data, handle authentication, parse responses, and use these tools effectively within PowerShell scripts.

Overview

Both Invoke-RestMethod and Invoke-WebRequest are used to interact with web services, but they serve slightly different purposes.
- Invoke-RestMethod is tailored for REST APIs and automatically processes JSON and XML responses into PowerShell objects.
- Invoke-WebRequest is more general-purpose, suitable for downloading files, parsing HTML content, and interacting with web pages.

Understanding when to use each can significantly streamline your scripting tasks.

Syntax and Parameters

Invoke-RestMethod

```
Invoke-RestMethod -Uri <string> [-Method <string>] [-Headers
<IDictionary>] [-Body <Object>] [-ContentType <string>] [-
Authentication <string>] [-Credential <pscredential>]
```

Invoke-WebRequest

```
Invoke-WebRequest -Uri <string> [-Method <string>] [-Headers
<IDictionary>] [-Body <Object>] [-ContentType <string>] [-
OutFile <string>] [-UseBasicParsing]
```

While the parameters look similar, the way each cmdlet handles the response can differ substantially.

Working with APIs Using Invoke-RestMethod

The Invoke-RestMethod cmdlet is ideal when you're working with modern web APIs that return data in structured formats such as JSON or XML.

Example: Fetching GitHub User Data

```
$uri = "https://api.github.com/users/octocat"
$response = Invoke-RestMethod -Uri $uri
$response.name
$response.public_repos
$response.followers
```

In this example, the JSON response from GitHub is automatically converted into a PowerShell object. You can then access its properties directly.

Sending Data with POST

```
$uri = "https://api.example.com/login"
$body = @{ username = "admin"; password = "password123" } |
ConvertTo-Json
$headers = @{ "Content-Type" = "application/json" }

$response = Invoke-RestMethod -Uri $uri -Method Post -Body
$body -Headers $headers
```

This is commonly used for authentication or creating resources on REST APIs.

Using Invoke-WebRequest for Web Interactions

While Invoke-RestMethod is optimized for APIs, Invoke-WebRequest shines when dealing with traditional web content such as HTML pages or downloading files.

Example: Downloading a File

```
Invoke-WebRequest -Uri "https://example.com/file.zip" -
OutFile "C:\Downloads\file.zip"
```

Parsing HTML Content

```
$response = Invoke-WebRequest -Uri "https://example.com"
$links = $response.Links
foreach ($link in $links) {
    Write-Output $link.href
}
```

This can be useful for scraping data or automating web interactions.

Authentication Methods

Both cmdlets support several types of authentication, including:

- Basic
- OAuth
- API Key via headers
- Windows Integrated (NTLM/Kerberos)

Basic Authentication

```
$cred = Get-Credential
Invoke-RestMethod -Uri "https://api.example.com/data" -
Credential $cred
```

API Key in Headers

```
$headers = @{ "x-api-key" = "your_api_key_here" }
Invoke-RestMethod -Uri "https://api.example.com/data" -
Headers $headers
```

Authentication requirements vary by API, so always consult the API documentation.

Error Handling and Status Codes

When calling web services, it's essential to handle errors properly.

Try/Catch Block

```
try {
```

```
    $response = Invoke-RestMethod -Uri "https://
api.example.com/data"
} catch {
    Write-Error "Request failed: $_"
}
```

Inspecting Status Codes

With Invoke-WebRequest, the StatusCode and StatusDescription properties are available:

```
$response = Invoke-WebRequest -Uri "https://example.com"
$response.StatusCode
$response.StatusDescription
```

Working with JSON and XML

PowerShell makes it easy to serialize and deserialize data.

JSON

```
$json = '{"name":"John","age":30}' | ConvertFrom-Json
$json.name
```

XML

```
$xml = '<person><name>John</name><age>30</age></person>'
[xml]$doc = $xml
$doc.person.name
```

These are particularly useful when sending structured data in API calls.

Common Use Cases

Here are some scenarios where Invoke-RestMethod and Invoke-WebRequest are particularly valuable:

- **Monitoring Services**: Periodically query a REST API for service health.
- **Automation**: Create or update cloud resources via API (e.g., AWS, Azure, or custom SaaS tools).
- **Integration**: Sync data between internal systems and external services.
- **Data Collection**: Gather metrics or user data from web services.
- **File Operations**: Downloading updates, configuration files, or

logs.

Choosing Between the Two

- Use Invoke-RestMethod when you're working with APIs that return structured data.
- Use Invoke-WebRequest when you're interacting with general web pages, downloading content, or need HTML parsing features.

For example, if you're calling a weather API, use Invoke-RestMethod. If you're downloading a log file or HTML report, go with Invoke-WebRequest.

Best Practices

1. **Always Handle Errors Gracefully**: Wrap API calls in try/catch blocks.
2. **Use ConvertTo-Json for Request Bodies**: This ensures the API receives valid JSON.
3. **Avoid Hardcoding Credentials**: Use Get-Credential or secure vaults.
4. **Respect Rate Limits**: Many APIs impose limits; handle 429 Too Many Requests responses accordingly.
5. **Log Interactions**: Keep records of requests and responses for troubleshooting.
6. **Use Headers Intelligently**: Set User-Agent and Content-Type appropriately to avoid server rejections.

Summary

PowerShell's Invoke-RestMethod and Invoke-WebRequest are essential tools for modern scripting. Whether you are managing cloud services, downloading content, or integrating systems via REST APIs, these cmdlets give you the flexibility and power you need.

Mastering them will allow you to build powerful scripts that bridge the gap between local automation and web-based services, empowering your scripts to be both smarter and more connected.

In the next section, we'll explore how to authenticate and manage sessions when working with more complex API workflows, such as those involving OAuth tokens or multi-step transactions.

HEADERS, TOKENS, AND JSON HANDLING

In PowerShell scripting, especially when dealing with APIs or web-based services, it's crucial to understand how to work with HTTP headers, tokens for authentication, and JSON-formatted data. These elements form the backbone of web requests and are essential for integrating PowerShell with external systems. This chapter will break down the importance of headers and tokens, and demonstrate how to parse and manipulate JSON effectively in PowerShell.

Understanding HTTP Headers

HTTP headers are key-value pairs sent between the client and server with HTTP requests and responses. Headers convey metadata such as authentication credentials, content types, and user-agent information.

Common Headers You Might Use

- **Authorization**: Carries credentials (tokens or username/ password) to authenticate the client.
- **Content-Type**: Specifies the format of the request body. Common types include application/json and application/x-www-form-urlencoded.
- **Accept**: Informs the server of the content types the client can process.

In PowerShell, you can create headers as a hashtable:

```
$headers = @{
    'Authorization' = 'Bearer your-token-here'
    'Content-Type'  = 'application/json'
    'Accept'        = 'application/json'
}
```

This $headers variable can then be passed to Invoke-RestMethod or Invoke-WebRequest using the -Headers parameter.

Authentication Tokens

Most modern APIs require some form of authentication. A common method is using a bearer token, often obtained by logging in or registering an app with the service.

Retrieving a Token

Typically, you will send a POST request to the API's authentication endpoint, passing a username and password or client credentials.

Example:

```
$body = @{
    username = 'your-username'
    password = 'your-password'
} | ConvertTo-Json

$response = Invoke-RestMethod -Uri 'https://api.example.com/auth/token' -Method Post -Body $body -ContentType 'application/json'

$token = $response.access_token
```

Once retrieved, the token is included in the header for subsequent requests:

```
$headers = @{ Authorization = "Bearer $token" }
```

This token typically expires, so your scripts may need logic to refresh it periodically.

JSON Handling in PowerShell

JSON (JavaScript Object Notation) is the most widely-used format for exchanging data between APIs and clients. PowerShell makes working with JSON straightforward through its built-in cmdlets.

Converting PowerShell Objects to JSON

Use ConvertTo-Json to serialize a PowerShell object into a JSON-formatted string:

```
$person = [PSCustomObject]@{
    FirstName = 'John'
    LastName  = 'Doe'
```

```
    Age        = 30
}

$json = $person | ConvertTo-Json
```

The $json variable now holds a string that looks like this:

```
{
    "FirstName": "John",
    "LastName": "Doe",
    "Age": 30
}
```

Converting JSON to PowerShell Objects

Use ConvertFrom-Json to deserialize a JSON string into a PowerShell object:

```
$jsonString = '{"FirstName": "John", "LastName": "Doe", "Age": 30}'

$personObj = $jsonString | ConvertFrom-Json

Write-Output $personObj.FirstName   # Outputs: John
```

Working with Nested JSON

JSON data often comes in nested structures. PowerShell handles this gracefully, allowing dot notation to access properties:

```
$json = '{ "user": { "name": "Alice", "email": "alice@example.com" } }'

$obj = $json | ConvertFrom-Json

Write-Output $obj.user.name   # Outputs: Alice
```

Pretty-Printing JSON

Sometimes, for readability or logging, you want pretty-printed JSON. The -Depth parameter in ConvertTo-Json controls how deeply nested objects are represented:

```
$object | ConvertTo-Json -Depth 5
```

Without the proper depth, deeply nested objects may be truncated.

Real-World API Interaction Example

Let's walk through a full example where we:
1. Authenticate with an API.
2. Retrieve a list of users.
3. Parse the JSON response.

```
# Step 1: Authenticate and get a token
$authBody = @{
    client_id     = 'abc123'
    client_secret = 'xyz789'
    grant_type    = 'client_credentials'
} | ConvertTo-Json

$authResponse = Invoke-RestMethod -Uri 'https://
api.service.com/token' -Method Post -Body $authBody -
ContentType 'application/json'

$token = $authResponse.access_token

# Step 2: Set headers with the token
$headers = @{
    Authorization = "Bearer $token"
    Accept        = 'application/json'
}

# Step 3: Make a GET request
$response = Invoke-RestMethod -Uri 'https://api.service.com/
users' -Headers $headers -Method Get

# Step 4: Parse the response
foreach ($user in $response.users) {
    Write-Output "$($user.name) <$($user.email)>"
}
```

Tips and Best Practices

Use -Verbose to Troubleshoot

Many cmdlets, including Invoke-RestMethod, support the -

Verbose flag. This can help you inspect the HTTP request/response details.

```
Invoke-RestMethod -Uri 'https://api.service.com/data' -
Method Get -Verbose
```

Secure Your Tokens

Avoid hardcoding tokens or passwords directly in your scripts. Use secure methods like Windows Credential Manager, environment variables, or Azure Key Vault.

Respect API Rate Limits

Many APIs enforce rate limits. Monitor headers like X-RateLimit-Remaining and implement retry logic if needed.

Automate Token Renewal

If your token expires after a certain time, write a function that checks the token's age and automatically requests a new one.

Handle Errors Gracefully

Use try/catch blocks around your API calls to capture and log errors, making your scripts more robust:

```
try {
    $response = Invoke-RestMethod -Uri $uri -Headers
$headers -Method Get
} catch {
    Write-Error "Failed to retrieve data: $_"
}
```

Conclusion

Mastering headers, tokens, and JSON is essential for modern PowerShell scripting. Whether you're querying a REST API, posting data to a web service, or handling responses, these tools enable you to interact confidently with web-based services. With the examples and best practices provided in this chapter, you'll be equipped to build secure, dynamic, and scalable scripts that interface with the modern web.

PowerShell and Azure

SETTING UP AZURE POWERSHELL MODULE

PowerShell has become a crucial tool for system administrators and cloud engineers, and its integration with Microsoft Azure is no exception. The Azure PowerShell module enables users to manage Azure resources directly from the command line, allowing for automation, scripting, and repeatable infrastructure deployment. In this chapter, we will walk through the steps to set up the Azure PowerShell module, including installation, configuration, authentication, and verification.

What Is the Azure PowerShell Module?

Azure PowerShell is a set of cmdlets for managing Azure resources directly from PowerShell. It supports a wide variety of Azure services including virtual machines, storage accounts, networking, and resource groups. It enables infrastructure-as-code and fits seamlessly into DevOps pipelines, making it essential for managing cloud environments efficiently.

The Azure PowerShell module is built on top of the .NET Standard, allowing cross-platform usage on Windows, macOS, and Linux.

Prerequisites

Before setting up the Azure PowerShell module, ensure the following prerequisites are in place:
1. **Operating System**:
    ◦ Windows 10/11, Windows Server 2016 or later
    ◦ macOS 10.12+ or most recent Linux distributions
2. **PowerShell Version**:

- ◦ PowerShell 7.x or Windows PowerShell 5.1
- ◦ You can check your version using:
  `$PSVersionTable.PSVersion`
3. **.NET Core** (if using PowerShell 7+):
   - ◦ Usually bundled with PowerShell 7+, but make sure it's updated.
4. **Administrator Privileges**:
   - ◦ Some installation steps require admin permissions.

Installing PowerShell (If Not Installed)

Windows

If you are running Windows 10 or later, Windows PowerShell 5.1 is already installed. However, it's recommended to use PowerShell 7+ for better compatibility and cross-platform scripting.

Install PowerShell 7 using the MSI installer from the official GitHub releases page.

macOS and Linux

You can use the package manager to install PowerShell:

macOS:

```
brew install --cask powershell
```

Ubuntu:

```
sudo apt-get update
sudo apt-get install -y wget apt-transport-https software-
properties-common
wget -q https://packages.microsoft.com/config/ubuntu/$
(lsb_release -rs)/packages-microsoft-prod.deb
sudo dpkg -i packages-microsoft-prod.deb
sudo apt-get update
sudo apt-get install -y powershell
```

Launch PowerShell by typing pwsh.

Installing the Azure PowerShell Module

Microsoft recommends using the Az module, which is the latest and replaces the older AzureRM module.

Step 1: Open PowerShell as Administrator

Step 2: Install the Az Module

```
Install-Module -Name Az -AllowClobber -Scope CurrentUser
```
- ◦ -AllowClobber ensures that any conflicting cmdlets are overwritten.
- ◦ -Scope CurrentUser installs the module only for the current user, which avoids the need for administrative privileges.

Step 3: Import the Module (Optional)

```
Import-Module Az
```
PowerShell automatically loads modules when you use a cmdlet from them, but manually importing can speed up scripts.

Step 4: Verify Installation

```
Get-InstalledModule -Name Az
```
This command shows the version of the Az module installed.

Authenticating to Azure

To perform any actions in Azure, you must authenticate with your Azure account.

Sign in Interactively

```
Connect-AzAccount
```
A web-based authentication window will pop up. Enter your Azure credentials here.

Sign in Using a Service Principal

Service principals are ideal for automated scripts and CI/CD pipelines.

```
$sp = Connect-AzAccount -ServicePrincipal -Tenant <TenantID>
-ApplicationId <AppID> -Credential (Get-Credential)
```
Make sure the service principal has the necessary permissions in the Azure AD and subscription.

Selecting a Subscription

If your account has access to multiple Azure subscriptions, you need to select the correct one.

List Available Subscriptions

```
Get-AzSubscription
```

Set a Specific Subscription
```
Set-AzContext -SubscriptionId <SubscriptionID>
```

Common Azure PowerShell Cmdlets

Here are a few common cmdlets to verify and practice your Azure PowerShell setup:

List All Resource Groups
```
Get-AzResourceGroup
```
Create a New Resource Group
```
New-AzResourceGroup -Name "TestRG" -Location "EastUS"
```
List All VMs
```
Get-AzVM
```
Start a VM
```
Start-AzVM -ResourceGroupName "TestRG" -Name "MyVM"
```
Stop a VM
```
Stop-AzVM -ResourceGroupName "TestRG" -Name "MyVM" -Force
```

Updating the Azure PowerShell Module

To keep the module up to date:
```
Update-Module -Name Az
```
This command will fetch and install the latest version of the module.

Troubleshooting Installation Issues

Module Not Found
If you get an error that the Az module is not recognized, ensure it is installed correctly and that your $env:PSModulePath includes the install location.

Authentication Issues
If login fails with Connect-AzAccount, verify that you have:
- Internet access
- Correct credentials

- Proper Azure permissions

Proxy Issues

If you're behind a corporate proxy, use:

```
[System.Net.WebRequest]::DefaultWebProxy.Credentials =
[System.Net.CredentialCache]::DefaultNetworkCredentials
```

Summary

The Azure PowerShell module provides a powerful interface for managing Azure resources programmatically. In this chapter, we've walked through how to:

- Install PowerShell (if needed)
- Install and import the Az module
- Authenticate using interactive or service principal methods
- Select and set your Azure subscription
- Run basic Azure management commands
- Troubleshoot common issues

With this setup complete, you're now ready to begin automating Azure infrastructure and building scalable, repeatable cloud environments using PowerShell.

In the next chapter, we'll dive deeper into scripting techniques and explore real-world scenarios such as creating VMs, configuring storage accounts, and managing networking using Azure PowerShell cmdlets.

MANAGING AZURE RESOURCES (VMS, STORAGE, USERS)

PowerShell is an invaluable tool for managing resources in Microsoft Azure. Whether you're a system administrator, DevOps engineer, or simply a curious learner, understanding how to script interactions with Azure services can save time, reduce errors, and unlock powerful automation. This section explores how to use PowerShell to manage three of the most common Azure resource types: Virtual Machines (VMs), Storage Accounts, and Users.

Prerequisites

Before diving into Azure resource management with PowerShell, make sure you have the following:

- An active Azure subscription.
- PowerShell 7+ installed on your machine.
- The Azure PowerShell module installed. You can install it with:

```
Install-Module -Name Az -Scope CurrentUser -Repository PSGallery -Force
```

- Sign in to your Azure account using:

```
Connect-AzAccount
```

Once authenticated, you can start scripting against your Azure resources.

Managing Azure Virtual Machines (VMs)

Azure Virtual Machines provide scalable computing resources. You can manage them entirely through PowerShell.

Listing Existing VMs

To retrieve all VMs in your current subscription:

```
Get-AzVM
```

To list VMs in a specific resource group:

```
Get-AzVM -ResourceGroupName "MyResourceGroup"
```

Creating a New VM

Creating a VM involves multiple steps, such as creating a resource group, virtual network, and specifying credentials:

```
$resourceGroup = "MyResourceGroup"
$location = "EastUS"

New-AzResourceGroup -Name $resourceGroup -Location $location

$cred = Get-Credential

New-AzVM -ResourceGroupName $resourceGroup -Name "MyVM" -Location $location `
    -VirtualNetworkName "MyVnet" -SubnetName "MySubnet" -SecurityGroupName "MyNSG" `
    -PublicIpAddressName "MyPublicIP" -Credential $cred
```

Starting, Stopping, and Restarting VMs

You can control VM state using the following commands:

```
Start-AzVM -Name "MyVM" -ResourceGroupName "MyResourceGroup"
Stop-AzVM -Name "MyVM" -ResourceGroupName "MyResourceGroup"
-Force
Restart-AzVM -Name "MyVM" -ResourceGroupName
"MyResourceGroup"
```

Deleting a VM

To remove a VM:

```
Remove-AzVM -Name "MyVM" -ResourceGroupName
"MyResourceGroup"
```

Managing Azure Storage Accounts

Storage accounts are crucial for data storage, backups, and logs.

Listing Storage Accounts

```
Get-AzStorageAccount
```

To view accounts in a specific resource group:

```
Get-AzStorageAccount -ResourceGroupName "MyResourceGroup"
```

Creating a Storage Account

```
New-AzStorageAccount -ResourceGroupName "MyResourceGroup" -
Name "mystorageacct123" `
    -Location "EastUS" -SkuName "Standard_LRS" -Kind
"StorageV2"
```

Getting Access Keys

To retrieve the keys needed to access the storage account programmatically:

```
$keys = Get-AzStorageAccountKey -ResourceGroupName
"MyResourceGroup" -Name "mystorageacct123"
$keys[0].Value
```

Working with Blob Containers

Once you have a key, you can create a context and start working with blob storage:

```
$context = New-AzStorageContext -StorageAccountName
"mystorageacct123" -StorageAccountKey $keys[0].Value
New-AzStorageContainer -Name "mycontainer" -Context $context
-Permission Blob
```

Uploading and Downloading Blobs

```
Set-AzStorageBlobContent -File "C:\MyData.txt" -Container
```

```
"mycontainer" -Blob "MyData.txt" -Context $context
Get-AzStorageBlobContent -Container "mycontainer" -Blob
"MyData.txt" -Destination "C:\Downloaded.txt" -Context
$context
```

Deleting a Storage Account

```
Remove-AzStorageAccount -ResourceGroupName "MyResourceGroup"
-Name "mystorageacct123"
```

Managing Azure Users (Azure AD)

Azure Active Directory (Azure AD) allows you to manage users and groups in the cloud. Managing Azure AD via PowerShell is slightly different—it uses the AzureAD or Microsoft Graph module.

Installing AzureAD Module

```
Install-Module -Name AzureAD
Connect-AzureAD
```

Listing Users

```
Get-AzureADUser
```

Creating a New User

```
New-AzureADUser -DisplayName "John Doe" -UserPrincipalName
"jdoe@yourdomain.com" `
    -AccountEnabled $true -PasswordProfile @{Password =
"ComplexP@ss123"; ForceChangePasswordNextLogin = $true} `
    -MailNickname "jdoe"
```

Updating User Information

```
Set-AzureADUser -ObjectId "jdoe@yourdomain.com" -JobTitle
"System Administrator"
```

Deleting a User

```
Remove-AzureADUser -ObjectId "jdoe@yourdomain.com"
```

Automating Resource Management

PowerShell excels at automation. You can chain tasks together to deploy entire environments.

Example: Daily VM Shutdown

Use a scheduled task or Azure Automation to run a script that shuts down all VMs at 7 PM:

```
$vms = Get-AzVM
foreach ($vm in $vms) {
```

```
    Stop-AzVM -Name $vm.Name -ResourceGroupName
$vm.ResourceGroupName -Force
}
```

Example: Monthly Storage Audit

Generate a report of all storage accounts and their usage:

```
$storageAccounts = Get-AzStorageAccount

foreach ($account in $storageAccounts) {
    Write-Output "Storage Account: $
($account.StorageAccountName), Location: $
($account.Location)"
}
```

Final Thoughts

PowerShell's ability to script, manage, and automate Azure resources empowers both individuals and organizations to maintain control, efficiency, and scalability. Once you're familiar with the basics of managing VMs, Storage Accounts, and Azure AD Users through PowerShell, you can expand into more complex areas such as:

- Role-Based Access Control (RBAC)
- Virtual Network (VNet) management
- Azure Resource Manager (ARM) templates integration
- Azure Policy and Compliance scripts

Mastering these concepts with PowerShell not only makes routine administrative tasks easier—it also positions you for advanced DevOps and cloud engineering roles.

Continue experimenting, scripting, and automating. Azure is a vast ecosystem, and PowerShell is your key to navigating it with precision.

SCRIPTED DEPLOYMENTS

One of the most powerful and practical uses of PowerShell is the ability to automate software and configuration deployments across multiple machines. Scripted deployments allow system administrators to roll out changes, install or update software, and configure settings in a repeatable, scalable, and error-free manner.

In this chapter, we'll explore what scripted deployments are, the advantages they offer, real-world use cases, and how to create and customize your own deployment scripts using PowerShell. We'll also cover best practices and provide several working examples you can adapt to your own environment.

What Are Scripted Deployments?

Scripted deployments refer to the automation of application installations, updates, configuration changes, or system provisioning through scripts. Instead of manually installing software or changing settings on each computer, administrators can write PowerShell scripts to perform these tasks programmatically.

These scripts can be executed locally, remotely, or across an entire network of machines using tools like PowerShell Remoting, Group Policy, or System Center Configuration Manager (SCCM).

Benefits of Scripted Deployments

1. **Consistency**: Every machine receives the exact same configuration and software versions.
2. **Speed**: Deployments that would take hours manually can be executed in minutes or seconds.
3. **Scalability**: Easily deploy across dozens, hundreds, or thousands of systems.
4. **Repeatability**: Run the same script multiple times with identical results.
5. **Error Reduction**: Automates complex steps, reducing the chance of human error.
6. **Auditability**: Log output for documentation and compliance.
7. **Flexibility**: Customize deployments based on system roles, locations, or environments.

Common Use Cases

- Installing required software on new employee workstations
- Deploying security patches or application updates
- Changing system settings or applying group policies
- Pushing new configuration files or registry changes
- Setting up a development or test environment
- Provisioning cloud-based VMs or containers

Essential PowerShell Concepts for Deployments

Before diving into scripting, it's important to understand the PowerShell concepts that make scripted deployments effective:

- **Cmdlets**: Command-line tools like Install-Package, Invoke-Command, Start-Process, and Copy-Item are essential.
- **Variables and Parameters**: Reuse values and allow scripts to be flexible.
- **Conditionals and Loops**: Execute logic based on the environment or data.
- **Remote Execution**: Use Invoke-Command or Enter-PSSession for deploying to remote machines.
- **Modules**: Use community or Microsoft-provided modules such as PSWindowsUpdate, PackageManagement, or AzureAD.
- **Error Handling**: Use try/catch blocks and logging to handle failures gracefully.

Building a Basic Deployment Script

Here's a simple example that installs Notepad++ on a list of remote computers:

```
$computers = Get-Content -Path "C:\Scripts\computers.txt"
$installerUrl = "https://github.com/notepad-plus-plus/
notepad-plus-plus/releases/download/v8.5/npp.
8.5.Installer.x64.exe"
$installerPath = "C:\Temp\nppInstaller.exe"

Invoke-WebRequest -Uri $installerUrl -OutFile $installerPath
```

```
foreach ($computer in $computers) {
    Copy-Item -Path $installerPath -Destination "\\
$computer\C$\Temp" -Force
    Invoke-Command -ComputerName $computer -ScriptBlock {
        Start-Process "C:\Temp\nppInstaller.exe" -
ArgumentList "/S" -Wait
    }
    Write-Host "Installed on $computer"
}
```

This script does the following:
1. Loads a list of computer names from a text file.
2. Downloads the Notepad++ installer.
3. Copies the installer to each remote machine.
4. Runs the installer silently.
5. Confirms deployment with a message.

Parameterizing the Script

Add flexibility by converting hardcoded values into parameters:

```
param(
    [string]$InstallerUrl,
    [string]$InstallerName,
    [string]$ComputerListPath
)

$computers = Get-Content -Path $ComputerListPath
$installerPath = "C:\Temp\$InstallerName"

Invoke-WebRequest -Uri $InstallerUrl -OutFile $installerPath

foreach ($computer in $computers) {
    Copy-Item -Path $installerPath -Destination "\\
$computer\C$\Temp" -Force
    Invoke-Command -ComputerName $computer -ScriptBlock {
        param($InstallerName)
        Start-Process "C:\Temp\$InstallerName" -ArgumentList
"/S" -Wait
    } -ArgumentList $InstallerName
```

```
    Write-Host "Installed on $computer"
}
```

Run it like this:
```
.\Deploy-Software.ps1 -InstallerUrl "https://example.com/
app.exe" -InstallerName "app.exe" -ComputerListPath "C:
\Scripts\computers.txt"
```

Handling Errors and Logging

Error handling is crucial for large-scale deployments:
```
try {
    Invoke-Command -ComputerName $computer -ScriptBlock {
        Start-Process "C:\Temp\$InstallerName" -ArgumentList
"/S" -Wait
    } -ErrorAction Stop
    Add-Content -Path "C:\Logs\DeploymentSuccess.log" -Value
"$computer: Success"
} catch {
    Add-Content -Path "C:\Logs\DeploymentErrors.log" -Value
"$computer: $_"
}
```

Advanced Scenarios

Deploying Configuration Files
```
$source = "C:\Scripts\config.xml"
foreach ($computer in $computers) {
    Copy-Item -Path $source -Destination "\\$computer\C$
\App\config.xml" -Force
}
```

Registry Changes
```
Invoke-Command -ComputerName $computers -ScriptBlock {
    Set-ItemProperty -Path "HKLM:\Software\MyCompany" -Name
"Setting" -Value 1
}
```

Running Scripts on Remote Computers
```
Invoke-Command -ComputerName $computers -FilePath "C:
```

```
\Scripts\PostInstall.ps1"
```

Security Considerations

- Use signed scripts where possible.
- Store credentials securely with Get-Credential or encrypted credential stores.
- Limit administrative access on the network.
- Always validate downloads (e.g., hash checks) before executing.

Best Practices

- **Test in a staging environment** before production deployment.
- **Log everything**: success, failure, timestamps.
- **Use version control** for your scripts (e.g., Git).
- **Document assumptions** and required permissions.
- **Use verbose output** when troubleshooting.
- **Create reusable functions** or modules for common tasks.

Summary

Scripted deployments can drastically reduce the effort and risk involved in managing large IT environments. PowerShell makes it possible to install software, push updates, and configure machines programmatically and reliably. By learning to write effective deployment scripts, you'll enhance your ability to support both small teams and enterprise-scale networks.

In the next chapter, we'll cover how to monitor and report on the success of these deployments using PowerShell logging, transcript files, and custom dashboards.

PowerShell and AWS

AWS TOOLS FOR POWERSHELL

Amazon Web Services (AWS) is the most widely adopted cloud platform, offering over 200 fully featured services from data centers globally. For Windows administrators and PowerShell users, AWS provides a robust command-line interface known as AWS Tools for PowerShell. This module allows administrators to interact with AWS services directly from PowerShell, enabling automation, scripting, and streamlined management of cloud resources.

In this section, we will explore the AWS Tools for PowerShell, covering its installation, authentication methods, common use cases, practical examples, and best practices. Whether you're a seasoned sysadmin transitioning to cloud infrastructure or a beginner exploring PowerShell in the cloud, this section will equip you with the knowledge to manage AWS using the language you already know.

What Are AWS Tools for PowerShell?

AWS Tools for PowerShell is a collection of PowerShell modules that allow you to script operations against AWS services. It acts as a wrapper around the AWS SDK for .NET, exposing AWS functionality through PowerShell cmdlets.

There are two primary versions:

- **AWSPowerShell**: The original version, compatible with Windows PowerShell 5.1 and earlier.
- **AWS.Tools**: A modular version recommended for PowerShell Core (v6+) and future development. It allows you to install only the modules you need.

AWS.Tools is generally preferred because of its modular design, smaller footprint, and support for cross-platform scripting.

Installing AWS Tools for PowerShell

Prerequisites

- PowerShell 5.1 or later (including PowerShell Core on macOS/ Linux)
- .NET Core (for non-Windows platforms)
- AWS account with access credentials

Installation Using PowerShell Gallery

You can install AWS.Tools using the Install-Module cmdlet from the PowerShell Gallery:

```
# Install the core AWS.Tools module
Install-Module -Name AWS.Tools.Installer -Scope CurrentUser

# Use the installer to install specific service modules
Install-AWSToolsModule -Name AWS.Tools.S3, AWS.Tools.EC2,
AWS.Tools.IAM
```

To install the legacy monolithic module:

```
Install-Module -Name AWSPowerShell -Scope CurrentUser
```

To verify installation:

```
Get-Module -ListAvailable AWS*
```

Configuring Credentials

AWS Tools for PowerShell require authentication using IAM credentials. There are multiple ways to authenticate:

1. Using Set-AWSCredential

```
$creds = Set-AWSCredential -AccessKey 'AKIA...' -SecretKey
'abc123...' -StoreAs 'MyProfile'
```

2. Using Credential Profiles

You can use the AWS CLI to configure a profile:

```
aws configure --profile MyProfile
```

Then reference it in PowerShell:

```
Set-AWSCredential -ProfileName 'MyProfile'
```

3. Using Environment Variables

Set these environment variables before starting your PowerShell session:

```
$env:AWS_ACCESS_KEY_ID = "AKIA..."
```

```
$env:AWS_SECRET_ACCESS_KEY = "abc123..."
```

Common Use Cases

Managing EC2 Instances

Start, stop, describe, and terminate EC2 instances with simple commands:

```
# List running EC2 instances
Get-EC2Instance | Where-Object { $_.State.Name -eq 'running'
}

# Start an instance
Start-EC2Instance -InstanceId i-0123456789abcdef0

# Stop an instance
Stop-EC2Instance -InstanceId i-0123456789abcdef0
```

Managing S3 Buckets and Objects

```
# List all S3 buckets
Get-S3Bucket

# Create a new bucket
New-S3Bucket -BucketName 'my-new-powershell-bucket'

# Upload a file
Write-S3Object -BucketName 'my-new-powershell-bucket' -File
'C:\temp\data.csv' -Key 'data.csv'

# Download a file
Read-S3Object -BucketName 'my-new-powershell-bucket' -Key
'data.csv' -File 'C:\downloads\data.csv'
```

IAM User Management

```
# Create a new IAM user
New-IAMUser -UserName 'powershell-user'

# Attach a policy
Register-IAMUserPolicy -UserName 'powershell-user' -
PolicyName 'S3FullAccess' -PolicyDocument (Get-Content '.
\s3-policy.json' -Raw)
```

CloudWatch Logs

```
# List log groups
```

```
Get-CWLogGroup

# List log streams in a group
Get-CWLogStream -LogGroupName '/aws/lambda/my-function'

# Get log events
Get-CWLogEvent -LogGroupName '/aws/lambda/my-function' -
LogStreamName '2025/04/11/[$LATEST]abc123...'
```

Scripting and Automation

One of the biggest advantages of AWS Tools for PowerShell is the ability to automate tasks. For example:

Scheduled Backup Script

```
$bucket = "daily-backup-bucket"
$file = "C:\Backups\db_backup_$(Get-Date -Format
yyyyMMdd).zip"

# Create the backup (mock example)
Compress-Archive -Path "C:\Database\*.bak" -DestinationPath
$file

# Upload to S3
Write-S3Object -BucketName $bucket -File $file -Key (Split-
Path $file -Leaf)
```

This script could be scheduled using Task Scheduler or cron (on Linux/macOS) to run nightly.

Best Practices

Use Named Profiles

Avoid hardcoding credentials in scripts. Use named profiles or managed identities when possible.

Modular Installations

Only install the AWS.Tools modules you need. This keeps your environment lean and reduces update overhead.

Secure Your Credentials

Never share your access keys. Rotate them regularly and use IAM policies to enforce least privilege.

Logging and Error Handling

Wrap critical code blocks with try/catch and log outputs to a file:

```
try {
    Write-S3Object -BucketName 'backup-bucket' -File $file -
Key 'db.zip'
} catch {
    Write-Error "Failed to upload to S3: $_"
}
```

Cross-Platform Support

AWS Tools for PowerShell work across Windows, macOS, and Linux using PowerShell Core. This makes it an ideal tool for cross-platform DevOps workflows, allowing you to maintain the same automation scripts regardless of the host OS.

Real-World Scenario: Provisioning a Web Server

Here's a simplified example of provisioning and preparing an EC2 instance for a web application using PowerShell:

```
# Step 1: Launch an EC2 instance
$instance = New-EC2Instance -ImageId 'ami-0abcdef1234567890'
-InstanceType 't2.micro' -KeyName 'MyKeyPair' -
SecurityGroupId 'sg-0123456789abcdef0' -SubnetId
'subnet-0123456789abcdef0' -MinCount 1 -MaxCount 1

# Step 2: Wait until the instance is running
Start-Sleep -Seconds 60

# Step 3: Tag the instance
New-EC2Tag -Resource $instance.Instances.InstanceId -Tag
@{Key='Name';Value='WebServer01'}
```

Add more steps to install IIS or deploy your application using Invoke-Command and remote PowerShell sessions if needed.

Summary

AWS Tools for PowerShell is a powerful asset in the cloud administrator's toolkit. It bridges the gap between cloud infrastructure and Windows scripting, making it easier for PowerShell users to leverage AWS. Whether you're spinning up new servers, managing backups, auditing IAM roles, or automating deployments, the AWS PowerShell module lets you do it all in a familiar syntax.

By mastering these tools, you extend the reach of your PowerShell scripts to the cloud, creating scalable, repeatable, and secure infrastructure automation workflows. Start with simple tasks and build up to more complex orchestrations as your confidence grows.

IAM, EC2, AND S3 OPERATIONS

PowerShell is a powerful tool for managing AWS resources when combined with the AWS Tools for PowerShell module. In this section, we'll cover how to perform common operations involving Identity and Access Management (IAM), Elastic Compute Cloud (EC2), and Simple Storage Service (S3). These services are core components of AWS, and learning to manage them with PowerShell enables automation, consistency, and efficiency.

Prerequisites

Before performing any AWS operations with PowerShell, ensure the following prerequisites are in place:

- **AWS Tools for PowerShell**: Install with Install-Module -Name AWSPowerShell.
- **AWS Credentials**: Either configure using the Set-AWSCredential cmdlet or use the AWS CLI with aws configure to store your credentials.
- **Appropriate IAM Permissions**: The IAM user you authenticate with must have permissions for the resources you'll manage.

EC2 Operations with PowerShell

EC2 allows you to run virtual machines in the cloud. PowerShell can manage EC2 lifecycle actions, security groups, and more.

Launching a New EC2 Instance

```
New-EC2Instance -ImageId "ami-0abcdef1234567890" -
InstanceType "t2.micro" -MinCount 1 -MaxCount 1 -KeyName
"MyKeyPair" -SecurityGroups "MySecurityGroup"
```

Stopping and Starting an Instance

```
Stop-EC2Instance -InstanceId "i-0123456789abcdef0"
Start-EC2Instance -InstanceId "i-0123456789abcdef0"
```

Describing EC2 Instances

```
Get-EC2Instance | Select-Object -ExpandProperty Instances |
Format-Table InstanceId, State, InstanceType,
PublicIpAddress
```

Terminating an Instance

```
Remove-EC2Instance -InstanceId "i-0123456789abcdef0"
```

Creating a Security Group

```
New-EC2SecurityGroup -GroupName "MySecurityGroup" -
Description "Allow SSH access"
```

Authorizing Inbound SSH Rule

```
Grant-EC2SecurityGroupIngress -GroupName "MySecurityGroup" -
IpProtocol "tcp" -FromPort 22 -ToPort 22 -CidrIp "0.0.0.0/0"
```

IAM Operations with PowerShell

IAM allows you to securely control access to AWS services and resources. Here's how to manage IAM users, groups, and roles.

Creating an IAM User

```
New-IAMUser -UserName "newuser"
```

Creating a Login Profile (for Console Access)

```
New-IAMLoginProfile -UserName "newuser" -Password
"ComplexPassword123!" -PasswordResetRequired $true
```

Attaching a Policy to a User

```
Register-IAMUserPolicy -UserName "newuser" -PolicyName
"AllowS3" -PolicyDocument '{
  "Version": "2012-10-17",
  "Statement": [
    {
      "Effect": "Allow",
      "Action": "s3:*",
      "Resource": "*"
```

```
    }
  ]
}'
```

Creating a Group and Adding Users

```
New-IAMGroup -GroupName "Developers"
Add-IAMUserToGroup -GroupName "Developers" -UserName
"newuser"
```

Creating and Attaching an IAM Role

```
New-IAMRole -RoleName "EC2S3AccessRole" -
AssumeRolePolicyDocument '{
  "Version": "2012-10-17",
  "Statement": [
    {
      "Effect": "Allow",
      "Principal": {"Service": "ec2.amazonaws.com"},
      "Action": "sts:AssumeRole"
    }
  ]
}'
```

S3 Operations with PowerShell

S3 is used for object storage. PowerShell enables creation, file uploads, and bucket management.

Creating a Bucket

```
New-S3Bucket -BucketName "my-unique-bucket-name"
```

Listing Buckets

```
Get-S3Bucket
```

Uploading a File to S3

```
Write-S3Object -BucketName "my-unique-bucket-name" -File "C:
\localpath\myfile.txt" -Key "myfile.txt"
```

Downloading a File from S3

```
Read-S3Object -BucketName "my-unique-bucket-name" -Key
"myfile.txt" -File "C:\localpath\myfile-downloaded.txt"
```

Listing Files in a Bucket

```
Get-S3Object -BucketName "my-unique-bucket-name"
```

Deleting a File

```
Remove-S3Object -BucketName "my-unique-bucket-name" -Key
"myfile.txt"
```

Scripting Real-World Scenarios

Scenario 1: Automating EC2 Startup

Suppose you have a development server that only needs to run during business hours. You could schedule a PowerShell script using Task Scheduler:

```
# StartDevServer.ps1
Start-EC2Instance -InstanceId "i-0123456789abcdef0"
```

And another script to stop it after hours:

```
# StopDevServer.ps1
Stop-EC2Instance -InstanceId "i-0123456789abcdef0"
```

Scenario 2: Backing Up Logs to S3

```
$source = "C:\Logs\application.log"
$bucket = "my-log-backups"
$key = "$(Get-Date -Format 'yyyy-MM-dd')_application.log"
Write-S3Object -BucketName $bucket -File $source -Key $key
```

A common real-world use case is setting up EC2 instances that can automatically back up files to S3 without manually managing credentials. This requires:

1. An IAM Role with permissions to access S3.
2. An EC2 instance launched with that role.
3. A script on the EC2 instance that copies data to S3.

IAM Role Policy

```
{
  "Version": "2012-10-17",
  "Statement": [
    {
      "Effect": "Allow",
      "Action": ["s3:PutObject", "s3:GetObject"],
      "Resource": "arn:aws:s3:::my-unique-bucket-name/*"
    }
  ]
}
```

Launch EC2 with Role

Use the AWS Console or PowerShell to associate the IAM role.

Upload Script (on EC2)

```
$localFile = "C:\data\report.csv"
$bucketName = "my-unique-bucket-name"
$key = "daily/report.csv"
Write-S3Object -BucketName $bucketName -File $localFile -Key $key
```

Summary

With PowerShell and the AWS Tools module, you can:
- Manage IAM identities securely and script user/group creation.
- Automate EC2 instance provisioning, management, and cost-saving operations.
- Upload, download, and manage files in S3.

This integration makes it easy to build repeatable infrastructure scripts for development, backup, and operations. Once you've grasped these basics, you can explore more advanced scripting techniques like parameterized scripts, modules, and dynamic role assumption for temporary credentials.

In the next chapter, we'll explore error handling and logging to ensure your automation scripts are resilient and easy to troubleshoot.

COMPARING POWERSHELL WITH TERRAFORM AND BICEP

As the demand for Infrastructure as Code (IaC) grows in modern IT environments, it has become critical for professionals to understand the nuances between various tools used to automate the provisioning and management of infrastructure. PowerShell, Terraform, and Bicep each offer unique capabilities and strengths. This section explores these tools in depth, comparing their syntax, use cases, platform compatibility, community support, extensibility, and integration within cloud ecosystems—particularly Azure.

PowerShell: A General-Purpose Scripting Language

PowerShell is a cross-platform task automation framework consisting of a command-line shell and a scripting language. Developed by Microsoft, it was originally designed to automate administrative tasks for Windows systems. Over time, PowerShell has evolved to support Linux, macOS, and a wide range of cloud platforms.

One of PowerShell's primary strengths is its versatility. It is not strictly an IaC tool but rather a general-purpose language capable of automating virtually any task across systems, applications, and cloud services. With modules like Az and AWS.Tools, PowerShell can interact with cloud platforms like Microsoft Azure and Amazon Web Services to create, manage, and delete infrastructure resources.

PowerShell scripts are procedural by nature, meaning they execute tasks step-by-step. This makes them highly flexible but also requires more manual effort when managing state or dependencies between resources. For example, if you script the creation of a virtual machine and its associated network interface, you need to explicitly define the order and ensure each step completes successfully.

Terraform: A Declarative IaC Tool

Terraform, developed by HashiCorp, is an open-source declarative IaC tool used to provision and manage infrastructure across a wide variety of cloud providers. It employs a high-level configuration language known as HCL (HashiCorp Configuration Language).

Terraform's declarative approach means you define *what* the infrastructure should look like, not *how* to build it. Terraform figures out the steps to take in order to reach the desired state from the current state. This is made possible through its built-in state management and execution plan features.

Terraform is highly modular and extensible. Providers enable Terraform to interact with cloud platforms, SaaS products, and even on-prem systems. Modules allow users to encapsulate reusable infrastructure components, which promotes maintainability and consistency across deployments.

One of Terraform's standout features is its terraform plan command, which previews changes before applying them. This helps avoid unintended consequences and gives teams a clear understanding of how the infrastructure will be modified.

Bicep: Azure's Native IaC Language

Bicep is a domain-specific language (DSL) developed by Microsoft as a more readable and maintainable alternative to Azure Resource Manager (ARM) templates. It is designed exclusively for Azure and provides a simpler, cleaner syntax than its JSON-based predecessor.

Bicep is fully declarative and integrates natively with the Azure ecosystem. Its syntax is minimal, with built-in support for type safety, code completion, and modularization. It also allows developers to reuse code through modules and parameter files.

Unlike Terraform, which requires a state file to manage infrastructure state, Bicep leverages Azure's own resource manager to maintain state. This removes the complexity of managing state files and makes Bicep a more straightforward option for teams focused solely on Azure.

Bicep files are transpiled into ARM templates, which are then deployed by Azure. Despite this intermediate step, users rarely need to interact with the underlying JSON. Microsoft actively maintains Bicep, ensuring that it supports all Azure resource types as soon as they become available.

Syntax Comparison and Learning Curve

PowerShell's syntax is more verbose and procedural, which can be both a strength and a weakness. While it offers granular control, it can also lead to more complex scripts with greater room for error. PowerShell is easier for system administrators familiar with scripting to pick up quickly, especially those coming from a Windows background.

Terraform's HCL syntax is concise and highly readable. The learning curve for new users is manageable, and extensive documentation and examples are available. However, understanding concepts like providers, resources, modules, and state management may require some initial investment.

Bicep offers a shallow learning curve for users already familiar with Azure. Its syntax is the most concise of the three and is purpose-built to simplify the creation of Azure resources. Visual Studio Code with the Bicep extension offers a first-class development experience, including syntax highlighting, autocompletion, and real-time validation.

Ecosystem and Integration

PowerShell's ecosystem is vast, with modules available for nearly every system, application, or cloud provider. This makes it an excellent choice for hybrid environments. For example, a script might automate user provisioning in Active Directory, perform security scans, and deploy cloud infrastructure—all in one workflow.

Terraform supports multi-cloud and hybrid-cloud strategies with its extensive set of providers. This makes it ideal for organizations looking to maintain consistent practices across AWS, Azure, GCP, and more. Terraform Cloud and Terraform Enterprise further extend its capabilities with collaboration features, policy enforcement, and secure state storage.

Bicep is Azure-specific and tightly integrated with the Azure platform. It offers the best experience for organizations that are all-in on Azure, particularly those leveraging Azure DevOps and GitHub Actions for CI/CD. Azure CLI and Azure PowerShell support direct deployment of Bicep files, making automation seamless.

State Management and Idempotency

PowerShell does not maintain infrastructure state inherently. You must handle idempotency and state tracking manually, often by checking for the existence of resources before creating or modifying them. While this provides flexibility, it can lead to more complex and error-prone scripts.

Terraform's state management is one of its core strengths. It tracks the current infrastructure state and determines the minimal changes required to reach the desired configuration. Remote state storage solutions allow teams to collaborate effectively and ensure consistency.

Bicep delegates state management to Azure Resource Manager. As such, deployments are idempotent, and the Azure platform ensures that resources are only changed when necessary. This greatly simplifies repeatable deployments and reduces the likelihood of drift between environments.

Use Case Scenarios

PowerShell is best suited for:
- Hybrid automation involving systems and infrastructure
- Tasks that require conditional logic and looping
- Administrators familiar with Windows environments
- Interfacing with both on-premises and cloud services

Terraform is ideal for:

- Multi-cloud infrastructure provisioning
- Teams requiring collaborative state management
- Reusable infrastructure components via modules
- Scalable, complex cloud environments

Bicep is optimal for:

- Azure-exclusive infrastructure deployments
- Teams leveraging Azure-native tooling
- Developers prioritizing rapid, readable configurations
- Organizations avoiding third-party tooling dependencies

Community and Support

PowerShell has a mature community with extensive documentation, forums, and PowerShell Gallery modules. It is supported by Microsoft and widely adopted in enterprise environments.

Terraform has a large and active open-source community. HashiCorp provides comprehensive documentation, forums, and commercial support through Terraform Cloud. The ecosystem continues to grow rapidly with contributions from the community and cloud providers.

Bicep is newer but benefits from Microsoft's full support and integration into Azure. Its community is growing, and official documentation, tutorials, and GitHub discussions are readily available. Microsoft ensures day-one support for new Azure resources.

Conclusion

PowerShell, Terraform, and Bicep are all powerful tools, but they serve different purposes. PowerShell excels in automation and orchestration across various platforms. Terraform shines in its ability to manage infrastructure declaratively across multiple clouds. Bicep offers an elegant, Azure-native solution for simplifying ARM template development.

Choosing the right tool depends on your environment, your

team's familiarity, and your infrastructure goals. In many cases, these tools can complement each other. For example, PowerShell can trigger Terraform or Bicep deployments as part of a broader automation pipeline. Understanding when and how to use each tool can significantly enhance your ability to manage modern infrastructure efficiently and reliably.

INFRASTRUCTURE DEPLOYMENT USE CASES

Infrastructure deployment is one of the most powerful applications of PowerShell, especially when managing environments at scale. Whether you're provisioning virtual machines (VMs), setting up cloud infrastructure, or configuring on-premises servers, PowerShell offers a versatile, repeatable, and efficient way to automate deployment tasks. In this chapter, we'll explore several real-world infrastructure deployment use cases that highlight the strengths of PowerShell scripting for IT professionals and system administrators.

Azure Resource Deployment Using ARM Templates

Azure Resource Manager (ARM) templates define infrastructure as code. PowerShell enables the deployment of these templates through automation scripts.

Scenario: You need to deploy a web app, SQL database, and storage account into Azure as part of a repeatable CI/CD pipeline.

Solution:

```
$templateFile = "C:\Templates\infrastructure.json"
$resourceGroup = "WebAppRG"
$location = "EastUS"

New-AzResourceGroup -Name $resourceGroup -Location $location
New-AzResourceGroupDeployment -ResourceGroupName $resourceGroup -TemplateFile $templateFile
```

Outcome: Rapid deployment of complex, multi-component Azure solutions with a single command.

311

Automating Domain Controller Promotion

Deploying a new Domain Controller (DC) manually is time-consuming. PowerShell simplifies and speeds up the process.

Scenario: As part of a branch office rollout, a new DC needs to be deployed.

Solution:

```
Install-WindowsFeature -Name AD-Domain-Services -
IncludeManagementTools


Import-Module ADDSDeployment
Install-ADDSDomainController -DomainName "corp.local" -
InstallDns -Credential (Get-Credential) -SiteName
"BranchOffice" -NoGlobalCatalog:$false -Force:$true
```

Outcome: Consistent DC installation that aligns with corporate security and topology standards.

Deploying IIS and Configuring a Web Server

Web server configuration is another excellent use case for deployment automation.

Scenario: A new internal web application requires deployment across 10 servers.

Solution:

```
$servers = @("Web01", "Web02", "Web03", "Web04", "Web05",
"Web06", "Web07", "Web08", "Web09", "Web10")


foreach ($server in $servers) {
    Invoke-Command -ComputerName $server -ScriptBlock {
        Install-WindowsFeature -Name Web-Server -
IncludeManagementTools
        New-Item -Path "C:\inetpub\wwwroot\internalapp" -
ItemType Directory
        Set-Content -Path "C:
\inetpub\wwwroot\internalapp\index.html" -Value
"<h1>Internal Application Deployed</h1>"
    }
}
```

Outcome: All web servers are identically configured and ready to serve traffic.

Provisioning Virtual Machines in Hyper-V

PowerShell allows you to create and configure Hyper-V virtual machines rapidly. Here's how it fits into a deployment use case:

Scenario: Your team needs to set up a test lab with five identical Windows Server VMs.

Solution:

```
$VMNamePrefix = "LabVM"
$VMPath = "D:\VMs"
$VHDPath = "D:\BaseImages\WindowsServer2019.vhdx"
$SwitchName = "InternalSwitch"

for ($i = 1; $i -le 5; $i++) {
    $VMName = "$VMNamePrefix$i"
    New-VM -Name $VMName -MemoryStartupBytes 2GB -VHDPath $VHDPath -Path $VMPath -SwitchName $SwitchName
    Start-VM -Name $VMName
}
```

Outcome: Five fully operational test VMs with minimal effort and consistent configuration.

Infrastructure Configuration with Desired State Configuration (DSC)

DSC enables declarative configurations that continuously enforce compliance.

Scenario: Ensure that a fleet of servers maintains consistent system settings and software.

Solution:

```
Configuration WebServerSetup {
    Node "Server01", "Server02" {
        WindowsFeature WebServer {
            Name = "Web-Server"
            Ensure = "Present"
        }
```

```
        File Homepage {
            DestinationPath = "C:
\inetpub\wwwroot\index.html"
            Contents = "<html><body><h1>Compliant Server</
h1></body></html>"
            Type = "File"
            Ensure = "Present"
        }
    }
}
```

```
WebServerSetup
Start-DscConfiguration -Path .\WebServerSetup -Wait -Verbose
-Force
```

Outcome: Your servers self-heal and stay in a compliant state regardless of drift.

Cloud-Native Infrastructure with Terraform and PowerShell

Terraform is a powerful tool for infrastructure provisioning. Combined with PowerShell, it becomes scriptable and automatable.

Scenario: Automate AWS EC2 instance deployment triggered from a Windows-based pipeline.

Solution:

```
Start-Process -NoNewWindow -FilePath "terraform.exe" -
ArgumentList "init"
Start-Process -NoNewWindow -FilePath "terraform.exe" -
ArgumentList "apply -auto-approve"
```

Outcome: Cross-platform and cross-cloud infrastructure deployment using a consistent PowerShell wrapper.

Multi-Tenant Office 365 Tenant Provisioning

Provisioning Microsoft 365 tenants and configuring policies manually is inefficient. PowerShell helps scale the process.

Scenario: Your MSP onboards multiple new small business clients monthly.

Solution:

```
$tenantDomains = @("client1.com", "client2.com")

foreach ($domain in $tenantDomains) {
    Connect-MsolService
    New-MsolUser -UserPrincipalName "admin@$domain" -
DisplayName "Admin User" -FirstName "Admin" -LastName "User"
-UsageLocation "US" -LicenseAssignment
"contoso:STANDARDPACK"
    Set-MsolUserPassword -UserPrincipalName "admin@$domain"
-NewPassword "P@ssw0rd!" -ForceChangePassword $true
}
```

Outcome: Rapid Office 365 tenant initialization, including users and licensing.

Automating Infrastructure Health Checks Post-Deployment

Infrastructure deployment isn't complete without validation.

Scenario: Ensure all deployed services are reachable and healthy after deployment.

Solution:

```
$servers = Get-Content .\serverlist.txt
foreach ($server in $servers) {
    Test-Connection -ComputerName $server -Count 2 -
ErrorAction SilentlyContinue
    Invoke-Command -ComputerName $server -ScriptBlock {
        Get-Service -Name w3svc
    }
}
```

Outcome: Quick verification that deployment was successful and all key services are operational.

Summary

Infrastructure deployment via PowerShell isn't just about spinning up machines—it's about enabling reliable, repeatable, and scalable environments that support business objectives. From Hyper-V VMs and Azure resources to Office 365 and AWS environments, PowerShell is a universal tool in the modern DevOps and SysAdmin toolkit. Use the scenarios in this chapter as templates, inspiration, or starting points to develop your own automation scripts tailored to your environment.

As you grow in proficiency, you'll find that integrating PowerShell with CI/CD tools, source control, and infrastructure-as-code platforms can unlock massive efficiency gains. PowerShell isn't just for one-off tasks anymore—it's a cornerstone of enterprise-grade automation.

CI/CD and Git Integration

POWERSHELL IN GITHUB ACTIONS AND AZURE DEVOPS

PowerShell has become a cornerstone scripting language for DevOps engineers, system administrators, and developers working within the Microsoft ecosystem. With the evolution of Continuous Integration and Continuous Deployment (CI/CD) practices, tools like GitHub Actions and Azure DevOps have made it easier to automate complex workflows. PowerShell fits perfectly into these environments by providing powerful, consistent scripting capabilities.

In this section, we explore how to leverage PowerShell effectively within GitHub Actions and Azure DevOps. We'll cover basic concepts, real-world scenarios, best practices, and integration tips to help you get the most from your CI/CD pipelines.

Understanding GitHub Actions and Azure DevOps

Before diving into PowerShell specifics, it's important to understand the platforms themselves.

GitHub Actions is GitHub's built-in automation framework that allows you to define workflows triggered by GitHub events, such as pushes, pull requests, or even scheduled cron jobs. These workflows are defined in YAML and executed in virtual environments provided by GitHub.

Azure DevOps offers a more comprehensive suite of development tools, including Boards, Repos, Pipelines, Test Plans, and Artifacts. Azure Pipelines, in particular, provides a robust CI/CD system that supports both YAML and classic visual editor pipelines. Like GitHub Actions, it supports multiple scripting languages including PowerShell.

Why Use PowerShell in CI/CD Pipelines?

PowerShell offers several advantages when used in GitHub Actions or Azure DevOps:

- **Cross-platform compatibility** with PowerShell Core
- **Rich scripting capabilities** with access to .NET libraries
- **Ease of automation** for Windows-centric tasks
- **Consistent syntax and behavior** across environments
- **Direct support for REST APIs and JSON manipulation**

Getting Started with PowerShell in GitHub Actions

Workflow Structure

A typical GitHub Actions workflow is defined in a .yml file inside the .github/workflows/ directory. Here is a basic example of using PowerShell in a GitHub Actions workflow:

```
name: PowerShell CI

on: [push]

jobs:
  build:
    runs-on: windows-latest

    steps:
      - name: Checkout code
        uses: actions/checkout@v3

      - name: Run PowerShell script
        run: |
           Write-Host "Running PowerShell from GitHub
Actions"
           Get-ChildItem -Path .
        shell: pwsh
```

Tips for GitHub Actions

- Always specify shell: pwsh to ensure that PowerShell Core is used.

- Use the windows-latest runner if your script depends on Windows features.
- Secrets can be accessed using the $env:GITHUB_TOKEN or custom secret environment variables.
- You can include inline scripts or reference .ps1 files stored in your repo.

PowerShell in Azure DevOps Pipelines

YAML Pipeline Example

Here's how you can include PowerShell in an Azure DevOps YAML pipeline:

```
trigger:
  branches:
    include:
      - main

pool:
  vmImage: 'windows-latest'

steps:
- task: PowerShell@2
  inputs:
    targetType: 'inline'
    script: |
      Write-Output "Running PowerShell in Azure DevOps"
      Get-Date
```

Classic Pipeline Integration

In a classic (GUI-based) pipeline, you can:
- Add a "PowerShell Script" task
- Choose between inline script or file path
- Configure error handling and logging options

Tips for Azure DevOps
- Azure DevOps provides both PowerShell@1 and PowerShell@2 tasks; the latter supports PowerShell Core.
- You can store and access secrets using Azure Key Vault or pipeline variables.
- Use Write-Host for colorized logging or Write-Output for clean

- Consider modularizing scripts and placing them in a shared repository or feed.

Use Cases for PowerShell in CI/CD

Build Automation

PowerShell can be used to compile code, run linters, or transform configuration files.

Test Orchestration

You can run unit tests, integration tests, or even UI tests with frameworks like Pester.

Infrastructure Automation

Use PowerShell to interact with Azure resources via Azure PowerShell or the Az CLI.

Artifact Management

Download or upload build artifacts, generate version tags, or archive logs.

Deployment Automation

Push builds to servers, run database migrations, and manage application lifecycles.

PowerShell and Secrets Management

When automating tasks, handling secrets securely is critical.

GitHub Actions Secrets

- Define secrets in your repository settings.
- Access them in scripts using environment variables.
- Example: $env:MY_SECRET

Azure DevOps Secrets

- Use the built-in variable group features.
- Store secrets in Azure Key Vault and link to pipelines.
- Example: $(mySecret) in YAML will be replaced at runtime.

Avoid hardcoding any sensitive data in your scripts or YAML

files.

Best Practices

Use Modular Scripts

Avoid writing long inline scripts. Instead, commit .ps1 scripts and call them with ./script.ps1.

Error Handling

Implement try/catch blocks and set $ErrorActionPreference = 'Stop' to catch failures early.

Logging

Use Write-Host, Write-Verbose, and Write-Warning to add clarity to logs. Azure DevOps and GitHub Actions support colored outputs.

Testing

Use tools like Pester to write tests for your PowerShell modules and run them in your pipeline.

Versioning

Pin versions of tools, modules, and actions to avoid breaking changes.

Advanced Tips

Use PowerShell Modules

Load custom or community modules from the PowerShell Gallery using Install-Module. You can cache these steps in GitHub Actions or Azure DevOps to improve performance.

```
Install-Module -Name Az -Scope CurrentUser -Force
```

REST API Integration

PowerShell's Invoke-RestMethod makes it easy to integrate with external APIs.

```
$response = Invoke-RestMethod -Uri "https://api.example.com"
-Headers @{ Authorization = "Bearer $token" }
```

Multi-Platform Support

PowerShell Core runs on Windows, Linux, and macOS. Structure your workflows to be OS-agnostic where possible.

```
runs-on: ${{ matrix.os }}
strategy:
```

```
matrix:
    os: [windows-latest, ubuntu-latest, macos-latest]
```

Secure File Handling

When using secrets or configuration files, always delete them securely after use.

```
Remove-Item -Path "./config.json" -Force
```

Conclusion

PowerShell brings flexibility, power, and consistency to CI/CD workflows in both GitHub Actions and Azure DevOps. Whether you're deploying infrastructure, running tests, or packaging applications, PowerShell offers a scriptable, maintainable approach to automation. By combining PowerShell with these modern DevOps tools, you can create robust, secure, and efficient pipelines that accelerate your development lifecycle.

The key to success is modularization, secure practices, and continuous learning. By mastering PowerShell in CI/CD contexts, you're not just writing scripts — you're building the backbone of modern DevOps automation.

SCRIPTING CODE PIPELINES

In modern DevOps practices, automation is key to maintaining a streamlined and efficient software delivery process. One of the most critical components in this ecosystem is the **code pipeline**. A code pipeline automates the build, test, and deployment phases of your application, ensuring consistency, speed, and reliability. With PowerShell, you can script these pipelines effectively, integrating seamlessly with various tools and platforms. This chapter explores how to script code pipelines using PowerShell, covering concepts, tools, examples, and best practices.

Understanding Code Pipelines

A **code pipeline** is a series of automated steps that software goes through on its way to being released. The main stages typically include:

1. **Source** – Where your code resides (e.g., GitHub, Bitbucket, Azure Repos).
2. **Build** – Compiling the code, running linters, and packaging.
3. **Test** – Running automated tests such as unit tests or integration tests.
4. **Deploy** – Moving the code to environments like staging or production.

Automation ensures that each stage executes consistently and quickly. PowerShell scripts can be integrated at every stage to facilitate and customize operations.

Why Use PowerShell for Code Pipelines?

PowerShell is a powerful scripting language that is:

- **Cross-platform** (PowerShell Core)
- **Extensible** through modules and community tools
- **Easily integrated** with CI/CD tools (e.g., Azure DevOps, GitHub Actions, Jenkins)
- **Capable of accessing APIs, system functions, and cloud resources**

PowerShell is especially useful in Windows environments but is also robust enough for Linux/macOS operations via PowerShell Core.

Building Blocks of a PowerShell Code Pipeline

To create a PowerShell-based code pipeline, you should structure your script with modular, testable components:

1. **Functions** – Reusable blocks for common tasks (e.g., Build-App, Run-Tests, Deploy-App)
2. **Configuration Files** – Store environment variables and secrets securely.
3. **Logging and Error Handling** – Capture outputs and track failures.
4. **Parameterization** – Accept dynamic input for flexibility.

Example function structure:

```
function Build-App {
    param (
        [string]$SourcePath,
        [string]$BuildOutputPath
    )

    Write-Output "Building app from $SourcePath..."
    # Simulate build
    Copy-Item -Path "$SourcePath\*" -Destination
$BuildOutputPath -Recurse
    Write-Output "Build complete. Output in
$BuildOutputPath"
}
```

Example Pipeline Script

Here is a simplified example of a PowerShell script that simulates a code pipeline:

```
param (
    [string]$RepoUrl,
    [string]$BuildDir = "C:\Build",
    [string]$TestScript = "C:\Tests\RunTests.ps1",
    [string]$DeployScript = "C:\Deploy\DeployApp.ps1"
)

function Clone-Repository {
    Write-Output "Cloning repository from $RepoUrl..."
    git clone $RepoUrl $BuildDir
}

function Run-Build {
    Write-Output "Running build..."
    # Insert build logic here
}

function Run-Tests {
    Write-Output "Running tests..."
    & $TestScript
}
```

```
function Deploy-App {
    Write-Output "Deploying application..."
    & $DeployScript
}

try {
    Clone-Repository
    Run-Build
    Run-Tests
    Deploy-App
    Write-Output "Pipeline execution complete."
} catch {
    Write-Error "Pipeline failed: $_"
    exit 1
}
```

This script outlines a basic four-step pipeline and highlights modular function usage and error handling.

Integrating with CI/CD Platforms

Azure DevOps

Azure DevOps pipelines can execute PowerShell scripts using the built-in task:

```
- task: PowerShell@2
  inputs:
    targetType: 'filePath'
    filePath: 'scripts\build.ps1'
```

Ensure your PowerShell script uses parameters to accept inputs from the pipeline YAML.

GitHub Actions

GitHub Actions allows you to run PowerShell using the pwsh shell:

```
jobs:
  build:
    runs-on: windows-latest
    steps:
      - name: Checkout code
```

```
uses: actions/checkout@v2

- name: Run PowerShell Script
  run: ./scripts/build.ps1
  shell: pwsh
```

Jenkins

You can invoke PowerShell scripts in Jenkins pipelines using:

```
powershell '''
  ./scripts/build.ps1
'''
```

Be sure to install the PowerShell plugin for Jenkins first.

Security Considerations

When scripting code pipelines with PowerShell, keep the following in mind:

- **Secrets Management**: Use secure variables or secret stores (e.g., Azure Key Vault, GitHub Secrets).
- **Execution Policy**: Ensure execution policies allow your script to run in your CI environment.
- **Input Validation**: Validate all user input to prevent injection attacks.
- **Error Handling**: Use try/catch and log all exceptions.

Advanced Features

Parallel Execution

Use PowerShell Jobs or ForEach-Object -Parallel (in PowerShell 7+) to run tasks concurrently:

```
$tasks = 1..3 | ForEach-Object -Parallel {
    Start-Sleep -Seconds $_
    "Task $_ complete"
}
```

API Integration

Use Invoke-RestMethod or Invoke-WebRequest to interact with external services:

```
$response = Invoke-RestMethod -Uri "https://api.example.com/
```

```
builds" -Method Post -Body $jsonData
```

Best Practices

- Keep scripts modular and reusable
- Use consistent naming conventions
- Log all important events and errors
- Store pipeline scripts in version control
- Test scripts in isolated environments before production use

Conclusion

Scripting code pipelines with PowerShell enables powerful, flexible automation across development workflows. By modularizing functionality, integrating with CI/CD tools, and implementing robust error handling and security practices, PowerShell can become the backbone of your automated deployment strategy. Whether deploying to local servers, cloud environments, or hybrid infrastructures, PowerShell equips you with the tools to script your entire delivery lifecycle efficiently and effectively.

In the next chapter, we'll explore how to **monitor your scripts and deployments using logs and alerting systems**, ensuring transparency and rapid response to failures.

USING GIT IN POWERSHELL

Version control is an essential component of modern software development, and Git has become the de facto standard for managing source code across projects, teams, and organizations. PowerShell, with its robust scripting capabilities and deep integration with the Windows operating system, provides an ideal environment for interacting with Git. In this section, we will explore how to use Git within PowerShell, covering setup, common commands, scripting workflows, and automation strategies.

Introduction to Git and PowerShell Integration

Git is a distributed version control system designed to track changes in source code during software development. While Git itself is command-line based, it can be easily integrated into PowerShell workflows, offering both flexibility and power. Whether you're managing your own scripts, contributing to open source, or collaborating in a corporate environment, using Git in PowerShell can streamline your development process.

PowerShell, on the other hand, is a task automation framework consisting of a command-line shell and scripting language. It is particularly powerful for system administrators and developers working on Windows environments, although it is also available cross-platform.

Installing Git for PowerShell

Before you can use Git in PowerShell, you need to install Git for Windows:

1. Visit https://git-scm.com and download the latest version for Windows.
2. Run the installer and accept the default options. Be sure to select the option that adds Git to your system PATH.
3. After installation, open PowerShell and type git --version to verify that Git is properly installed and available from your terminal.

Additionally, consider installing Windows Terminal from the Microsoft Store for a more enhanced terminal experience.

Configuring Git in PowerShell

Once Git is installed, the next step is to configure it with your user information. This ensures your commits are correctly attributed.

```
# Set your name
git config --global user.name "Your Name"
```

```
# Set your email
git config --global user.email "youremail@example.com"
```
You can verify your configuration with:
```
git config --list
```
These settings are stored in a .gitconfig file in your user profile directory and apply globally unless overridden in a specific repository.

Basic Git Commands in PowerShell

Once Git is set up, you can begin using it directly in PowerShell. Here are some of the most commonly used commands:

Cloning a Repository
```
git clone https://github.com/username/repository.git
```
This command copies the repository to your local machine.

Checking Repository Status
```
git status
```
This shows the current state of the working directory and staging area.

Adding Changes
```
git add .
```
Adds all modified and new files to the staging area.

Committing Changes
```
git commit -m "Your commit message"
```
Commits the staged changes with a message.

Pushing Changes
```
git push origin main
```
Sends your commits to the remote repository.

Pulling Updates
```
git pull origin main
```
Fetches and merges changes from the remote repository.

Creating and Switching Branches

Working with branches is a core part of Git workflows:

Create a New Branch

```
git checkout -b feature/new-feature
```
Switch to an Existing Branch
```
git checkout develop
```
Merge a Branch
```
git checkout main
git merge feature/new-feature
```

Git Aliases in PowerShell

To save time, you can create aliases in PowerShell for your frequently used Git commands:
```
Set-Alias gs git status
Set-Alias ga git add
Set-Alias gc git commit
Set-Alias gp git push
```
To make these persistent, add them to your PowerShell profile script (usually located at $PROFILE).

Using Git in PowerShell Scripts

PowerShell scripts can call Git commands just like any other executable. This is useful for automation, CI/CD workflows, and bulk operations.

Example: Automating Git Pull and Build
```
$repoPath = "C:\Projects\MyRepo"
cd $repoPath

# Pull latest changes
git pull origin main

# Build the project
.\build.ps1
```
This script ensures your repository is up-to-date before running a build script.

Git Credential Management

When using Git over HTTPS, you'll often need to authenticate.

Credential Manager integration on Windows can store your credentials:

1. During the first push, Git will prompt for your credentials.
2. You can choose to remember them via the credential manager.
3. Alternatively, use SSH for a more secure, seamless experience.

Setting Up SSH

```
ssh-keygen -t ed25519 -C "youremail@example.com"
```

Add the key to your Git provider (e.g., GitHub) and test it:

```
ssh -T git@github.com
```

Git GUIs and PowerShell

While command-line Git is powerful, you may also want to use GUI tools such as:

- **Git GUI**: Installed with Git for Windows.
- **Sourcetree**: A free Git GUI from Atlassian.
- **GitKraken**: Cross-platform Git GUI.

These tools can be used alongside PowerShell workflows to provide a visual representation of repositories.

Handling Merge Conflicts in PowerShell

Merge conflicts can occur during collaboration. Git will notify you and mark the conflicted files. To resolve them:

1. Open the conflicting files.
2. Edit to resolve conflicts, then save.
3. Mark the conflict as resolved:

   git add filename
4. Commit the merge:

   git commit

You can also configure a merge tool like VS Code to help with resolving conflicts:

```
git config --global merge.tool vscode
git config --global mergetool.vscode.cmd "code --wait
$MERGED"
```

Using Modules: posh-git

Posh-Git is a PowerShell module that enhances the Git experience:

Install posh-git

```
Install-Module posh-git -Scope CurrentUser
```

Import it into your session

```
Import-Module posh-git
```

It provides tab completion, enhanced prompt info, and Git status indicators directly in your PowerShell prompt.

Automating Workflows with Git Hooks

Git hooks allow you to automate tasks during Git events like commits or pushes.

Example: Pre-commit Hook

Create a script at .git/hooks/pre-commit:

```
#!/bin/sh
pwsh ./scripts/lint.ps1
```

Make it executable:

```
chmod +x .git/hooks/pre-commit
```

This runs your PowerShell linter before each commit.

Best Practices for Using Git in PowerShell

- **Commit Often**: Small, focused commits make history easier to manage.
- **Write Meaningful Messages**: Describe what and why, not just how.
- **Use Branches**: Avoid working on main for new features.
- **Sync Regularly**: Pull before pushing to avoid conflicts.
- **Secure Your Credentials**: Use SSH or credential managers.
- **Leverage Aliases and Scripts**: Save time with automation.

Conclusion

Using Git in PowerShell unlocks the full potential of both tools for managing your scripts, infrastructure-as-code, and development projects. By combining Git's powerful version control capabilities with PowerShell's scripting and automation features, you can create efficient, repeatable, and collaborative workflows.

Whether you're a solo developer, a systems administrator, or part of a large team, mastering Git in PowerShell is a crucial step in becoming a more effective technologist. Embrace it, script it, and automate your way to a smoother development experience.

Modules and Script Organization

CREATING, IMPORTING, AND PUBLISHING MODULES

PowerShell modules are essential building blocks for organizing reusable scripts and functions. As your scripting skill evolves, the ability to create, import, and publish your own modules becomes vital for scalable automation, code reuse, and professional development. In this chapter, we will explore everything you need to know to get started with PowerShell modules.

What Is a PowerShell Module?

A PowerShell module is a package that contains PowerShell code in the form of functions, cmdlets, variables, and workflows. Modules help encapsulate logic and make it portable, manageable, and reusable across different projects or environments.

There are several types of modules:

- **Script Modules** (.psm1) — These are the most common and contain plain PowerShell scripts.
- **Binary Modules** — Written in C# or another .NET language, compiled into DLLs.
- **Manifest Modules** (.psd1) — Contain metadata about the module, such as version, dependencies, and author information.
- **Dynamic Modules** — Created at runtime using New-Module.

For beginners, script and manifest modules are most relevant.

Creating a Script Module

To begin, we'll create a simple script module that contains a couple of functions.

Step 1: Create the Module Folder

Every module should live in its own directory named after the

module.
```
New-Item -Path
"$HOME\Documents\PowerShell\Modules\MyFirstModule" -ItemType
Directory
```

Step 2: Write the Functions

Create a .psm1 file. This file will hold your functions:
```
# File: MyFirstModule.psm1

function Get-HelloWorld {
    return "Hello, World!"
}

function Get-DateFormatted {
    param(
        [string]$Format = "yyyy-MM-dd"
    )
    return (Get-Date).ToString($Format)
}
```

Save this file inside your module folder as MyFirstModule.psm1.

Creating a Module Manifest

A manifest is a .psd1 file that describes the contents of your module and helps manage dependencies and compatibility.

Step 1: Generate the Manifest

Use the New-ModuleManifest cmdlet:
```
New-ModuleManifest -Path
"$HOME\Documents\PowerShell\Modules\MyFirstModule\MyFirstMod
ule.psd1" `
                    -RootModule "MyFirstModule.psm1" `
                    -Author "Your Name" `
                    -Description "A simple module for
demonstration purposes"
                    -ModuleVersion "1.0.0"
```

This creates a manifest file with metadata, which PowerShell uses when loading and managing modules.

Step 2: Review the Manifest File

Open the .psd1 file. You'll see fields like:

```
@{
    RootModule          = 'MyFirstModule.psm1'
    ModuleVersion       = '1.0.0'
    GUID                = '...'  # Unique identifier
    Author              = 'Your Name'
    Description         = 'A simple module for demonstration
purposes'
    FunctionsToExport = @('Get-HelloWorld', 'Get-
DateFormatted')
    CmdletsToExport   = @()
    VariablesToExport = @()
    AliasesToExport   = @()
}
```

Fill in or adjust these fields as needed.

Importing a Module

After creating a module, you can import it manually or automatically.

Importing Manually

Use Import-Module:

```
Import-Module
"$HOME\Documents\PowerShell\Modules\MyFirstModule\MyFirstMod
ule.psm1"
```

You can confirm it loaded using Get-Module:

```
Get-Module -Name MyFirstModule
```

Importing Automatically

Place the module in one of the paths listed in $env:PSModulePath. For example:

```
$env:PSModulePath -split ';'
```

Putting the module in Documents\PowerShell\Modules ensures it is available for automatic loading when you call any exported function.

Testing Your Module

Once imported, test your functions:

```
Get-HelloWorld
Get-DateFormatted -Format 'MM/dd/yyyy'
```

If the module is well-written and your functions are defined correctly, you'll see the expected outputs.

Versioning and Updating Modules

As your module evolves, versioning helps manage dependencies and deployments.

Updating Version Number

Each time you make a significant change:

1. Update the version in the .psd1 manifest.
2. Consider following Semantic Versioning: MAJOR.MINOR.PATCH.

For example:

- 1.0.0 – Initial release
- 1.1.0 – New function added
- 1.1.1 – Bug fix

Changelog File

Maintain a CHANGELOG.md file to document updates. This is especially helpful when publishing or collaborating.

Publishing Modules

Publishing your module makes it accessible to others. PowerShell modules are typically published to the PowerShell Gallery.

Step 1: Set Up PowerShellGet

Ensure you have the PowerShellGet module:

```
Install-Module -Name PowerShellGet -Force -AllowClobber
```

Step 2: Register and Authenticate

Create an account at PowerShellGallery.com.

Authenticate with an API key:

```
Set-PSRepository -Name 'PSGallery' -InstallationPolicy Trusted
Publish-Module -Path 'C:\Path\To\MyFirstModule' -NuGetApiKey 'your-api-key'
```

Note: Store API keys securely using credential managers or

environment variables.

Step 3: Verify Upload

Search for your module:

```
Find-Module -Name MyFirstModule
```

Best Practices for Module Development

To ensure your modules are maintainable and reliable, follow these guidelines:

- **Consistent Naming**: Use verb-noun format (Get-, Set-, Invoke-).
- **Comment-Based Help**: Add help comments to all functions.
- **Export Explicitly**: Only export functions you want to expose.
- **Use Manifest Metadata**: Document author, version, and compatibility.
- **Write Tests**: Validate functions using Pester or other test frameworks.
- **Avoid Hardcoding Paths**: Use $PSScriptRoot for relative paths.

Troubleshooting Tips

- **Module Not Loading?**
  - Check $env:PSModulePath.
  - Ensure manifest and .psm1 file are present.
- **Functions Not Found?**
  - Ensure they are defined in the .psm1 file.
  - Confirm FunctionsToExport in the manifest.
- **Cannot Publish?**
  - Check for missing metadata.
  - Validate module with Test-ModuleManifest.

Summary

Modules transform your PowerShell scripts into scalable, reusable components. By mastering the creation, importing, and publishing of modules, you empower yourself to build more robust automation solutions and contribute to the broader PowerShell ecosystem. Whether for personal productivity, team collaboration, or public sharing, knowing how to develop and manage modules is a key milestone in becoming an advanced PowerShell scripter.

Start simple, follow best practices, and with time, your modules will become invaluable tools in your scripting toolkit.

STRUCTURING SCRIPTS FOR REUSE

In PowerShell scripting, the ability to reuse code is one of the most valuable practices you can develop. Whether you're a solo admin managing a few servers or part of a DevOps team responsible for complex infrastructures, reusable scripts enhance efficiency, maintainability, scalability, and collaboration. This chapter focuses on how to properly structure PowerShell scripts for maximum reusability.

Why Reusability Matters

Reusable scripts allow you to write code once and use it in multiple contexts, saving time and reducing errors. This practice also encourages consistency across your scripts and systems. Here are some of the core benefits:

- **Time Efficiency:** Reuse reduces the need to rewrite code.
- **Consistency:** Standard functions provide uniform behavior.
- **Easier Maintenance:** Fixes and updates need only be made in one place.
- **Scalability:** A well-structured script can easily scale to larger tasks.
- **Collaboration:** Team members can understand and build upon reusable components.

Fundamental Principles of Reusability

Before diving into structure, it's important to understand the core

principles behind reusable scripts:
1. **Modularity:** Break scripts into smaller, focused components.
2. **Encapsulation:** Each script or function should handle a single responsibility.
3. **Parameterization:** Avoid hardcoding. Instead, use parameters to make scripts flexible.
4. **Documentation:** Properly document your scripts and functions.
5. **Version Control:** Maintain a version history and track changes for future reuse.

Building Blocks of Reusable Scripts

Functions First

Reusable scripts almost always revolve around functions. These are modular blocks that encapsulate logic and can be invoked anywhere.

```
function Get-DiskSpace {
    param(
        [string]$ComputerName = $env:COMPUTERNAME
    )
    Get-WmiObject -Class Win32_LogicalDisk -ComputerName
$ComputerName -Filter "DriveType=3" |
    Select-Object DeviceID,
@{Name='FreeSpace(GB)';Expression={"{0:N2}" -f ($_.FreeSpace
/ 1GB)}}
}
```

This function can be copied into other scripts or saved in a module.

Script Layout

A typical reusable script should follow this structure:

```
<### SCRIPT HEADER ###>
# Script Name: ExampleScript.ps1
# Description: Describe what it does
# Author: Your Name
# Version: 1.0
# Last Modified: Date
<####################>

# Import Modules
```

```
Import-Module MyCustomFunctions

# Define Parameters
param(
    [string]$TargetServer,
    [string]$OutputPath
)


# Main Logic
Initialize-Logging -Path $OutputPath
$data = Get-ServerData -Server $TargetServer
Export-Data -InputObject $data -Path $OutputPath
```

Each part is logically separated, making it easy to understand, maintain, and reuse.

Parameter Blocks

Avoid using hardcoded values. Instead, make your scripts accept parameters:

```
param(
    [Parameter(Mandatory=$true)]
    [string]$ComputerName,

    [Parameter(Mandatory=$false)]
    [switch]$Verbose
)
```

This allows the script to be used in different contexts without editing the code.

Creating Script Modules

When you find yourself copying functions between scripts, it's time to make a module. A PowerShell module is simply a .psm1 file containing your functions, which can then be imported into any script.

Step 1: Create a .psm1 file.

```
# MyUtilities.psm1
function Get-SystemInfo {
    Get-ComputerInfo
}
```

```
function Restart-Services {
    param([string[]]$ServiceNames)
    foreach ($service in $ServiceNames) {
        Restart-Service -Name $service -Force
    }
}
```

Step 2: Create a module manifest with New-ModuleManifest.

```
New-ModuleManifest -Path .\MyUtilities.psd1 -RootModule
'MyUtilities.psm1' -Author 'Your Name'
```

Step 3: Import the module in your script.

```
Import-Module .\MyUtilities.psd1
```

Now you can use Get-SystemInfo and Restart-Services anywhere.

Logging and Error Handling

Reusable scripts should include standard logging and error handling to ensure they work reliably in any environment.

```
function Write-Log {
    param(
        [string]$Message,
        [string]$Level = 'INFO'
    )
    $timestamp = Get-Date -Format 'yyyy-MM-dd HH:mm:ss'
    "$timestamp [$Level] $Message" | Out-File -Append -
FilePath "C:\Logs\script.log"
}
```

Error handling can be added via try/catch/finally blocks:

```
try {
    Restart-Service -Name 'Spooler' -ErrorAction Stop
    Write-Log -Message 'Spooler service restarted
successfully.'
} catch {
    Write-Log -Message $_.Exception.Message -Level 'ERROR'
}
```

External Configuration Files

To maximize reuse, extract configuration data (e.g., paths, server names, credentials) into a separate file like a .json or .xml.

Example config.json:

```
{
    "Servers": ["Server1", "Server2"],
    "LogPath": "C:\Logs",
    "OutputDirectory": "C:\Output"
}
```

Load it in PowerShell:

```
$config = Get-Content -Path .\config.json | ConvertFrom-Json
foreach ($server in $config.Servers) {
    Test-Connection -ComputerName $server
}
```

Naming Conventions and Documentation

Use clear, consistent naming for your functions and scripts. Prefix functions with verbs and nouns (e.g., Get-, Set-, Start-, Stop-):

- Good: Get-UserList, Start-BackupJob
- Bad: UserListFunction, BackupStart

Also, every function should have a comment-based help block:

```
function Get-UserList {
<#
.SYNOPSIS
    Retrieves a list of users from Active Directory.
.DESCRIPTION
    This function queries Active Directory and returns all
user objects.
.EXAMPLE
    Get-UserList -OU 'Sales'
#>
    param([string]$OU)
    # Logic here
}
```

Testing and Validation

Reusable scripts should include logic to validate input and ensure they're running in the expected environment:

```
if (-not (Test-Path $OutputPath)) {
    throw "Output path does not exist: $OutputPath"
}


if (-not (Get-Module -ListAvailable -Name
'ActiveDirectory')) {
    throw "Required module 'ActiveDirectory' is not
installed."
}
```

Consider creating unit tests using Pester for critical functions.

Summary

Structuring PowerShell scripts for reuse is about more than just convenience—it's a cornerstone of professional scripting. By following best practices like modularization, parameterization, using modules, externalizing configurations, and maintaining clear documentation, you ensure your scripts are flexible, reliable, and useful in a variety of contexts.

In the long run, these habits save time, reduce bugs, and foster a collaborative environment where your scripts can serve not only your needs but your team's and your organization's. Start small by refactoring your commonly used logic into functions and modules, and over time, you'll build a powerful toolkit that you can rely on for years to come.

Advanced Data Structures

WORKING WITH JSON AND XML

When working with PowerShell, especially in the context of automation, systems administration, or data exchange, two of the most common formats you'll encounter are JSON (JavaScript Object Notation) and XML (eXtensible Markup Language). Both formats are widely used for storing, transmitting, and structuring data. In this section, we will explore how PowerShell can work with these formats, parse them, create them, and manipulate their contents. Understanding how to interact with JSON and XML is essential for any PowerShell scripter.

Introduction to JSON and XML

JSON is a lightweight data-interchange format that is easy for humans to read and write and easy for machines to parse and generate. It is most commonly used in web APIs and configuration files. It represents data as key-value pairs and supports arrays and nested objects.

XML, on the other hand, is a markup language that defines a set of rules for encoding documents in a format both human-readable and machine-readable. XML is widely used in older systems and applications, especially in enterprise environments.

Reading and Parsing JSON in PowerShell

One of the easiest ways to work with JSON in PowerShell is to convert a JSON string into a PowerShell object using the ConvertFrom-Json cmdlet.

```
$json = '{"name": "John", "age": 30, "isEmployee": true}'
$person = $json | ConvertFrom-Json
```

```
Write-Output $person.name  # Outputs: John
```

Once converted, the $person variable becomes a PowerShell custom object, and you can access its properties just like any other object.

To read JSON from a file, you can use:

```
$jsonContent = Get-Content -Path 'C:\data\person.json' -Raw
$person = $jsonContent | ConvertFrom-Json
```

The -Raw flag ensures the file content is read as a single string, which is necessary for proper JSON parsing.

Creating JSON from PowerShell Objects

You can convert PowerShell objects into JSON strings using ConvertTo-Json.

```
$person = [PSCustomObject]@{
    name       = "Alice"
    age        = 28
    isEmployee = $true
}


$json = $person | ConvertTo-Json
Write-Output $json
```

To save this JSON to a file:

```
$person | ConvertTo-Json | Out-File -FilePath 'C:
\data\person.json'
```

This is extremely useful for exporting configuration settings or storing structured data from a script.

Working with Nested JSON

JSON objects can be deeply nested. PowerShell handles these gracefully by creating nested custom objects.

```
$json = '{"user": {"name": "Bob", "contact": {"email":
"bob@example.com"}}}'
$obj = $json | ConvertFrom-Json
Write-Output $obj.user.contact.email  # Outputs:
bob@example.com
```

You can manipulate nested structures using standard dot notation.

346

Dealing with Arrays in JSON

When JSON contains arrays, PowerShell treats them as object arrays.

```
$json = '{"employees": [ {"name": "Alice"}, {"name": "Bob"}
]}'
$data = $json | ConvertFrom-Json

foreach ($employee in $data.employees) {
    Write-Output $employee.name
}
```

This makes it easy to loop over items and perform bulk operations.

Reading and Parsing XML in PowerShell

PowerShell includes native support for XML through the [xml] type accelerator.

```
[xml]$xml = Get-Content -Path 'C:\data\example.xml'
Write-Output $xml.catalog.book[0].title
```

XML files can be deeply nested and often use attributes. Here's an example of reading XML content with attributes:

```
[xml]$xml = '<user id="123"><name>Jane</name><role>Admin</
role></user>'
Write-Output $xml.user.name
Write-Output $xml.user.role
Write-Output $xml.user.id  # May not work for attributes
```

To access attributes properly:

```
Write-Output $xml.user.'id'
```

Creating XML from PowerShell Objects

While JSON creation is straightforward in PowerShell, creating XML is more involved. You generally build an XML document using the System.Xml.XmlDocument class.

```
$xmlDoc = New-Object System.Xml.XmlDocument
$root = $xmlDoc.CreateElement("users")
$user = $xmlDoc.CreateElement("user")
```

```
$name = $xmlDoc.CreateElement("name")
$name.InnerText = "Alice"
$user.AppendChild($name)

$root.AppendChild($user)
$xmlDoc.AppendChild($root)
$xmlDoc.Save("C:\data\users.xml")
```

This method provides full control over the structure of your XML document.

Navigating XML with XPath

XPath is a language used for navigating through elements and attributes in XML documents. PowerShell allows you to use XPath queries on XML objects.

```
[xml]$xml = Get-Content -Path 'C:\data\example.xml'
$nodes = $xml.SelectNodes("//book[price>30]")
foreach ($node in $nodes) {
    Write-Output $node.title
}
```

XPath can dramatically simplify complex XML queries.

Converting Between JSON and XML

There is no built-in, seamless way to convert between JSON and XML in PowerShell because the formats differ fundamentally. However, you can manually convert by reading one format into an object and writing it out in the other format, bearing in mind structural differences.

```
# JSON to XML (simple example)
$json = '{"name": "Eve", "age": 34}'
$obj = $json | ConvertFrom-Json
```

```
$xmlDoc = New-Object System.Xml.XmlDocument
$root = $xmlDoc.CreateElement("person")
foreach ($property in $obj.PSObject.Properties) {
    $element = $xmlDoc.CreateElement($property.Name)
    $element.InnerText = $property.Value
    $root.AppendChild($element)
}
$xmlDoc.AppendChild($root)
$xmlDoc.Save("C:\data\person.xml")
```

This conversion requires building the XML structure manually.

Common Pitfalls and Tips

1. **JSON Depth**: PowerShell's ConvertTo-Json has a default depth of 2. Use the -Depth parameter to ensure deeper structures are fully serialized.

```
ConvertTo-Json -Depth 10
```

2. **Character Encoding**: Ensure the encoding of your input and output files is UTF-8 for maximum compatibility.
3. **XML Namespaces**: If your XML documents use namespaces, you'll need to handle those explicitly when querying with XPath. Use XmlNamespaceManager to manage them.
4. **Performance**: Parsing large JSON or XML files can be slow. In these cases, consider using streaming techniques or filtering the file before parsing.
5. **Validation**: Always validate input data when consuming JSON or XML from external sources to avoid injection or malformed content errors.

Summary

PowerShell's native support for JSON and XML makes it an excellent tool for systems integration, configuration management, and data transformation tasks. Whether you're consuming a REST API, managing a legacy configuration file, or automating cross-system communication, mastering JSON and XML handling in PowerShell equips you to deal with real-world scenarios effectively. As you progress, you'll find yourself combining these techniques with other PowerShell capabilities to build more powerful and flexible automation scripts.

NESTED HASHTABLES, CUSTOM OBJECTS

When working with PowerShell, you'll often find yourself needing to represent complex data structures. Whether it's hierarchical data, configuration settings, or the output from a script that should resemble a report, two essential tools come into play: **nested hashtables** and **custom objects**. This section provides a deep dive into these topics, exploring how they work, how to use them effectively, and practical scenarios that demonstrate their power in scripting.

Understanding Hashtables

A **hashtable** in PowerShell is a collection of key-value pairs, offering a simple way to store data where each item has a unique identifier (key). You define a hashtable using the @{} syntax:

```
$person = @{
    FirstName = "John"
    LastName = "Doe"
    Age = 30
}
```

Each key (e.g., FirstName, LastName, Age) maps to a specific value. Hashtables are flexible and support dynamic keys and values of any data type.

Introduction to Nested Hashtables

A **nested hashtable** is simply a hashtable within a hashtable. This allows for the representation of more complex structures, akin to JSON objects or dictionaries in other programming languages.

Example of a Nested Hashtable:

```
$employee = @{
    Name = "Alice"
    Department = @{
        Name = "IT"
        Location = "Building 1"
    }
    Contact = @{
        Email = "alice@example.com"
        Phone = "555-1234"
    }
}
```

Here, Department and Contact are themselves hashtables stored as values in the outer employee hashtable. Accessing nested data is straightforward:

```
$employee.Contact.Email  # Returns "alice@example.com"
```

Nested hashtables are ideal when modeling data that has multiple layers or when parsing structured output like JSON.

Practical Uses of Nested Hashtables

Configuration Files

One common use case is representing configuration data:

```
$config = @{
    Server = @{
        Hostname = "web01"
        Port = 443
    }
    Database = @{
        Name = "InventoryDB"
        User = "admin"
        Password = "P@ssw0rd"
    }
}
```

This kind of structure can be easily serialized to JSON or XML for configuration storage or communication with other systems.

User Profiles

In Active Directory scripting, you may need to build complex user profiles programmatically:

```
$userProfile = @{
    Username = "jsmith"
    Attributes = @{
        FirstName = "John"
        LastName = "Smith"
        Department = "Finance"
    }
    AccessRights = @{
        Mailbox = $true
        VPN = $false
        FileShare = $true
    }
}
```

Such structures allow for cleaner, readable, and maintainable code.

Limitations of Nested Hashtables

While nested hashtables are powerful, they lack the strong structure and clarity of **custom objects**, especially when passing data between functions or outputting to a report. This is where custom objects shine.

Custom Objects in PowerShell

PowerShell allows you to define your own objects using [PSCustomObject]. These objects are more structured and provide better integration with cmdlets that expect objects.

Creating a Simple Custom Object

```
$person = [PSCustomObject]@{
    FirstName = "John"
    LastName = "Doe"
    Age = 30
}
```

This is visually similar to a hashtable, but it creates a formal object with named properties. You can pass it through the pipeline, export it to CSV, JSON, or XML, and use it in reporting scripts more naturally than hashtables.

Nested Custom Objects

Just like hashtables, you can nest custom objects inside other custom objects. This is useful when working with structured data that should be treated as actual objects, not key-value stores.

Example:

```
$department = [PSCustomObject]@{
    Name = "IT"
    Location = "Building 1"
}

$contact = [PSCustomObject]@{
    Email = "alice@example.com"
    Phone = "555-1234"
}

$employee = [PSCustomObject]@{
    Name = "Alice"
    Department = $department
    Contact = $contact
}
```

Now, $employee.Department.Name returns "IT", just as it would with a hashtable, but the structure is object-based.

Benefits of Custom Objects Over Hashtables

1. **Pipeline Friendly**: Custom objects can be easily piped to Export-Csv, ConvertTo-Json, or consumed by other cmdlets.
2. **Intellisense Support**: Many editors like VS Code provide auto-completion for custom object properties.
3. **Stronger Typing**: Helps enforce structure and prevent errors.

4. **Readable Output**: When printed, custom objects are easier to read than hashtables, especially when nested.

Mixing Hashtables and Custom Objects

You're not limited to one or the other. In many cases, it's beneficial to use hashtables internally and then convert the result to a custom object for output.

Example:

```
function Get-UserSummary {
    param($username)

    $profile = @{
        Username = $username
        Details = @{
            FirstName = "Jane"
            LastName = "Doe"
        }
        Enabled = $true
    }

    return [PSCustomObject]@{
        Username = $profile.Username
        FirstName = $profile.Details.FirstName
        LastName = $profile.Details.LastName
        Enabled = $profile.Enabled
    }
}
```

This approach keeps your logic flexible and your output clean.

Enumerating Nested Structures

Working with nested structures means you'll often need to iterate through them.

Looping Through Nested Hashtables

```
foreach ($key in $employee.Contact.Keys) {
    "$key: $($employee.Contact[$key])"
}
```

Looping Through Arrays of Custom Objects

```
$employees = @()

$employees += [PSCustomObject]@{
    Name = "Alice"
    Department = "IT"
}

$employees += [PSCustomObject]@{
    Name = "Bob"
    Department = "HR"
}

foreach ($emp in $employees) {
    Write-Host "$($emp.Name) works in $($emp.Department)"
}
```

Real-World Script Example

Here's a script that uses nested hashtables and returns structured custom objects.

```
function Get-ServerConfig {
    $servers = @(
        @{ Name = "Web01"; IP = "10.0.0.1"; Services = @{
HTTP = $true; HTTPS = $true; FTP = $false } },
        @{ Name = "File01"; IP = "10.0.0.2"; Services = @{
SMB = $true; FTP = $true } }
    )

    $output = @()

    foreach ($server in $servers) {
        $output += [PSCustomObject]@{
            Name = $server.Name
            IP = $server.IP
            Services = [PSCustomObject]$server.Services
        }
    }

    return $output
}
```

```
Get-ServerConfig | Format-Table -AutoSize
```

This produces a readable list of servers with their IP addresses and services.

Conclusion

Nested hashtables and custom objects are foundational to writing effective PowerShell scripts. Hashtables offer dynamic, flexible data structures that are perfect for logic-heavy portions of code or temporary data collections. Custom objects, on the other hand, provide formality, structure, and improved interoperability with other tools and cmdlets.

By mastering both—and knowing when to use each—you equip yourself with powerful tools for building scalable, readable, and maintainable PowerShell scripts. Whether you're scripting a user import tool, an automated reporting solution, or cloud infrastructure deployments, these structures will elevate the quality and functionality of your work.

As a best practice, start with hashtables when prototyping or working with highly dynamic data, and move to custom objects when your data structure stabilizes or when preparing for output and reporting. This hybrid approach will give you the best of both worlds.

Logging, Debugging, and Testing

SCRIPT LOGGING TECHNIQUES

Logging is an essential part of any robust PowerShell script. Whether you're troubleshooting, auditing, or simply ensuring transparency in your script's execution, logging provides a record of activity that can help you or others understand what happened, when it happened, and why. In this section, we will explore various script logging techniques for PowerShell, from basic methods to more advanced strategies, including examples and best practices.

Why Logging Matters

Before we dive into the techniques, it's worth emphasizing why logging is important:

- **Troubleshooting**: Logs help identify what went wrong and where.
- **Auditing and Compliance**: Logs serve as an audit trail for security and compliance reviews.
- **Monitoring**: Logs can be monitored by systems to detect errors or important events.
- **Documentation**: Logs serve as a living record of script activity.

Without proper logging, troubleshooting failures can feel like chasing ghosts. With logs, you're looking at a roadmap.

Basic Logging with Out-File

The most straightforward way to implement logging in PowerShell is by redirecting output to a file.

```
"Starting script..." | Out-File -FilePath "C:
```

```
\Logs\MyScript.log" -Append
```

Pros:

- Simple and quick to implement.

Cons:

- Lacks structure.
- Not ideal for complex or multi-step processes.

Using Add-Content

Add-Content allows you to append lines to a file, often more readable and flexible than Out-File for basic logging.

```
$logPath = "C:\Logs\MyScript.log"
Add-Content -Path $logPath -Value "[$(Get-Date -Format
'yyyy-MM-dd HH:mm:ss')] Script started."
```

Tip: Always include a timestamp to indicate when each action occurred.

Building a Custom Logging Function

Creating a reusable function for logging helps enforce consistency throughout your scripts.

```
function Write-Log {
    param (
        [string]$Message,
        [string]$Level = "INFO",
        [string]$LogFile = "C:\Logs\MyScript.log"
    )

    $timestamp = Get-Date -Format 'yyyy-MM-dd HH:mm:ss'
    $logEntry = "[$timestamp] [$Level] $Message"
    Add-Content -Path $LogFile -Value $logEntry
}

# Example usage
Write-Log -Message "Initialization complete."
Write-Log -Message "An error occurred." -Level "ERROR"
```

Benefits:
- Modular and reusable.
- Supports different log levels (INFO, ERROR, WARNING, etc.).
- Easy to extend with more features later (e.g., rotating logs, alerting).

Logging Errors with Try/Catch

Capturing exceptions and logging them is a must for robustness.

```
try {
    # Simulated risky operation
    Get-Item "C:\NonExistentFile.txt"
} catch {
    Write-Log -Message "Failed to find file: $_" -Level
"ERROR"
}
```

By using try/catch, you ensure that your script doesn't simply fail silently or crash without context.

Structured Logging with JSON

If your logs need to be machine-readable (e.g., for ingestion by log analysis tools), consider logging in JSON format.

```
function Write-JsonLog {
    param (
        [string]$Message,
        [string]$Level = "INFO",
        [string]$LogFile = "C:\Logs\MyScript.json"
    )

    $entry = [PSCustomObject]@{
        Timestamp = Get-Date -Format 'yyyy-MM-
ddTHH:mm:ss.fffZ'
        Level    = $Level
        Message  = $Message
    }

    $json = $entry | ConvertTo-Json -Compress
    Add-Content -Path $LogFile -Value $json
```

```
}
```

```
Write-JsonLog -Message "Script started."
```
Pros:
- Easier integration with monitoring and SIEM tools.
- Enables structured querying.

Cons:
- Slightly more complex to read manually.

Rotating Log Files

Large log files can become difficult to manage. Implement log rotation by checking the file size and renaming or archiving when necessary.

```
function Rotate-Log {
    param (
        [string]$LogPath,
        [int]$MaxSizeMB = 5
    )

    if ((Test-Path $LogPath) -and ((Get-Item
$LogPath).Length -gt ($MaxSizeMB * 1MB))) {
        $archivePath = $LogPath.Replace(".log", "_$(Get-Date
-Format 'yyyyMMddHHmmss').log")
        Rename-Item -Path $LogPath -NewName $archivePath
    }
}


# Use before writing to the log
Rotate-Log -LogPath "C:\Logs\MyScript.log"
```


Writing to the Windows Event Log

In enterprise environments, writing directly to the Windows Event Log is a more secure and standardized way to track script behavior.

```
if (-not (Get-EventLog -LogName Application -Source
"MyScript" -ErrorAction SilentlyContinue)) {
    New-EventLog -LogName Application -Source "MyScript"
}
```

```
Write-EventLog -LogName Application -Source "MyScript" -
EntryType Information -EventId 1000 -Message "Script
executed successfully."
```

Pros:

- Centralized and secure.
- Integrates with existing monitoring tools.

Cons:

- Requires administrative privileges.
- Less portable across environments.

Using Transcripts

PowerShell offers a built-in way to log the full console output using Start-Transcript.

```
Start-Transcript -Path "C:\Logs\MyScriptTranscript.txt"

# Your script logic here

Stop-Transcript
```

Note: This captures everything sent to the host, including errors and verbose output. Great for debugging, but be cautious about sensitive data.

Best Practices for Logging

- **Consistency**: Use a centralized function like Write-Log for all log entries.
- **Timestamp Everything**: Every log entry should include a precise timestamp.
- **Use Log Levels**: Define and use log levels like DEBUG, INFO, WARNING, and ERROR.
- **Sanitize Inputs**: Avoid logging passwords or sensitive data.
- **Automate Cleanup**: Schedule jobs to archive or delete old logs.
- **Document Log Locations**: Make it easy for others to know where to find logs.

Summary

Logging transforms your PowerShell scripts from ephemeral, black-box processes into traceable, maintainable, and reliable systems. Whether you're a beginner writing your first admin script or an advanced user automating complex infrastructure, implementing good logging practices will elevate your work and make it sustainable.

From simple Add-Content lines to full-fledged JSON logging and Windows Event Log integration, PowerShell gives you the tools to keep your execution traceable and transparent. Start with something simple, and as your scripts grow in complexity, so too should your logging techniques.

WRITE-DEBUG, WRITE-VERBOSE

When scripting in PowerShell, especially at scale or in production-level environments, the ability to track, monitor, and understand script behavior is invaluable. While Write-Output and Write-Host are common methods for outputting information, they aren't ideal for debugging or creating maintainable, well-structured scripts. That's where Write-Debug and Write-Verbose come into play. These cmdlets offer a more flexible and controllable way to provide insight into script execution without polluting standard output.

In this section, we'll cover the purpose of each cmdlet, their differences, how and when to use them, and best practices for incorporating them into your scripts.

What is Write-Debug?

Write-Debug is a cmdlet used to output diagnostic information useful during the development and troubleshooting of scripts. Unlike standard output, debug messages are suppressed by default and only shown when explicitly enabled.

```
Write-Debug "This is a debug message."
```

To view the output of Write-Debug, you must enable the debug stream:

```
$DebugPreference = 'Continue'
```

Alternatively, you can use the -Debug switch when running a script or function that supports it:

```
.\MyScript.ps1 -Debug
```

This flexibility allows you to keep the debugging information out of the way until it's needed, making scripts cleaner and easier to read during standard execution.

What is Write-Verbose?

Write-Verbose is used to output detailed information about the progress or internal workings of a script. Like Write-Debug, its output is suppressed by default and only displayed when enabled.

```
Write-Verbose "Starting file copy operation..."
```

To display verbose output, use the -Verbose parameter:

```
.\MyScript.ps1 -Verbose
```

This is particularly useful for operations that take time or involve multiple steps. It gives users or administrators visibility into what the script is doing without overwhelming them with information unless they ask for it.

Key Differences Between Write-Debug and Write-Verbose

While these cmdlets may seem similar, they serve distinct purposes:

- **Audience**:
- Write-Debug is intended for script developers. It's used to diagnose script issues during development or advanced troubleshooting.
- Write-Verbose is aimed at script users or administrators who need insight into script progress or flow.
- **Behavior**:
- Write-Debug can pause script execution if $DebugPreference is set to Inquire, allowing step-by-step review.
- Write-Verbose does not pause execution.
- **Enablement**:
- Write-Debug output is controlled via the $DebugPreference variable or -Debug switch.
- Write-Verbose output is controlled by the $VerbosePreference

variable or -Verbose switch.

Understanding when to use one or the other—or both—is crucial for writing intuitive and helpful scripts.

When to Use Write-Debug

Use Write-Debug for output that is specifically intended to help you understand *why* something went wrong:

- Diagnosing logic errors
- Checking variable states during loop iterations
- Identifying branching problems in if/else logic
- Investigating unexpected behavior

Because Write-Debug output can be conditionally enabled, it's perfect for adding rich diagnostic content without cluttering normal output.

Example: Debugging a Loop

```
function Test-Loop {
    [CmdletBinding()]
    param ()

    for ($i = 0; $i -lt 5; $i++) {
        Write-Debug "Loop iteration: $i"
        # Simulated operation
    }
}

Test-Loop -Debug
```

When to Use Write-Verbose

Use Write-Verbose to give users or yourself insight into what a script is doing while it's running:

- Announcing major steps or stages
- Informing the user about file paths, operation summaries, etc.
- Confirming successful completion of sub-tasks

Verbose messages can reassure users that a long-running script is still working or help them understand its execution path.

Example: Verbose Output for File Copy

```
function Copy-Files {
  [CmdletBinding()]
  param (
    [Parameter(Mandatory)]
    [string]$Source,

[Parameter(Mandatory)]
    [string]$Destination
  )

  Write-Verbose "Copying from $Source to $Destination"
      Copy-Item -Path $Source -Destination $Destination -Recurse
      Write-Verbose "Copy completed."
  }

Copy-Files -Source "C:\Temp" -Destination "D:\Backup" -Verbose
```

Combining Both for Maximum Effect

In more sophisticated scripts, you can use both cmdlets to provide layers of insight:

- Use Write-Verbose to describe what the script is *trying* to do
- Use Write-Debug to show what actually *happened* at a detailed, technical level

This layered approach is invaluable for support and troubleshooting, particularly when someone else is running your script.

Example:

```
function Process-Data {
```

```
[CmdletBinding()]
param (
  [Parameter(Mandatory)]
  [string]$InputFile
)

Write-Verbose "Loading file: $InputFile"

if (-Not (Test-Path $InputFile)) {
    Write-Debug "File not found: $InputFile"
    throw "Input file does not exist."
}

$content = Get-Content $InputFile
    Write-Verbose "File loaded. Processing lines..."

foreach ($line in $content) {
    Write-Debug "Processing line: $line"
    # Do some processing here
}

Write-Verbose "Processing complete."
  }

Process-Data -InputFile "C:\data.txt" -Verbose -Debug
```

Best Practices

1. **Always Include CmdletBinding**: Use [CmdletBinding()] at the top of your functions to enable automatic support for -Verbose and -Debug.
2. **Use Conditional Logic Sparingly**: Don't rely on if ($VerbosePreference -eq 'Continue') to write verbose messages. Just use Write-Verbose.
3. **Be Descriptive**: Verbose and debug messages should be clear and informative, not just placeholders.

4. **Avoid Write-Host**: Unlike Write-Verbose and Write-Debug, Write-Host sends output directly to the console, making it difficult to suppress or redirect.

5. **Use -Debug and -Verbose switches** when testing scripts to see what's happening under the hood.

6. **Don't Overdo It**: Too many verbose or debug messages can be as unhelpful as too few. Strike a balance.

7. **Document Expected Output**: In comments or accompanying documentation, indicate what kinds of messages can be expected when verbose or debug output is enabled.

Summary

Write-Debug and Write-Verbose are indispensable tools in the PowerShell scripter's toolkit. They let you peer into the inner workings of your script without overwhelming the end user. Write-Debug is your go-to for development and troubleshooting, giving you a magnifying glass to inspect variables and flow. Write-Verbose is your communication line to the user, keeping them informed without overwhelming them.

Used correctly, these cmdlets promote transparency, accountability, and professionalism in your scripting. They are the keys to building scripts that not only work—but are easy to understand, maintain, and support.

PESTER TESTING FRAMEWORK

PowerShell is not just a scripting language; it's a platform for building robust automation workflows. Like any development platform, testing is crucial to ensure the reliability, functionality, and maintainability of scripts and modules. For PowerShell, the de facto standard for testing is **Pester**.

This section will introduce you to the Pester testing framework, walk you through writing your first tests, and guide you in adopting best practices for test-driven development (TDD) in your PowerShell scripting journey.

What is Pester?

Pester is a test framework for PowerShell. It allows you to write unit tests, integration tests, and even acceptance tests for your scripts and modules. With Pester, you can validate output, check the existence of objects, mock commands, and ensure your code behaves exactly as expected.

Pester is built into Windows 10 and later versions of PowerShell (5.1+), but it's also available via the PowerShell Gallery, making it easy to update or install in earlier versions or non-Windows environments.

Why Use Pester?

Writing tests with Pester offers many benefits:
- **Reliability:** Ensure your scripts do what they're supposed to.
- **Regression Testing:** Catch unintended changes early.
- **Documentation:** Your tests describe what your code is *supposed* to do.
- **Refactoring Safety:** Make changes with confidence.
- **Automation-Ready:** Integrates well with CI/CD pipelines.

Installing Pester

If you're using PowerShell 5.1 or later, Pester may already be installed. To check the installed version:

```
Get-Module -Name Pester -ListAvailable
```

To install or update Pester from the PowerShell Gallery:

```
Install-Module -Name Pester -Force -SkipPublisherCheck
```

This installs the latest version available. If you want a specific version:

```
Install-Module -Name Pester -RequiredVersion 5.5.0
```

Structure of a Pester Test

Pester tests use a behavior-driven development (BDD) style syntax. Here's a breakdown:

```
Describe 'FunctionName' {
    It 'Does something expected' {
        # Your test here
    }
}
```

- **Describe**: Groups related tests.
- **It**: Individual test cases.

You can write assertions using Should:

```
$actual = 2 + 2
$actual | Should -Be 4
```

Writing Your First Pester Test

Suppose you have a function that multiplies two numbers:

```
function Multiply-Numbers {
    param (
        [int]$a,
        [int]$b
    )
    return $a * $b
}
```

Let's write a test for it:

```
Describe 'Multiply-Numbers' {
    It 'Returns the product of two numbers' {
        Multiply-Numbers -a 3 -b 4 | Should -Be 12
    }
    It 'Returns 0 when one number is 0' {
        Multiply-Numbers -a 0 -b 5 | Should -Be 0
    }
}
```

Save this test in a file like Multiply-Numbers.Tests.ps1 and run it:

```
Invoke-Pester -Path ./Multiply-Numbers.Tests.ps1
```

Using Mocks in Pester

Mocks let you isolate the function you're testing. Suppose your function calls Get-ADUser, but you don't want to hit the real Active

Directory during tests:

```
Describe 'Get-UserInfo' {
    Mock -CommandName Get-ADUser -MockWith {
        return @{Name='TestUser'}
    }

    It 'Returns mocked user data' {
        $result = Get-UserInfo -Username 'TestUser'
        $result.Name | Should -Be 'TestUser'
    }
}
```

Mocking is especially useful for testing code with external dependencies (e.g., databases, APIs, AD).

Advanced Features

TestDrive:

Use TestDrive: to safely test file system changes:

```
Describe 'File creation test' {
    It 'Creates a file in the test drive' {
        New-Item -Path "TestDrive:\temp.txt" -ItemType File
        Test-Path "TestDrive:\temp.txt" | Should -BeTrue
    }
}
```

BeforeAll / BeforeEach / AfterEach / AfterAll:

Setup or teardown logic around tests:

```
Describe 'Sample tests' {
    BeforeAll { "Starting tests" }
    BeforeEach { $global:x = 5 }

    It 'Checks if x equals 5' {
        $x | Should -Be 5
    }

    AfterEach { Remove-Variable -Name x -Scope Global }
    AfterAll { "Finished tests" }
}
```

Tags:

Run only specific subsets of tests:

```
It 'Performs fast check' -Tag 'Fast' {
    1 | Should -Be 1
}

Invoke-Pester -Tag Fast
```

Organizing Tests

Keep your tests in a dedicated folder like Tests/ or alongside the code. Naming convention:

```
MyFunction.ps1
MyFunction.Tests.ps1
```

This helps identify related tests and keeps your codebase clean.

Integrating with CI/CD

Pester fits neatly into DevOps workflows. In tools like Azure DevOps, GitHub Actions, or Jenkins, you can add a PowerShell task that runs Pester tests.

```
- task: PowerShell@2
  inputs:
    targetType: 'inline'
    script: |
      Install-Module -Name Pester -Force
      Invoke-Pester -Path './Tests'
```

This ensures that new code merges or releases only happen when tests pass.

Test-Driven Development (TDD) with Pester

TDD is the practice of writing your tests *before* the code. The cycle is:

1. **Write a failing test.**
2. **Write just enough code to pass.**
3. **Refactor and optimize.**

Example:

Test First:

```
Describe 'Add-Numbers' {
    It 'Adds two numbers correctly' {
        Add-Numbers -a 2 -b 3 | Should -Be 5
    }
}
```

Then Code:

```
function Add-Numbers {
    param ([int]$a, [int]$b)
    return $a + $b
}
```

This approach ensures focused, testable code and reduces bugs.

Best Practices

- **Write small, focused tests.**
- **Mock external dependencies.**
- **Automate test execution in your CI/CD.**
- **Use tags to organize test categories.**
- **Always test before deploying.**

Summary

Pester is an essential tool for any serious PowerShell scripter. It promotes clean code, encourages best practices, and gives you confidence that your scripts behave as intended. Whether you're managing infrastructure, automating deployments, or building PowerShell modules, learning Pester and using it daily will make you a better, more professional scripter.

In the world of infrastructure as code, testing is no longer optional —it's expected. With Pester in your toolkit, you're fully equipped to meet that expectation.

Security and Best Practices

SECURE CREDENTIAL STORAGE

One of the fundamental principles of secure scripting in PowerShell is protecting sensitive information such as usernames, passwords, API keys, and other credentials. Storing credentials in plain text is a significant security risk, especially in automated scripts that run on production systems or access cloud resources. This chapter explores how to securely store, retrieve, and manage credentials in PowerShell, ensuring your scripts are both functional and secure.

Why Credential Security Matters

Whenever a script interacts with systems requiring authentication— whether it's connecting to Active Directory, Exchange, Azure, or a SQL database—it needs credentials. If these credentials are hardcoded or stored insecurely, malicious actors who gain access to the scripts or systems could exploit them, leading to data breaches, privilege escalation, or worse.

Common Mistakes
- **Hardcoding credentials** in scripts
- **Storing passwords in plain text** files
- **Using weak or default credentials**
- **Neglecting to rotate credentials**
- **Sharing unencrypted scripts among teams**

These pitfalls can be avoided by adopting PowerShell's built-in tools for secure credential handling.

PowerShell's Native Credential Handling

PowerShell provides several mechanisms to store and retrieve credentials securely using the System.Security namespace.

The Get-Credential Cmdlet

The Get-Credential cmdlet is a user-friendly method to collect credentials interactively:

```
$credential = Get-Credential
```

This command prompts the user with a secure dialog box to enter a username and password, storing them in a PSCredential object.

Using ConvertTo-SecureString

Passwords should never be stored in plaintext. The ConvertTo-SecureString cmdlet can encrypt strings:

```
$securePassword = ConvertTo-SecureString
"MyPlainTextPassword" -AsPlainText -Force
```

Note: While this encrypts the password, it's tied to the current user context and machine.

You can pair this with a username to create a full credential object:

```
$credential = New-Object
System.Management.Automation.PSCredential("username",
$securePassword)
```

Exporting and Importing Credentials Securely

To store credentials for later use, you can serialize and save the SecureString and reconstruct it when needed. Here's a common technique:

Exporting Credentials

$credential = Get-Credential

$credential.Password | ConvertFrom-SecureString | Set-Content "C:\scripts\password.txt"

$credential.UserName | Set-Content "C:\scripts\username.txt"

Importing Credentials

$username = Get-Content "C:\scripts\username.txt"

$securePassword = Get-Content "C:\scripts\password.txt" | ConvertTo-SecureString

$credential = New-Object System.Management.Automation.PSCredential($username,

$securePassword)

Pros and Cons
- **Pros:** Secure if run under the same user and on the same machine
- **Cons:** Not portable across users or systems. If the machine or user profile is compromised, so is the credential.

Using the Windows Credential Manager

Windows has a secure credential storage system that PowerShell can leverage via the Credential Manager. With the CredentialManager module, you can store credentials once and retrieve them securely as needed.

Installing the CredentialManager Module
```
Install-Module -Name CredentialManager
```
Storing a Credential
```
$cred = Get-Credential
New-StoredCredential -Target "MyAppCreds" -UserName
$cred.UserName -Password
($cred.GetNetworkCredential().Password) -Persist
LocalMachine
```
Retrieving a Credential
```
$cred = Get-StoredCredential -Target "MyAppCreds"
$psCred = New-Object
System.Management.Automation.PSCredential ($cred.UserName,
($cred.Password | ConvertTo-SecureString -AsPlainText -
Force))
```
This approach allows credentials to be securely stored in the Windows Credential Store and reused in scripts without storing them in files.

Advanced Option: Secret Management Module

For scripts that run across multiple machines or require a more advanced secret management solution, PowerShell 7 introduced the Microsoft.PowerShell.SecretManagement module.

Installing the Modules

```
Install-Module Microsoft.PowerShell.SecretManagement
Install-Module Microsoft.PowerShell.SecretStore
```

Registering a Vault

```
Register-SecretVault -Name MySecretVault -ModuleName
Microsoft.PowerShell.SecretStore -DefaultVault
```

Adding and Retrieving Secrets

```
Set-Secret -Name "MySqlAdminPassword" -Secret (ConvertTo-
SecureString "MySecretPwd" -AsPlainText -Force)
$secret = Get-Secret -Name "MySqlAdminPassword"
```

You can convert $secret to a PSCredential object as needed.

Best Practices for Secure Credential Handling

1. **Avoid Hardcoding Credentials:** Never write passwords or tokens directly into your scripts.
2. **Use Get-Credential for Interactive Scripts:** This ensures no secrets are exposed in code.
3. **Store Secure Strings Properly:** If exporting credentials, protect the files and use NTFS permissions.
4. **Use Windows Credential Manager:** A convenient and secure alternative that persists credentials safely.
5. **Adopt SecretManagement for Enterprise Use:** Ideal for cross-platform or DevOps use cases.
6. **Encrypt Your Scripts:** Consider signing and encrypting scripts using certificates to prevent tampering.
7. **Limit Scope and Privileges:** Credentials should have the minimum necessary permissions.
8. **Rotate Secrets Regularly:** Update passwords and API keys on a schedule.
9. **Audit and Monitor Usage:** Log and review when and where credentials are accessed in scripts.
10. **Test for Errors:** Always validate credential handling with error trapping to avoid security gaps.

Example: Using Secure Credentials in a Scheduled Task

You might want to run a PowerShell script that authenticates against

Exchange Online as a scheduled task without manual credential entry. Here's how you could do it securely:

Create and Export the Credential

```
$cred = Get-Credential
$cred.Password | ConvertFrom-SecureString | Set-Content "C:
\secure\password.txt"
$cred.UserName | Set-Content "C:\secure\username.txt"
```

In the Script

```
$username = Get-Content "C:\secure\username.txt"
$securePassword = Get-Content "C:\secure\password.txt" |
ConvertTo-SecureString
$cred = New-Object
System.Management.Automation.PSCredential($username,
$securePassword)
Connect-ExchangeOnline -Credential $cred
```

Ensure the folder is protected with strict NTFS permissions accessible only to the user running the task.

Conclusion

PowerShell provides multiple options for handling credentials securely. Whether you're an administrator writing internal scripts or an automation engineer deploying systems in production, understanding and applying secure credential storage techniques is crucial. By combining tools like SecureString, Credential Manager, and the Secret Management module, you can significantly reduce the security risks associated with automation.

As your scripts grow more complex and span across environments, prioritizing secure practices isn't just a best practice— it's a requirement. Secure your credentials now to avoid preventable security incidents later.

AVOIDING COMMON VULNERABILITIES

PowerShell is a powerful tool in the hands of system administrators and developers, but with great power comes the potential for great risk. Poorly written or misconfigured scripts can open up critical vulnerabilities in a system, leading to data loss, privilege escalation, or even full system compromise. This chapter will explore the most common vulnerabilities encountered in PowerShell scripting and how to avoid them with sound coding practices, awareness, and security hygiene.

Hardcoded Credentials

What It Is: Embedding usernames, passwords, or API keys directly into scripts.

Why It's Dangerous: Hardcoded credentials are often committed to version control systems or shared across environments, leaving sensitive data exposed. If an attacker gains access to the script, they gain access to systems as well.

How to Avoid It:
- Use the Windows Credential Manager or secure vaults like Azure Key Vault or HashiCorp Vault.
- Prompt users for credentials using Get-Credential.
- Store credentials in encrypted formats using Export-Clixml and Import-Clixml.

```
# Securely storing a credential
$cred = Get-Credential
$cred | Export-Clixml -Path "$env:USERPROFILE\mycred.xml"

# Reusing securely stored credential
$cred = Import-Clixml -Path "$env:USERPROFILE\mycred.xml"
```

Lack of Input Validation

What It Is: Scripts that don't validate or sanitize user input.

Why It's Dangerous: Improper input handling can lead to command injection, malformed data entries, and logic errors that attackers can exploit.

How to Avoid It:

- Always validate input types and expected values.
- Use regex to enforce input formatting.
- Avoid directly executing user-supplied input in commands or scripts.

```
# Input validation example
param (
    [Parameter(Mandatory=$true)]
    [ValidatePattern("^[a-zA-Z0-9_-]+$")]
    [string]$Username
)
```

Overuse of Invoke-Expression

What It Is: Running dynamically generated strings as PowerShell commands.

Why It's Dangerous: Invoke-Expression can be used to execute arbitrary code. If that string is built from user input, it's a critical security risk.

How to Avoid It:

- Don't use Invoke-Expression unless absolutely necessary.
- Use native cmdlets and structured code instead.
- For dynamic tasks, use splatting or functions rather than dynamic strings.

```
# Bad practice
Invoke-Expression "Remove-Item $userInput"


# Safer alternative
Remove-Item -Path $userInput -Force
```

Excessive Privilege Usage

What It Is: Running scripts or commands with administrator or domain-level privileges when not needed.

Why It's Dangerous: Running scripts with excessive privileges increases the blast radius of mistakes or malicious actions. A poorly written script could disable antivirus, delete important files, or add unauthorized users.

How to Avoid It:

- Follow the Principle of Least Privilege.
- Test scripts as standard users first.
- Use Start-Process -Verb RunAs only when elevation is necessary.

Improper Error Handling

What It Is: Scripts that fail silently or expose sensitive data in verbose error messages.

Why It's Dangerous: Errors that go unhandled may result in incomplete processes, broken configurations, or open attack surfaces. Overly verbose error logs may leak system paths, credentials, or internal logic.

How to Avoid It:

- Use try/catch/finally blocks.
- Suppress non-critical errors using -ErrorAction when appropriate.
- Log only what's necessary.

```
try {
    Remove-Item -Path $logPath -ErrorAction Stop
} catch {
    Write-Warning "Failed to remove log file: $
($_.Exception.Message)"
}
```

Improper Use of Remote Execution

What It Is: Using PowerShell Remoting or WinRM without encryption or authentication.

Why It's Dangerous: Transmitting sensitive data or commands over the network without encryption can expose systems to man-in-the-middle attacks.

How to Avoid It:

- Always use HTTPS for WinRM or PowerShell Remoting.
- Use Kerberos or certificate-based authentication.
- Use Just Enough Administration (JEA) to limit the scope of what remote users can do.

```
Enable-PSRemoting -Force
Set-Item WSMan:\localhost\Service\AllowUnencrypted -Value
$false
```

Insecure File Permissions

What It Is: Scripts and credential files stored with open or permissive file system access.

Why It's Dangerous: Anyone with access to the system could view or modify these files, leading to privilege escalation or information leaks.

How to Avoid It:

- Store scripts in protected directories.
- Use Get-Acl and Set-Acl to manage permissions.
- Use file encryption (e.g., EFS) when needed.

```
# Check file ACLs
(Get-Acl "C:\Scripts\SecureScript.ps1").Access
```

Not Signing Scripts

What It Is: Running unsigned scripts in environments with execution policy set to RemoteSigned or higher.

Why It's Dangerous: Unsigned scripts can be modified by an attacker and executed without detection.

How to Avoid It:

- Sign your scripts with a trusted code-signing certificate.
- Set and enforce execution policies using Group Policy.
- Use Get-AuthenticodeSignature to verify script integrity.

```
Set-ExecutionPolicy RemoteSigned -Scope LocalMachine
```

Ignoring Script Logging and Auditing

What It Is: Failing to implement logging in production scripts.

Why It's Dangerous: Lack of logging makes troubleshooting difficult and hampers forensic investigations during incidents.

How to Avoid It:

- Use logging frameworks like Start-Transcript, Write-EventLog,

or custom log files.
- Integrate with SIEMs for centralized logging.
- Log meaningful events, inputs, and errors.

```
Start-Transcript -Path "C:\Logs\DeployLog.txt"
```

Unpatched PowerShell Versions

What It Is: Using outdated versions of PowerShell with known security vulnerabilities.

Why It's Dangerous: Old versions may lack important security features and patches.

How to Avoid It:
- Stay current with PowerShell releases.
- Use PowerShell Core (7+) for cross-platform and modern scripting.
- Enable Microsoft Update to automatically patch Windows PowerShell.

Conclusion

Avoiding common vulnerabilities in PowerShell scripting is essential to maintaining secure, reliable, and professional automation. Always follow best practices such as secure credential storage, input validation, proper privilege management, and robust error handling. As PowerShell continues to evolve, staying informed about new security features and potential risks will empower you to write resilient scripts that stand up under scrutiny.

Security is not a checkbox—it's a mindset. Adopt it early and consistently, and your scripts will not only perform their intended tasks, but also uphold the integrity and security of your systems.

SIGNING SCRIPTS

PowerShell is a powerful scripting language and automation framework developed by Microsoft. With this power comes responsibility—especially when it comes to security. One of the most important practices in enterprise environments and secure script deployment is *script signing*. Signing scripts in PowerShell helps ensure the authenticity, integrity, and origin of the scripts being run. This chapter covers what script signing is, why it's important, how to sign scripts, and how to configure your environment for secure script execution.

What is Script Signing?

Script signing is the process of digitally signing your PowerShell scripts using a code-signing certificate. This signature acts as a proof that the script has not been tampered with and that it originated from a trusted source. When a signed script is executed, PowerShell checks the signature to ensure that:
- The signature is valid.
- The certificate used to sign the script is trusted.
- The script hasn't been altered since it was signed.

This process provides a crucial layer of security, especially in enterprise environments where scripts are distributed across multiple systems.

Why Sign Scripts?

There are several compelling reasons to sign your PowerShell scripts:
1. **Security**: Unsigned scripts can be modified by attackers. Signing helps ensure scripts haven't been altered since creation.
2. **Compliance**: Many organizations enforce strict security policies that require code to be signed to comply with regulatory requirements.
3. **Trust**: A signed script assures system administrators and users that the script comes from a known and trusted source.
4. **Execution Policy Enforcement**: PowerShell has different execution policies that affect how scripts are run. Some of these require scripts to be signed.

Understanding PowerShell Execution Policies

PowerShell has a built-in security mechanism called *execution policies*. These policies determine the conditions under which PowerShell loads configuration files and runs scripts. Here's a brief overview:

- **Restricted**: No scripts can run. PowerShell is in interactive mode only.
- **AllSigned**: Only scripts signed by a trusted publisher can be run.
- **RemoteSigned**: Downloaded scripts must be signed by a trusted publisher.
- **Unrestricted**: All scripts can run, but warnings are given for downloaded scripts.
- **Bypass**: No restrictions; typically used for automation.
- **Undefined**: No policy set at this level.

The AllSigned and RemoteSigned policies require you to sign your scripts before execution, making script signing a necessity in these environments.

You can check the current execution policy with:

```
Get-ExecutionPolicy
```

Or set it with:

```
Set-ExecutionPolicy RemoteSigned -Scope CurrentUser
```

Acquiring a Code Signing Certificate

Before you can sign your scripts, you need a code-signing certificate. There are two main options:

1. **Public Certificate Authority (CA)**: These certificates are issued by a trusted third-party vendor like DigiCert, GlobalSign, or Sectigo. They are ideal for scripts that will be used across many machines or by external users.
2. **Internal Certificate Authority**: In enterprise environments, many organizations use an internal CA (typically via Active Directory Certificate Services) to issue code-signing certificates.

You can also generate a **self-signed certificate** for testing purposes:

```
New-SelfSignedCertificate -Type CodeSigningCert -Subject
"CN=My Code Signing Cert" -CertStoreLocation "Cert:
```

```
\CurrentUser\My"
```

Exporting and Installing the Certificate

To sign scripts, the certificate needs to be present in the **Personal** store and trusted by the local machine or user. If you're using a self-signed certificate for testing, you must add it to the **Trusted Root Certification Authorities** and **Trusted Publishers**:

```
$cert = Get-ChildItem -Path Cert:\CurrentUser\My | Where-
Object { $_.Subject -eq "CN=My Code Signing Cert" }
Export-Certificate -Cert $cert -FilePath "C:\mycert.cer"
Import-Certificate -FilePath "C:\mycert.cer" -
CertStoreLocation Cert:\CurrentUser\TrustedPublisher
Import-Certificate -FilePath "C:\mycert.cer" -
CertStoreLocation Cert:\CurrentUser\Root
```

Signing a Script

Once the certificate is available, use the Set-AuthenticodeSignature cmdlet to sign a script:

```
$cert = Get-ChildItem -Path Cert:\CurrentUser\My | Where-
Object { $_.Subject -eq "CN=My Code Signing Cert" }
Set-AuthenticodeSignature -FilePath "C:
\Scripts\MyScript.ps1" -Certificate $cert
```

After signing, the script will include a signature block at the bottom. PowerShell verifies this signature whenever the script is run.

Verifying Script Signatures

To check if a script is signed and valid:

```
Get-AuthenticodeSignature -FilePath "C:
\Scripts\MyScript.ps1"
```

This returns an object with details like Status, SignerCertificate, and IsOSBinary. A Status of Valid means the script has not been tampered with and the certificate is trusted.

Best Practices for Script Signing

- **Use a Reputable CA**: For production use, always use certificates from a trusted CA.
- **Limit Certificate Use**: Restrict the usage of your code-signing certificate to reduce risk.
- **Protect Private Keys**: Store certificates on secure hardware (e.g., YubiKey or HSM) if possible.
- **Automate Signing**: Use a CI/CD pipeline to automatically sign scripts during the build process.
- **Revocation Awareness**: Ensure your environment checks certificate revocation lists (CRLs) to avoid running scripts signed with compromised certs.
- **Avoid Reusing Certificates for Multiple Purposes**: Separate your code signing, email, and SSL certs.

Troubleshooting Common Issues

1. **"Cannot be loaded because it is not digitally signed"**: Check your execution policy. If it's AllSigned, unsigned scripts will be blocked.
2. **Certificate Not Found**: Ensure the certificate is in the correct store.
3. **Invalid Signature**: Make sure the script wasn't modified after signing.
4. **CRL Check Fails**: Confirm that your environment has internet access or an accessible internal CRL server.

Summary

Signing PowerShell scripts is a vital step in building secure, trusted automation—especially in production environments or distributed enterprise systems. By using code-signing certificates, setting appropriate execution policies, and following best practices, you create a robust foundation for script security. Whether you're an individual developer or an IT administrator in a Fortune 500 company, integrating script signing into your workflow is a critical habit that enhances both credibility and protection.

As we continue through this book, you'll see real-world examples where signed scripts protect environments from accidental or malicious execution. Take the time to set up your environment for signing early—it's an investment in stability and trust.

Appendices

A. POWERSHELL CHEATSHEET

Welcome to the PowerShell Cheat Sheet, a practical quick-reference guide designed to help beginners and intermediate users recall essential PowerShell concepts, commands, and syntax. Whether you're automating a task, managing system resources, or writing a script, this section provides a concise overview of the most commonly used PowerShell features.

PowerShell Basics

Launching PowerShell
Start PowerShell by typing powershell into a Command Prompt or Run dialog (Win + R). To run as administrator, right-click PowerShell and choose "Run as administrator."

Running a Command
```
Get-Process
```

Running a Script File
```
.\myscript.ps1
```
Use Set-ExecutionPolicy to change script execution policy if blocked.

Comments
Single-line comment: # This is a comment
Multi-line comments:
```
<#
This is a
multi-line comment
#>
```

Common Cmdlets

System Information

```
Get-ComputerInfo
Get-Process
Get-Service
```

File System

```
Get-ChildItem          # List files and folders
Set-Location           # Change directory (alias: cd)
New-Item               # Create file or folder
Remove-Item            # Delete file or folder
Copy-Item              # Copy file or folder
Move-Item              # Move file or folder
```

Services and Processes

```
Get-Service
Start-Service -Name "wuauserv"
Stop-Service -Name "wuauserv"
Restart-Service -Name "spooler"
Get-Process
Stop-Process -Name "notepad"
```

Package Management

```
Get-Package
Find-Package
Install-Package -Name "7zip"
```

Variables and Data Types

Declaring Variables

```
$name = "John"
$age = 30
$items = @("Pen", "Notebook", "Laptop")
```

Data Types

```
[string]$city = "Chicago"
[int]$count = 5
[bool]$isEnabled = $true
```

Displaying Output

```
Write-Output "Hello, $name!"
Write-Host "Your age is $age"
```

Loops and Conditionals

If-Else Statement

```
if ($age -gt 18) {
```

```
    Write-Host "Adult"
} elseif ($age -eq 18) {
    Write-Host "Just turned adult"
} else {
    Write-Host "Minor"
}
```

For Loop

```
for ($i = 1; $i -le 5; $i++) {
    Write-Host "Number $i"
}
```

While Loop

```
$count = 1
while ($count -le 3) {
    Write-Host "Loop $count"
    $count++
}
```

Foreach Loop

```
$items = @("Apple", "Banana", "Cherry")
foreach ($item in $items) {
    Write-Host $item
}
```

Functions

Basic Function

```
function Say-Hello {
    Write-Host "Hello World"
}
Say-Hello
```

Function with Parameters

```
function Greet-User ($name) {
    Write-Host "Welcome, $name"
}
Greet-User -name "Alice"
```

Return Values

```
function Add-Numbers ($a, $b) {
    return $a + $b
}
```

```
$result = Add-Numbers 5 10
Write-Host $result
```

Error Handling

Try/Catch Block
```
try {
    Get-Item "C:\nonexistentfile.txt"
} catch {
    Write-Host "Error occurred: $_"
}
```
Finally Block
```
try {
    # Attempt
} catch {
    # Handle error
} finally {
    Write-Host "Cleanup finished."
}
```

Working with Objects

Select and Sort
```
Get-Process | Select-Object Name, CPU | Sort-Object CPU -
Descending
```
Filtering
```
Get-Service | Where-Object {$_.Status -eq "Running"}
```
Formatting Output
```
Format-Table Name, Status
Format-List
```

Pipelining and Filtering

Using the Pipeline
```
Get-Process | Where-Object {$_.CPU -gt 100} | Sort-Object
CPU -Descending
```
Pipeline with Formatting
```
Get-Service | Where-Object {$_.Status -eq "Stopped"} |
Format-Table Name, DisplayName
```

Modules and Importing

Import a Module

```
Import-Module ActiveDirectory
```

List Available Modules

```
Get-Module -ListAvailable
```

Create Your Own Module Save a .psm1 file and place it in a folder named after your module. Import using Import-Module.

Scripting Essentials

Read Input from User

```
$name = Read-Host "Enter your name"
Write-Host "Hello, $name"
```

Check If File Exists

```
if (Test-Path "C:\data.txt") {
    Write-Host "File found."
}
```

Schedule a Task

```
$action = New-ScheduledTaskAction -Execute "PowerShell.exe"
-Argument "-File C:\script.ps1"
Register-ScheduledTask -Action $action -Trigger $trigger -
TaskName "MyScriptTask" -Description "Runs my script"
```

Security and Permissions

Set Execution Policy

```
Set-ExecutionPolicy RemoteSigned -Scope CurrentUser
```

Run as Administrator Make sure your script has privileges when modifying system settings or services.

Digital Signing You can sign your scripts using a code signing certificate to ensure integrity.

Active Directory (If Module Installed)

Get User

```
Get-ADUser -Identity jsmith
```
Create User
```
New-ADUser -Name "John Smith" -SamAccountName jsmith -
AccountPassword (ConvertTo-SecureString "P@ssw0rd!" -
AsPlainText -Force) -Enabled $true
```
Add User to Group
```
Add-ADGroupMember -Identity "HR Team" -Members jsmith
```

Network Cmdlets

Ping a Host
```
Test-Connection google.com
```
Get IP Configuration
```
Get-NetIPAddress
```
Firewall Rules
```
Get-NetFirewallRule
Enable-NetFirewallRule -DisplayName "Remote Desktop"
```

Helpful Tips

- Use Get-Help <cmdlet> to read detailed documentation.
- Use Get-Command to discover available commands.
- Use Get-Member to inspect object properties and methods.
- Scripts should include logging and error handling for production use.
- Test scripts in a safe environment before deploying them in production.

Aliases You Should Know

```
ls      -> Get-ChildItem
cd      -> Set-Location
dir     -> Get-ChildItem
rm      -> Remove-Item
mv      -> Move-Item
cp      -> Copy-Item
```

These are shorthand versions to make PowerShell more familiar to users coming from Linux or traditional shells.

This cheat sheet is not exhaustive but should serve as a solid reference foundation. As you become more comfortable with PowerShell, you'll find that the flexibility and power of the shell increase exponentially with experience and creativity.

B. USEFUL COMMUNITY RESOURCES

One of the greatest strengths of the PowerShell ecosystem is its active, vibrant, and knowledgeable community. Whether you are a beginner just getting started or an experienced scripter looking for advanced tips, the PowerShell community offers an abundance of free resources to support your growth. This section outlines a wide range of useful community-driven platforms, repositories, forums, and events that can dramatically accelerate your learning and help you stay up to date with best practices.

PowerShell GitHub Repositories

GitHub has become the central hub for open-source collaboration and the PowerShell community fully embraces it. Microsoft's official PowerShell repository is located at https://github.com/PowerShell/PowerShell, and it hosts the PowerShell engine itself. Browsing this repository is a fantastic way to:

- Understand the roadmap and ongoing development.
- Submit issues or feature requests.
- Review and contribute to the source code.
- Participate in discussions about enhancements and bugs.

In addition to the main repo, GitHub is full of community modules, tools, and script libraries. Searching with terms like "PowerShell module" or filtering by the PowerShell language tag often leads to high-quality projects.

Notable community repositories include:

- **PowerShell/PSReadLine**: For advanced command-line editing.
- **PowerShell/PSScriptAnalyzer**: For static code analysis and linting.

- **MicrosoftDocs/PowerShell-Docs**: Documentation repository you can contribute to.

PowerShell Gallery

The PowerShell Gallery is the official repository for sharing PowerShell modules, scripts, and DSC (Desired State Configuration) resources. It is integrated with PowerShell itself, allowing you to install modules directly from the command line:

```
Install-Module -Name ModuleName -Scope CurrentUser
```

The Gallery is useful for:

- Discovering community-maintained modules.
- Publishing your own reusable code.
- Finding up-to-date resources for automation, cloud tasks, and more.

PowerShell Gallery is heavily moderated and provides trust indicators like author profiles, download counts, and digital signatures.

PowerShell.org

PowerShell.org is a cornerstone of the PowerShell community. Operated by the DevOps Collective, the site provides a variety of helpful resources including:

- Daily blog posts from seasoned experts.
- Discussion forums for Q&A.
- E-books covering different PowerShell topics.
- Announcements about events and summits.
- Job postings for PowerShell roles.

Perhaps most importantly, the site hosts the **PowerShell + DevOps Global Summit**, an annual event where professionals from around the world gather to present, network, and learn.

Reddit Communities

Reddit has two active subreddits that provide crowdsourced support and inspiration:

- r/PowerShell: General scripting help, career advice, showcase of scripts, and best practices.
- r/sysadmin: Broader IT operations discussions where PowerShell topics frequently arise.

The PowerShell subreddit is particularly beginner-friendly. Users often post helpful walkthroughs, and there is a "Daily Q&A" thread where newcomers can ask any question, no matter how basic.

Stack Overflow

Stack Overflow is one of the most useful platforms for practical PowerShell problem-solving. The PowerShell tag has tens of thousands of questions with detailed answers. It is a great place to:

- Search for solutions to common errors.
- Review patterns and idioms used by experienced scripters.
- Learn how to write clearer, more maintainable code.

When posting questions, be sure to include clear problem descriptions and sample code. The community appreciates specific, well-researched questions.

Microsoft Learn

Microsoft Learn offers official, interactive, and beginner-friendly tutorials for PowerShell. These modules are structured like lessons and cover topics such as:

- Basic syntax and objects.
- Managing files and folders.
- Writing and running scripts.
- Automating administrative tasks.

They are ideal for learners who prefer structured, self-paced instruction and are integrated with browser-based labs that let you practice without installing anything.

YouTube Channels

Many PowerShell experts and organizations maintain YouTube channels with free training videos. Some popular ones include:

- **TechThoughts** – Practical use cases for PowerShell automation.
- **Adam Driscoll** – Creator of PowerShell Universal, provides walkthroughs and tips.
- **Don Jones** – Co-founder of PowerShell.org, and one of the original evangelists.
- **I.T. Career Questions** – While broader in focus, includes PowerShell learning paths.

Watching real-time demonstrations can be an effective way to absorb syntax and understand how scripts are built.

Discord Servers

Discord has emerged as a popular platform for real-time discussion among IT professionals. Several servers offer dedicated PowerShell channels where you can:

- Ask quick questions.
- Join voice-based study sessions.
- Get feedback on scripts.
- Make professional connections.

Notable servers include:

- **PowerShell Discord** (linked from PowerShell.org)
- **Tech Discords** with general IT topics and specific scripting rooms

Unlike forums, Discord offers faster replies and more informal dialogue, making it ideal for learners who prefer real-time support.

Twitter (X) and LinkedIn

Social media can be surprisingly rich in PowerShell content. Many scripters and Microsoft MVPs regularly share code snippets, updates, and opinion pieces.

Follow These Notable Contributors:

- **Jeffrey Snover** – Inventor of PowerShell.
- **Don Jones** – Educator and community leader.

- **Chrissy LeMaire** – Founder of dbatools.
- **Boe Prox** – Microsoft MVP, prolific script writer.

Use hashtags like #PowerShell, #SysAdmin, and #DevOps to surface new posts. On LinkedIn, you can also join professional PowerShell groups for curated posts and event announcements.

Community Blogs

There are dozens of high-quality blogs maintained by PowerShell enthusiasts. These blogs often share real-world scripts, lessons learned, and nuanced advice not found in textbooks. A few well-regarded ones include:

- **4sysops.com** – Community of IT professionals, includes PowerShell walkthroughs.
- **Scripting Blog (TechNet Archive)** – Though no longer updated, still a valuable reference.
- **FoxDeploy.com** – Run by Stephen Owen, offering enterprise-grade scripts and theory.
- **The Lazy Administrator** – Focused on modern management with practical scripts.

You can use RSS feeds or tools like Feedly to stay updated with these sites.

Podcasts

PowerShell and DevOps-focused podcasts allow you to learn while commuting or doing chores. Recommended podcasts include:

- **The PowerShell Podcast** – Interviews, news, and educational episodes.
- **SysAdmin Today** – General systems administration topics with regular PowerShell discussion.
- **Microsoft Cloud IT Pro Podcast** – Covers Azure, M365, and PowerShell integration.

Podcasts can offer unique insights into career development, tool adoption, and industry trends.

Conferences and Meetups

Nothing beats in-person or virtual engagement when it comes to community-building. Consider attending or watching recordings from:

- **PowerShell + DevOps Global Summit** – The premier event for PowerShell users.
- **PowerShell Saturday** – Local events in various cities.
- **Microsoft Ignite** – While broader in focus, often includes PowerShell workshops.

Use Meetup.com to find local PowerShell groups. Many meet virtually and welcome newcomers.

Final Thoughts

While this book provides a structured path for learning PowerShell, real growth happens when you interact with the wider community. The most successful PowerShell users are not lone wolves—they are collaborators, learners, and contributors. Whether you prefer forums, social media, podcasts, or meetups, there is a place in the PowerShell community for you. Dive in, ask questions, and don't hesitate to share what you've learned.

The community doesn't just make PowerShell easier to learn—it makes it more fun, more powerful, and more rewarding.

C. GLOSSARY OF TERMS

This section serves as a comprehensive glossary of terms used throughout the "Beginner's Guide to PowerShell Scripting." Whether you're new to scripting or brushing up on concepts, this glossary is designed to provide clear and concise definitions for both fundamental and advanced PowerShell-related terms.

Alias: A shorthand or nickname for a cmdlet or command. For example, ls is an alias for Get-ChildItem. Aliases allow for quicker command entry but can be confusing in scripts intended for others to read.

Array: A data structure that holds a fixed number of items. Arrays can store multiple values in a single variable. Example: $array = @(1, 2, 3).

Boolean: A data type that represents one of two values: $true or $false. Useful in conditional logic and loops.

Break: A keyword used to exit a loop or switch statement prematurely.

Catch: Part of the try/catch/finally block. It handles exceptions that occur in the try block.

Cmdlet: Pronounced "command-let," this is a lightweight command used in PowerShell, typically written in C#. Cmdlets follow a Verb-Noun naming pattern (e.g., Get-Process, Set-Date).

Comment: Text in a script ignored during execution. Denoted by # for single-line or <# ... #> for multi-line comments.

Comparison Operators: Operators used to compare values, such as -eq (equal), -ne (not equal), -lt (less than), and -gt (greater than).

Conditional Statement: Logic that executes code only if certain conditions are met. The if/elseif/else structure is a common example.

Console: The PowerShell interface where commands are entered and executed. Also called the command line interface (CLI).

Constant: A variable whose value cannot be changed once defined. Defined using [const] keyword.

Continue: Used inside a loop to skip the remaining code in the current iteration and proceed with the next iteration.

Credential Object: An object that stores a username and password securely. Created using Get-Credential.

Data Type: Defines what kind of data a variable can hold. Examples include [string], [int], [datetime], [bool], etc.

Default Parameter: A pre-assigned value to a parameter if no other value is provided when the script is executed.

Directory: A folder in the file system. PowerShell can navigate and manipulate directories using commands like Set-Location and Get-ChildItem.

Dot Sourcing: A technique used to run a script within the current scope so that functions and variables defined within it remain accessible after execution.

Dynamic Parameter: A parameter that is added to a function or cmdlet dynamically at runtime, typically based on some condition.

Environment Variable: A system-wide or user-specific variable available in the shell environment. Accessed in PowerShell using $env:VARIABLENAME.

Error Handling: The process of anticipating, catching, and resolving errors in scripts using try/catch/finally blocks.

Escape Character: A special character used to represent characters that have special meaning, such as the backtick (`) in PowerShell.

Execution Policy: A security feature that determines which scripts can run on your system. Policies include Restricted, RemoteSigned, Unrestricted, etc.

Expression: A combination of values, variables, operators, and functions that are evaluated to produce another value.

Filter: A specialized function that processes objects passed through the pipeline.

Foreach: A loop that processes each item in a collection. There are two versions: foreach (statement) and ForEach-Object (cmdlet).

Format Cmdlet: Cmdlets like Format-Table and Format-List used to control how output is displayed.

Function: A reusable block of code defined using the function keyword. Functions may accept parameters and return values.

Hashtable: A collection of key-value pairs. Defined using @{} syntax. Example: $hash = @{Name="Paul"; Age=30}.

Host: The application that hosts the PowerShell engine, such as the PowerShell console, Windows Terminal, or Visual Studio Code.

Import-Module: A cmdlet used to load a module and make its functions and cmdlets available in the session.

Integrated Scripting Environment (ISE): A GUI-based PowerShell editor provided by Microsoft. It has been largely replaced by Visual Studio Code.

Loop: A control structure used to repeat a block of code. Includes for, foreach, while, and do-until loops.

Module: A package of related functions, cmdlets, variables, and other elements that can be loaded into PowerShell using Import-Module.

Object: Everything in PowerShell is an object, even simple outputs. Objects have properties and methods.

Output: The result produced by a command or script. Output can be displayed, saved, or passed through the pipeline.

Parameter: An input value that customizes a function or script's behavior. Parameters are declared within a function block.

Parameter Set: A group of parameters that work together. Only one parameter set can be used per function call.

Parse: The process of analyzing a string to extract specific data types or values, often using methods like .Parse() or regular expressions.

Pipeline: A chain of cmdlets connected by the | (pipe) symbol, where the output of one cmdlet is passed as input to the next.

Profile: A script that runs every time PowerShell starts. Used to customize the environment.

Property: A value associated with an object. Accessed using the dot (.) notation, like $object.Name.

Provider: A .NET-based interface that allows access to different data stores (like the registry, file system, or certificates) as if they were directories.

Regex (Regular Expression): A powerful pattern-matching syntax used for searching and manipulating strings.

Remoting: Running commands on remote computers. Enabled using Enable-PSRemoting and accessed via Invoke-Command or Enter-PSSession.

Return: Used in a function to send a value back to the caller.

Script Block: A block of code enclosed in {} that can be stored in a variable, passed to cmdlets, or executed.

Scope: The context in which variables and functions exist. Common scopes include global, script, local, and private.

Secure String: A string that is encrypted in memory. Used for storing sensitive information like passwords.

Select-Object: A cmdlet used to select specific properties from an object or to limit the number of items in output.

Session: An instance of a PowerShell environment. Remoting sessions are called PSSessions.

Splatting: A technique for passing parameters to a function or cmdlet using a hashtable or array.

Standard Output (stdout): The default destination for output data, usually the console.

String: A data type used to represent text. Strings can be enclosed in either single or double quotes.

Switch: A control statement that handles multiple conditions, replacing complex if/elseif structures.

Syntax: The rules that define the structure of PowerShell code. Correct syntax is essential to avoid errors.

Try: Used in error handling to define a block of code to attempt. Used with catch and optionally finally.

Variable: A named storage location for data. Defined using the $ symbol, such as $name = "Paul".

Verb-Noun Naming: The naming convention for cmdlets and functions. The verb describes the action, and the noun describes the target (e.g., Get-Help).

Where-Object: A cmdlet used to filter objects based on specified conditions.

While Loop: A loop that runs as long as the specified condition is true.

Wildcard: Characters used to substitute part of a string. Common wildcards include * (zero or more characters) and ? (one character).

Workflow: A sequence of automated steps or tasks. PowerShell workflows allow for parallel execution and persistence.

This glossary is intended to be a living reference. As you deepen your knowledge of PowerShell scripting, you'll continue to encounter new terms and patterns. Always take time to understand unfamiliar terms as they appear—they are the building blocks of your scripting expertise.

D. PRACTICE EXERCISES BY CHAPTER

This section provides a curated set of practice exercises for each chapter in the book *Beginner's Guide To PowerShell Scripting*. These exercises are designed to reinforce the concepts covered, provide hands-on experience, and help readers develop a deeper understanding of PowerShell scripting. The difficulty level increases gradually, allowing beginners to build confidence and proficiency.

Chapter 1: Introduction to PowerShell

Objective: Familiarize yourself with the PowerShell interface and basic command structure.

Exercises:
1. Launch PowerShell as Administrator and run your first command: Get-Help.
2. Explore a command: Run Get-Help Get-Process and summarize its syntax and parameters.
3. Use Get-Command to list all available cmdlets on your system.
4. Identify your PowerShell version using Get-Host.
5. Navigate the file system: Use Get-ChildItem, Set-Location, and Clear-Host.

Chapter 2: PowerShell Syntax and Variables

Objective: Learn PowerShell syntax, how to define and manipulate variables.

Exercises:
1. Create three variables: $name, $age, $city, and assign values.
2. Concatenate strings using the + operator and string interpolation.
3. Use Get-Member to inspect variable types.
4. Practice arithmetic using numeric variables.
5. Use Write-Host and Write-Output to display information.

Chapter 3: Conditional Statements and Loops

Objective: Understand how to use if, switch, for, foreach, and while loops.

Exercises:
1. Write a script that checks if a number is even or odd.
2. Create a switch statement to return the name of a weekday based on a number input.
3. Write a for loop that prints numbers 1 through 10.
4. Use a foreach loop to iterate over a list of colors.
5. Create a while loop that counts down from 5 to 1.

Chapter 4: Working with Objects and the Pipeline

Objective: Practice working with object properties and pipeline filtering.

Exercises:

1. Use Get-Process | Select-Object Name, Id to display running processes.
2. Pipe Get-Service results through Where-Object to show stopped services.
3. Sort a list of services by status using Sort-Object.
4. Export a list of running processes to a CSV file using Export-Csv.
5. Import a CSV and display it using Import-Csv.

Chapter 5: Functions and Scripting Basics

Objective: Learn how to define and use functions in PowerShell scripts.

Exercises:

1. Write a function called Say-Hello that accepts a name and prints a greeting.
2. Modify the function to return the value instead of printing.
3. Write a function that takes two numbers and returns their sum.
4. Save a script containing multiple functions in a .ps1 file and run it.
5. Use param() to define parameters for a script.

Chapter 6: Working with Files and Directories

Objective: Practice file and directory manipulation with PowerShell.

Exercises:

1. Use New-Item to create a text file and a folder.
2. Write content to a file using Out-File.
3. Append text to an existing file with Add-Content.
4. Copy a file to a new location with Copy-Item.
5. Delete files or directories with Remove-Item.

Chapter 7: Bulk User Creation

Objective: Automate user creation using input files.

Exercises:

1. Create a CSV file with columns: FirstName, LastName, Username.

2. Write a script that reads the CSV and outputs the intended usernames.
3. Modify the script to simulate user creation using New-ADUser (commented out if not in domain).
4. Add error checking to ensure all required fields are populated.
5. Log the results to a new CSV file.

Chapter 8: Last Login Report

Objective: Gather login activity and export a report.

Exercises:
1. Use Get-ADUser -Properties LastLogonDate to fetch user login data.
2. Filter out disabled accounts.
3. Create a report of users who haven't logged in for 90+ days.
4. Export the report to CSV.
5. Add a parameterized date filter to your script.

Chapter 9: Querying Installed Software

Objective: Retrieve and export a list of installed software on a local or remote system.

Exercises:
1. Use Get-WmiObject -Class Win32_Product to list software.
2. Filter results to only show software installed in the last 30 days.
3. Export the output to CSV.
4. Write a function Get-InstalledSoftware that accepts a computer name.
5. Schedule the script using Task Scheduler.

Chapter 10: Scripted Deployments

Objective: Automate deployment tasks such as software installs or system configuration.

Exercises:
1. Write a script that installs an MSI package using Start-Process.
2. Add logging for start and end time of installation.
3. Include a check to see if the software is already installed.
4. Create a configuration baseline with Set-ItemProperty for registry edits.

5. Deploy a set of tools to a remote machine using Invoke-Command.

Chapter 11: IAM, EC2, and S3 Operations

Objective: Use AWS tools with PowerShell to manage cloud resources.

Exercises:

1. Install and configure the AWS PowerShell module.
2. List IAM users using Get-IAMUsers.
3. Create an EC2 instance using New-EC2Instance.
4. Upload a file to an S3 bucket.
5. Write a script to backup local files to S3 daily.

Chapter 12: Scripting Code Pipelines

Objective: Build and manage automated CI/CD pipelines using PowerShell.

Exercises:

1. Define a function to package and zip code for deployment.
2. Create a script that uploads code to a repository.
3. Integrate PowerShell with a CI tool like Jenkins or GitHub Actions.
4. Write a deployment script that triggers when a new version is detected.
5. Include rollback logic in case of failure.

Chapter 13: Creating, Importing, and Publishing Modules

Objective: Organize reusable scripts as PowerShell modules.

Exercises:

1. Create a module folder and .psm1 file with at least two functions.
2. Create a .psd1 manifest file for the module.
3. Import your module using Import-Module.
4. Publish your module to a local or private repository.
5. Add help documentation using comment-based help.

Chapter 14: Error Handling and Logging

Objective: Implement structured error handling and logging mechanisms.

Exercises:

1. Use Try, Catch, and Finally in a script that opens a file.
2. Log errors to a text file with timestamps.
3. Create a custom error message for a failed condition.
4. Practice using $ErrorActionPreference.
5. Build a logging function that accepts severity levels.

Chapter 15: Advanced Scripting and Real-World Scenarios

Objective: Tackle complex scripts that mirror real-world administrative tasks.

Exercises:

1. Build a script that audits local user accounts and group memberships.
2. Create a script that checks disk space and emails a report.
3. Write a backup script that compresses a directory and stores it remotely.
4. Schedule a PowerShell script to run weekly and log its results.
5. Develop a script that parses event logs for login failures.

By completing these exercises, readers will solidify their understanding of PowerShell scripting and gain the confidence needed to apply their skills in real-world environments. Repetition, experimentation, and curiosity are key—there is no substitute for hands-on practice when learning to script in PowerShell.

E. SAMPLE PROJECTS

One of the best ways to learn PowerShell scripting is by engaging with real-world projects. Sample projects allow you to apply the concepts you've learned in practical, relevant scenarios. This chapter will walk you through several projects of increasing complexity, each designed to give you hands-on experience with PowerShell. These projects cover administrative automation, reporting, cloud interactions, and more.

Project 1: Bulk User Account Creation in Active Directory

Objective: Automate the process of creating multiple user accounts in Active Directory (AD) from a CSV file.

Requirements
- Windows Server with Active Directory installed
- PowerShell Active Directory module
- CSV file containing user information

CSV Format Example
FirstName,LastName,Username,OU,Password

John,Doe,jdoe,OU=Sales,Password123

Jane,Smith,jsmith,OU=Marketing,Password123

Script Overview

```
Import-Module ActiveDirectory
$users = Import-Csv -Path "C:\UsersToCreate.csv"

foreach ($user in $users) {
    $name = "$($user.FirstName) $($user.LastName)"
    $username = $user.Username
        $password = ConvertTo-SecureString $user.Password -AsPlainText -Force
    $ou = $user.OU

    New-ADUser -Name $name -GivenName $user.FirstName -Surname $user.LastName `
                -SamAccountName $username -UserPrincipalName "$username@domain.local" `
                -AccountPassword $password -Path $ou -Enabled $true
}
```

Key Takeaways
- Shows how to work with CSV input
- Demonstrates user creation via New-ADUser
- Emphasizes automation of repetitive administrative tasks

Project 2: Last Login Report for All Domain Users

Objective: Generate a report of the last login date for all users in the domain.

Script Overview

```
Import-Module ActiveDirectory
$users = Get-ADUser -Filter * -Properties LastLogonDate

$report = foreach ($user in $users) {
    [PSCustomObject]@{
      Name = $user.Name
      Username = $user.SamAccountName
      LastLogon = $user.LastLogonDate
    }
  }


$report  |  Export-Csv  -Path  "C:\LastLoginReport.csv"  -NoTypeInformation
```

Key Takeaways
- Introduces Get-ADUser with additional properties
- Teaches object creation using [PSCustomObject]
- Demonstrates exporting data to CSV

Project 3: Installed Software Inventory Script

Objective: Query a list of remote computers and generate a report of installed software.

Script Overview

```
$computers = Get-Content -Path "C:\ComputerList.txt"
$softwareReport = @()


foreach ($computer in $computers) {
    try {
            $software = Get-WmiObject -Class Win32_Product -ComputerName $computer
        foreach ($app in $software) {
          $softwareReport += [PSCustomObject]@{
            Computer = $computer
            Name    = $app.Name
            Version = $app.Version
          }
```

```
    }
  } catch {
    Write-Host "Failed to query $computer"
  }
}
```

$softwareReport | Export-Csv -Path "C:\SoftwareInventory.csv" -NoTypeInformation

Key Takeaways
- Introduces WMI (Get-WmiObject) for system-level queries
- Uses try/catch for error handling
- Builds a report from multiple machines

Project 4: Scripted Application Deployment
Objective: Deploy a software application via PowerShell script.

Example Scenario

Deploy Notepad++ silently across multiple endpoints.

Script Overview

```
$computers = Get-Content -Path "C:\ComputerList.txt"
$installerPath = "\\NetworkShare\Notepad++Installer.exe"

foreach ($computer in $computers) {
    Invoke-Command -ComputerName $computer -ScriptBlock {
        Start-Process -FilePath "C:\Installers\Notepad++Installer.exe" -ArgumentList "/S" -Wait
    } -Credential (Get-Credential)
}
```

Key Takeaways
- Demonstrates remote execution with Invoke-Command
- Covers silent installation with command-line arguments
- Shows credential usage for cross-machine tasks

Project 5: AWS IAM and S3 Automation
Objective: Use PowerShell to interact with AWS, creating IAM users and uploading files to an S3 bucket.

Prerequisites

- AWS PowerShell module installed
- AWS credentials configured

Script Overview

```
# Create IAM user
New-IAMUser -UserName "NewUser"

# Attach policy
Register-IAMUserPolicy -UserName "NewUser" -PolicyArn "arn:aws:iam::aws:policy/AmazonS3FullAccess"

# Upload file to S3
Write-S3Object -BucketName "my-bucket" -File "C:\Reports\monthly.pdf" -Key "reports/monthly.pdf"
```

Key Takeaways

- Teaches interaction with cloud platforms
- Demonstrates IAM and S3 operations
- Encourages exploration of cloud automation

Project 6: Scheduled Task Automation

Objective: Automatically create scheduled tasks on local or remote systems.

Script Overview

```
$action = New-ScheduledTaskAction -Execute "powershell.exe" -Argument "-File C:\Scripts\Backup.ps1"
$trigger = New-ScheduledTaskTrigger -Daily -At 2am

Register-ScheduledTask -Action $action -Trigger $trigger -TaskName "DailyBackup" -Description "Runs backup script daily" -User "SYSTEM" -RunLevel Highest
```

Key Takeaways

- Teaches use of ScheduledTasks module
- Reinforces daily operational scripting
- Helps automate tasks consistently and reliably

Project 7: Code Pipeline for Script Deployment

Objective: Automate deployment of scripts from version control to production.

Requirements
- Git installed
- Access to a deployment environment
- PowerShell

Script Overview
```
# Clone the repo if not already present
if (!(Test-Path "C:\Scripts\Repo")) {
    git clone https://github.com/yourorg/powershell-scripts.git C:\Scripts\Repo
}
```

```
# Pull the latest code
cd C:\Scripts\Repo
git pull
```

```
# Deploy to production folder
Copy-Item -Path "C:\Scripts\Repo\*.ps1" -Destination "\\ProdServer\Scripts" -Force
```

Key Takeaways
- Highlights DevOps principles
- Connects version control and deployment
- Encourages collaboration and version safety

Project 8: Custom PowerShell Module Creation
Objective: Package multiple functions into a reusable PowerShell module.

Example Structure
```
MyModule\
├── MyModule.psm1
└── MyModule.psd1
```

Module Script Example
```
# MyModule.psm1
function Get-HelloWorld {
  [CmdletBinding()]
  param ()
```

```
    "Hello, World!"
}
```

Export-ModuleMember -Function Get-HelloWorld

Manifest File

New-ModuleManifest -Path ".\MyModule.psd1" -RootModule "MyModule.psm1" -Author "Your Name" -Description "Sample module"

Import and Use

Import-Module "C:\Modules\MyModule"
Get-HelloWorld

Key Takeaways
- Encourages code reusability
- Demonstrates module structure and manifest creation
- Forms the basis for publishing to PowerShell Gallery

Summary

These sample projects provide a strong foundation for PowerShell scripting by solving real-world problems. They help reinforce core concepts like importing modules, working with objects, handling errors, exporting data, automating routine tasks, and even working with cloud environments. As you complete each project, consider adapting them to suit your specific IT environment, and experiment with adding features or improving their robustness. The more you practice with real tasks, the more proficient and confident you will become in PowerShell scripting.

F. INTERVIEW QUESTIONS AND PRACTICE TASKS

Breaking into a role that requires PowerShell knowledge often involves demonstrating both theoretical understanding and hands-on scripting capability. Whether you are preparing for an entry-level system administrator role, a DevOps position, or a cybersecurity analyst role, being able to confidently answer PowerShell-related interview questions—and prove your skills with real-world tasks—is essential.

This section provides you with a variety of commonly asked PowerShell interview questions, along with answers and practical tasks to sharpen your scripting skills. These are broken into three tiers: beginner, intermediate, and advanced.

Beginner-Level Interview Questions

These questions test fundamental PowerShell knowledge and basic command usage.

1. What is PowerShell, and how is it different from Command Prompt?

Answer: PowerShell is a task automation and configuration management framework from Microsoft, consisting of a command-line shell and scripting language. Unlike Command Prompt, PowerShell uses cmdlets (specialized .NET classes), supports object piping, and allows for complex scripting.

2. What is a cmdlet?

Answer: A cmdlet is a lightweight command used in the PowerShell environment. Cmdlets are instances of .NET classes and follow a verb-noun naming pattern like Get-Process or Set-Service.

3. How do you get help in PowerShell?

Answer: Use the Get-Help cmdlet. For example:

```
Get-Help Get-Process
```

Add -Full or -Examples for detailed help or sample usage.

4. How do you list all running services?

Answer:

```
Get-Service | Where-Object {$_.Status -eq 'Running'}
```

5. What is the difference between Write-Host, Write-Output, and Write-Verbose?

Answer:

- Write-Host: Writes directly to the console. Use for messages you don't need in the output stream.
- Write-Output: Sends data to the pipeline. Best for functions.
- Write-Verbose: Sends verbose messages when -Verbose is used.

Beginner Practice Tasks

Task 1: List all services that are not running.

```
Get-Service | Where-Object {$_.Status -ne 'Running'}
```

Task 2: Export a list of installed software to a CSV.

```
Get-ItemProperty HKLM:
\Software\Wow6432Node\Microsoft\Windows\CurrentVersion\Unins
tall\* | \
Select-Object DisplayName, DisplayVersion, Publisher | \
Export-Csv -Path "C:\InstalledSoftware.csv" -
NoTypeInformation
```

Task 3: Create a script that checks if a process is running.

```
$processName = "notepad"
if (Get-Process -Name $processName -ErrorAction
SilentlyContinue) {
    Write-Host "$processName is running."
} else {
    Write-Host "$processName is not running."
}
```

Intermediate-Level Interview Questions

These questions explore deeper PowerShell usage including loops, conditions, and functions.

1. What is a pipeline in PowerShell?

Answer: A pipeline (|) is used to pass the output of one command as input into another. It enables chaining commands efficiently.

2. How do you handle errors in PowerShell?

Answer: Use Try, Catch, and optionally Finally blocks. You can also use -ErrorAction to suppress or control error behavior.

3. How do you define a function in PowerShell?

Answer:

```
function Get-Greeting {
    param([string]$Name)
    return "Hello, $Name!"
}
```

4. How would you schedule a PowerShell script to run daily?

Answer: Use Task Scheduler to create a task that calls powershell.exe with the script path.

5. What is the $PSVersionTable variable?

Answer: It is an automatic variable that displays the current PowerShell version and environment information.

```
$PSVersionTable
```

Intermediate Practice Tasks

Task 1: Write a function that accepts a username and returns the user's SID.

```
function Get-UserSID {
    param([string]$username)
    $user = New-Object
System.Security.Principal.NTAccount($username)
    $sid =
$user.Translate([System.Security.Principal.SecurityIdentifie
r])
    return $sid.Value
}
```

Task 2: Create a script to back up a directory with a timestamp.

```
$source = "C:\Data"
$backup = "C:\Backups\Data_$(Get-Date -Format
'yyyyMMdd_HHmmss')"
Copy-Item -Path $source -Destination $backup -Recurse
```

Task 3: Log failed login attempts from the event log.

```
Get-WinEvent -FilterHashtable @{LogName='Security'; Id=4625}
| \
Select-Object TimeCreated, Message | \
Export-Csv -Path "C:\failed_logins.csv" -NoTypeInformation
```

Advanced-Level Interview Questions

These questions test knowledge of scripting at scale, automation integration, and infrastructure scripting.

1. How do you import a CSV and create users from it?

Answer:

```
Import-Csv -Path "C:\Users.csv" | ForEach-Object {
    New-ADUser -Name $_.Name -SamAccountName $_.Username -
UserPrincipalName $_.UPN -AccountPassword (ConvertTo-
SecureString $_.Password -AsPlainText -Force) -Enabled $true
}
```

2. Explain remoting and how to enable it.

Answer: PowerShell remoting uses WinRM to allow remote script execution. Enable it with:

```
Enable-PSRemoting -Force
```

Use Invoke-Command or Enter-PSSession to run scripts remotely.

3. What is DSC (Desired State Configuration)?

Answer: DSC is a configuration management platform built into PowerShell. It allows you to declaratively define and enforce system configuration states.

4. How can PowerShell be used with REST APIs?

Answer: Use Invoke-RestMethod or Invoke-WebRequest for REST calls. Example:

```
Invoke-RestMethod -Uri "https://api.example.com/data" -Method Get
```

5. How do you create and publish your own PowerShell module?
Answer:

1. Create a .psm1 file with functions.
2. Add a .psd1 manifest file.
3. Use Publish-Module if publishing to PowerShell Gallery.

Advanced Practice Tasks
Task 1: Script a report of last login for all domain users.

```
Get-ADUser -Filter * -Properties LastLogonDate | \
Select-Object Name, LastLogonDate | \
Export-Csv -Path "C:\UserLogins.csv" -NoTypeInformation
```

Task 2: Deploy software silently with PowerShell.

```
Start-Process -FilePath "msiexec.exe" -ArgumentList "/i \"C:\setup.msi\" /quiet /norestart" -Wait
```

Task 3: Rotate log files older than 30 days.

```
$logPath = "C:\Logs"
Get-ChildItem -Path $logPath -Recurse | \
Where-Object { $_.LastWriteTime -lt (Get-Date).AddDays(-30) } | \
Move-Item -Destination "C:\Logs\Archive"
```

Final Tips

- **Practice regularly** using the examples provided.
- **Document your scripts** with comments and help sections.
- **Use version control** (e.g., Git) to track changes.
- **Experiment safely** using virtual machines or containers.
- **Build your own PowerShell project portfolio** to showcase during interviews.

Being interview-ready requires a blend of knowledge and hands-on experience. Practice with intent, automate real-world tasks, and study the behavior of your scripts under various conditions to build confidence. Mastery is a result of consistency and curiosity.

This section provides a strong foundation for interview readiness. You can further build upon these exercises by customizing scripts to solve problems in your own environment, contributing to open-source projects, or challenging yourself to create reusable tools in PowerShell.